"Microsoft Excel is already installed on 750 million computers. But creating modern visualizations using Excel charts seems impossible. In this book, Jonathan Schwabish gives you the step-by-step instructions to make Excel charts do what most people (including me) previously thought was impossible in Excel. Every chapter, you will learn how to make visualizations that most people assume require Python or R."

*–**Bill Jelen**, Excel MVP and publisher of MrExcel.com*

"Those who expanded their graphicacy with Schwabish's *Better Data Visualizations* are going to love the follow up, in which Jon outlines how to make graphs using the ubiquitous Microsoft Excel. Readers will appreciate Jon's pragmatic examples, easy-to-follow instructions and entertaining writing. If you need to communicate with data and lack confidence making graphs in Excel, I urge you to add *Data Visualization in Excel* to your library!"

*–**Cole Nussbaumer Knaflic**, founder and CEO of storytelling with data (SWD)*

"Wow, just wow. One book that explains how to make all the fancy, powerful charts you see in good ol' Excel. If you want to impress your boss with Excel charting wizardry, this is THE BOOK for you. Not only does the book explain the chart construction process, it also provides guidance on designing great outputs. I wish I had this book when I started my data analyst journey. A must buy. Highly recommended."

*–**Chandoo (Purna Duggirala)**, Microsoft MVP, Chandoo.org*

"This book takes you well beyond the defaults of Excel charting. It shows you how to apply principles and best practices of data visualization in an accessible way. In the process it streamlines the use of Excel while enabling the creation of much more advanced graphics."

*–**Jon Peltier**, Peltier Technical Services*

"Thank you Jonathan Schwabish for giving us such a clear how-to book! Data Visualization in Excel shows us how far we can go with Excel to make data visualization insights accessible to a much broader audience! I am making this my go-to textbook for teaching myself and my students to create better, more effective, and different graphs in Excel to operationalize the data visualization concepts and strategies the earlier books have inspired in us."

*–**Kosali Simon**, Distinguished Professor, Indiana University, O'Neill School of Public and Environmental Affairs*

"There aren't many places where the cliché "think outside the box" can be applied with such propriety (and benefits) than when making charts in Excel. If you go beyond its poor chart library and defaults, there is a whole world to discover, and Jon's new book is a great journey companion. This detailed step-by-step tutorial will show you how to take advantage of Excel's flexibility, how to use design and formatting options far from their original intent and how to visualize data directly on the spreadsheet, going even further away from the chart library. On top of this, Jon is a communicator and a data visualization expert, so his many examples are relevant (many analytical tasks can benefit from them) and designed for effectiveness applying sound data visualization guidelines."

*–**Jorge Camões**, data visualization consultant, founder of Excelcharts.com*

"For data visualisation practitioners looking to hone their charting craft there are three core questions: what, when, and how. What different options exist. When should I use. How do I make them. Jon's bestseller "Better Data Visualizations: A Guide for Scholars, Researchers, and Wonks" addresses the first two of those enquiries, and much more besides, but this excellent new text gives explicit solutions for the matter of how. For Excel users, beginners or advanced, this book will become an essential practical companion. You'll learn how to elegantly master the standard charting functions in the most effective and efficient way, but you'll also discover how to truly make Excel sing, finding novel approaches and clever workarounds to expand your visual vocabulary even further."

*–**Andy Kirk**, independent consultant, educator, and author,*
founder of visualisingdata.com

"I found this book 20 years too late! Seriously, I wish I had this book a long time ago, for its rich collection of tutorials, best practices, lessons learned, and principles of data visualization using Excel. From broken stacked bars to Gantt charts, heatmaps, tile grid maps, and waffle plots (and so much more from A to Z), the many detailed visualization examples in this book will provide tremendous benefit in the workplace whenever and wherever data storytelling, visual analytics, or data-driven decision insights are required. Excel users from beginners to experts will discover useful data visualization examples, corresponding detailed instructions, and perhaps some secrets of Excel here in this wonderful book."

*–**Kirk Borne**, Chief Science Officer, DataPrime Inc.*

"Jonathan Schwabish taught me what constitutes a good chart. In this incredibly useful volume, he teaches me how to make a good chart in Excel. A step-by-step guide – practical, easy to follow and (of course) well-illustrated."

–**David Wessel**, *Director, Hutchins Center on Fiscal & Monetary Policy, The Brookings Institution*

"Finally, a comprehensive data visualisation book for Excel that's detailed enough that a relative beginner can use it, and extensive enough that an experienced user will also discover tips and learn valuable Excel techniques and data visualisation best practices."

–**Mynda Treacy**, *MyOnlineTrainingHub.com*

"Data visualization has an ever-growing toolbox of applications and programming languages for creating charts, but some may come with steep learning curves, some may require coding skills, and some resources may lack the full range of functionality we really need. The one, often overlooked tool familiar and often available to most of us is Microsoft Excel. In this companion book to *Better Data Visualizations: A Guide for Scholars, Researchers and Wonks*, Jon Schwabish systematically and expertly shows us how to create a wide variety of visualization types, from simple heatmaps right through to more complex examples such as raincloud plots and Marimekko charts, each with detailed tutorials and with all companion resources available via his website. This book first opens your eyes to the wide range of visualization possibilities that were most likely available to you all along in Excel, then promptly equips you with the skills to create them all."

–**Neil Richards**, *Lead Business Intelligence Analyst at JLL, former Knowledge Director for the Data Visualization Society*

Data Visualization in Excel

This book closes the gap between what people think Excel can do and what they can achieve in the tool. Over the past few years, recognition of the importance of effectively visualizing data has led to an explosion of data analysis and visualization software tools. But for many people, Microsoft Excel continues to be the workhorse for their data visualization needs, not to mention the only tool that many data workers have access to. Although Excel is not a specialist data visualization platform, it does have strong capabilities. The default chart types do not need to be the limit of the tool's data visualization capabilities, and users can extend its features by understanding some key elements and strategies. *Data Visualization in Excel* provides a step-by-step guide to creating more advanced and often more effective data visualizations in Excel and is the perfect guide for anyone who wants to create better, more effective, and more engaging data visualizations.

Jonathan Schwabish is an economist and data communication expert. Dr Schwabish is considered a leader in the data visualization field and is a leading voice for clarity and accessibility in research. He is a senior fellow at the Urban Institute, a non-profit research institution in Washington, D.C., and is the founder of the data visualization and presentation skills firm, PolicyViz.

AK Peters Visualization Series

Visualization plays an ever-more prominent role in the world, as we communicate about and analyze data. This series aims to capture what visualization is today in all its variety and diversity, giving voice to researchers, practitioners, designers, and enthusiasts. It encompasses books from all subfields of visualization, including visual analytics, information visualization, scientific visualization, data journalism, infographics, and their connection to adjacent areas such as text analysis, digital humanities, data art, or augmented and virtual reality.

SERIES EDITORS:

Tamara Munzner, *University of British Columbia, Vancouver, Canada*
Alberto Cairo, *University of Miami, USA*

RECENT TITLES:

Building Science Graphics

An illustrated guide to communicating science through diagrams and visualizations

Jen Christiansen

Joyful Infographics

A Friendly, Human Approach to Data

Nigel Holmes

Questions in Dataviz

A Design-Driven Process for Data Visualisation

Neil Richards

Making with Data

Physical Design and Craft in a Data-Driven World

Edited by Samuel Huron, Till Nagel, Lora Oehlberg, Wesley Willett

Mobile Data Visualization

Edited by Bongshin Lee, Raimund Dachselt, Petra Isenberg, Eun Kyoung Choe

Data Sketches

Nadieh Bremer, Shirley Wu

Visualizing with Text

Richard Brath

Interactive Visual Data Analysis

Christian Tominski, Heidrun Schumann

Data-Driven Storytelling

Nathalie Henry Riche, Christophe Hurter, Nicholas Diakopoulos, Sheelagh Carpendale

For more information about this series please visit: https://www.routledge.com/AK-Peters-Visualization-Series/book-series/CRCVIS

Data Visualization in Excel

A Guide for Beginners, Intermediates, and Wonks

Jonathan Schwabish

CRC Press
Taylor & Francis Group
Boca Raton London New York

CRC Press is an imprint of the
Taylor & Francis Group, an **informa** business

AN A K PETERS BOOK

First Edition published 2023
by CRC Press
6000 Broken Sound Parkway NW, Suite 300, Boca Raton, FL 33487-2742

and by CRC Press
4 Park Square, Milton Park, Abingdon, Oxon, OX14 4RN

CRC Press is an imprint of Taylor & Francis Group, LLC

© 2023 Jonathan Schwabish

Library of Congress Cataloging-in-Publication Data
Names: Schwabish, Jonathan A., author.
Title: Data visualization in Excel : a guide for beginners, intermediates, and wonks / Jonathan Schwabish.
Description: First edition. | Boca Raton : AK Peters/CRC Press, 2023. |
Series: AK Peters visualization series | Includes bibliographical references and index.
Identifiers: LCCN 2022055048 (print) | LCCN 2022055049 (ebook) | ISBN 9781032343280 (hbk) |
ISBN 9781032343266 (pbk) | ISBN 9781003321552 (ebk) | ISBN 9781032487823 (eBook+)
Subjects: LCSH: Information visualization—Data processing. | Visual analytics. |
Microsoft Excel (Computer file)
Classification: LCC QA76.9.I52 S394 2023 (print) | LCC QA76.9.I52 (ebook) | DDC 005.7/2—dc23/eng/20230104
LC record available at https://lccn.loc.gov/2022055048
LC ebook record available at https://lccn.loc.gov/2022055049

ISBN: 978-1-032-34328-0 (hbk)
ISBN: 978-1-032-34326-6 (pbk)
ISBN: 978-1-003-32155-2 (ebk)
ISBN: 978-1-032-48782-3 (eBook+)

DOI: 10.1201/9781003321552

Typeset in Minion
by codeMantra

Access the Support Materials: https://www.routledge.com/9781032343266

Dedication

For Ellie and Jack

Contents

To help guide you through the tutorials, each chapter is roughly classified by difficulty depending on the number of steps, how many different chart types are used, and how much data preparation is needed.

■ Beginner   ■■ Intermediate   ■■■ Advanced

PART THREE: MOVING VISUALS OUT OF EXCEL

Acknowledgements

After teaching any sort of introductory data visualization class or workshop, one of the first questions I hear is: How can I build data visualizations? Learning more about dot plots, slope charts, waffle charts, and others can expand a person's graphic toolbox, but how does someone *create* those visuals?

In response, I started teaching more about the technical aspects of building data visualizations in Excel. But an hour or two or four is still insufficient for folks to really level up their skills, so I wrote a step-by-step e-book (a fancy word for a PDF document) for people who needed extra support during the training.

This book is a better, more comprehensive version of that e-book. I thought it would be easy—just take the e-book, update a few steps, add a few more graphs, and it's all set! But it's never as easy as that. Even when I finished the first draft and asked my kids to take a first pass through the tutorials, I knew it needed a major revision. The steps were too much of a narrative—I needed to simplify, update, and streamline.

This book could not have been completed without the assistance of Glenna Shaw. Glenna outdid herself with this project. She worked tirelessly to capture all of the images, adding pointers and annotations, and correcting several mistakes. Without her help, this project would have taken twice as long and looked half as good.

I'm also thankful for the assistance of Michael Brenner and Wesley Jenkins. Michael, a designer with the incredible Data4Change organization, created the cover for the book and assisted with a variety of images. Wes is an expert editor and helped shepherd this project to its final completion. Writing a step-by-step book is not the most creative writing exercise in the world, but Wes stuck by me, making sure the writing was concise and clear.

A book like this needs to be tested. Each step. Over and over again. I am grateful to the people who spent time and effort testing each tutorial: Margot Hollick, Kyungmin (Mina) Lee, Cynthia Ma, Navya Patury, Charles Tang, and Steven Yates.

Big thanks are due to the publishing team at CRC Press—Randi Cohen, Sathya Devi, Mansi Kabra, Elliot Morsia and Todd Perry—and the series editors, Alberto Cairo and Tamara Munzner. I'm also thankful to the reviewers of early versions of this book, including Dave Bruns, Jorge Camões, and Jon Peltier.

The data visualization community is incredibly supportive, creative, and energetic. Without that creativity and desire to produce better, more effective ways to communicate data, this book would not have come to fruition. I hope that through this book readers will see it's not what tool you use to create your visualizations, but the care and creativity you bring to that work.

I'm also grateful for my Urban Institute colleagues who strive to make the world a better place through economic and social policy research. The diversity of perspectives, backgrounds, experiences, and skills has helped me to become a better researcher and better data communicator.

I'm especially thankful to friends inside and outside the data visualization field who have supported me while I worked on this book, either by answering questions about data or data visualization or simply grabbing a quick breakfast or a drink at the end of the day: Lindsay Betzendahl, Nayan Bhula, Matt Chase, Alice Feng, Kevin Flerlage, Francis Gagnon, Cole Knaflic, Ken Skaggs, Sharon Sotsky Ramirez, Alli Torban, and John Wehmann. Special thanks to my entire extended family for the endless supply of support and love.

Finally, as always, my most special thanks go to my wife and kids. Since Ellie and Jack have grown up, I have written four books; fortunately for me, they are now more active participants in the process. Both spent hours testing this book, trying to follow their dad's complicated instructions, looking through colors and fonts, cover drafts, and always offering constructive feedback and thoughtful opinions. I couldn't have completed this book without them. I hope they'll always know how they inspire me to do the work I do.

My deepest thanks go to my wife, Lauren. Let's always hold hands.

Part 1

Setting the Stage

Chapter **1**

Introduction

As a senior in college at the University of Wisconsin at Madison, my mentor and I worked on a project that looked at how the US poverty rate and US economic growth changed over time. For my part of the project, I compiled data from a number of government sources, from employment data at the Bureau of Labor Statistics to economic growth data at the Bureau of Economic Analysis. For each year in the dataset, I entered the values into several Excel workbooks, made a *lot* of charts, and even ran regressions (something I would never do now!).

The graphs were, let's just say, not inspired. I'm sure I used the Excel defaults (likely Excel 97) and just let the tool do what it wanted to do. But creating those graphs is my earliest memory of using Microsoft Excel for research, and it's a memory that has stuck with me ever since (Figure 1.1).

Several years later, while conducting my graduate work in economics at Syracuse University, I had another opportunity to explore the capabilities of Excel. I was assisting my graduate mentor with his work that measured earnings and income inequality in different countries around the world. We used the Luxembourg Income Study, an archive and research center that houses the largest database of cross-national data in the world. I compiled the estimates of certain measures of inequality—such as the 10th, 50th, and 90th percentiles and the Gini coefficient—to include in journal articles and reports. My mentor had already created a graph for this dataset, which strategically placed a bar

DOI: 10.1201/9781003321552-2

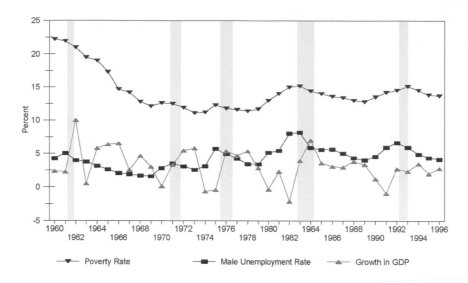

FIGURE 1.1   *Source: Robert Haveman and Jonathan Schwabish. 1999. "Macroeconomic Performance and the Poverty Rate: A Return to Normalcy?" IRP Discussion Paper No. 1187-99 (March).*

chart in the middle of the table so readers could see the exact values and the gap between the top and bottom of the income distribution.

By this time, I could write computer code using statistical packages like SAS and Stata, but I still used Excel to make my graphs and charts. This table was more inspired than my earlier attempts as an undergraduate, and it afforded me the exciting opportunity to explore Excel by recreating it and expanding the capabilities of the tool beyond the standard bar chart. Although I could likely improve this table now, it was perhaps the first time that I saw a more effective way to present complex data (Figure 1.2).

My interest in creating better, more effective graphs and tables would continue to grow as my career progressed. While working at the Congressional Budget Office—the budget arm of the US Congress—in Washington, DC, I investigated ways my colleagues and I could improve how we communicated our work to federal policymakers. We used Excel and several other tools to create clearer, more engaging, and more colorful graphs and diagrams in our reports, slide decks, and blog posts.

All the while, the landscape of data visualization tools was changing. In 2003, the dashboarding tool Tableau launched, allowing users to create interactive dashboards quickly and without computer code. Statistician and developer Hadley Wickham also released his *ggplot2* system for making data visualizations in the R programming language in 2003, immediately enabling users to make better graphs. Members of Stanford University's Visualization group— Mike Bostock, Jeffrey Heer, and Vadim Ogievetsky—released D3, a JavaScript

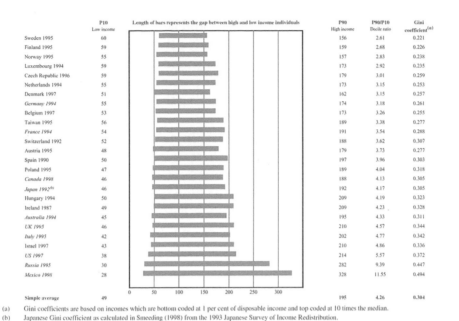

	P10 Low income	Length of bars represents the gap between high and low income individuals	P90 High income	P90/P10 Decile ratio	Gini coefficient[a]
Sweden 1995	60		156	2.61	0.221
Finland 1995	59		159	2.68	0.226
Norway 1995	55		157	2.83	0.238
Luxembourg 1994	59		173	2.92	0.235
Czech Republic 1996	59		179	3.01	0.259
Netherlands 1994	55		173	3.15	0.253
Denmark 1997	51		162	3.15	0.257
Germany 1994	55		174	3.18	0.261
Belgium 1997	53		173	3.26	0.255
Taiwan 1995	56		189	3.38	0.277
France 1994	54		191	3.54	0.288
Switzerland 1992	52		188	3.62	0.307
Austria 1995	48		179	3.73	0.277
Spain 1990	50		197	3.96	0.303
Poland 1995	47		189	4.04	0.318
Canada 1998	46		188	4.13	0.305
Japan 1992[b]	46		192	4.17	0.305
Hungary 1994	50		209	4.19	0.323
Ireland 1987	49		209	4.23	0.328
Australia 1994	45		195	4.33	0.311
UK 1995	46		210	4.57	0.344
Italy 1995	42		202	4.77	0.342
Israel 1997	43		210	4.86	0.336
US 1997	38		214	5.57	0.372
Russia 1995	30		282	9.39	0.447
Mexico 1998	28		328	11.55	0.494
Simple average	49		195	4.26	0.304

(a) Gini coefficients are based on incomes which are bottom coded at 1 per cent of disposable income and top coded at 10 times the median.
(b) Japanese Gini coefficient as calculated in Smeeding (1998) from the 1993 Japanese Survey of Income Redistribution.

FIGURE 1.2 *Source: Timothy M. Smeeding. 2002. "Globalisation, Inequality and the Rich Countries of the G-20: Evidence from the Luxembourg Income Study (LIS)." Reserve Bank of Australia Conference presentation. https://www.rba.gov.au/publications/confs/2002/smeeding. html.*

library used to produce interactive data visualizations on the web, in 2011. Later, more tools would show up on the scene, including Datawrapper (started in 2012), RAWGraphs (2013), PowerBI (2014), Google Data Studio (2016), and Flourish (2018) (Figure 1.3).

FIGURE 1.3

But I stuck with Excel. I tried to learn some of these other tools—I could code in SAS, Stata, and Fortran (yes, Fortran!), but a language like D3 was beyond my skills. Today, I use all of the tools mentioned above to some degree—maybe I make a map in R, a Sankey diagram in RAWGraphs, interactive tables in Google Data Studio—but Excel remains my workhorse and my go-to.

You might be thinking to yourself: Why would someone who spends so much of his time collecting, analyzing, and visualizing data use a tool that requires, at its core, manual processes? For one, it requires time and dedication to become proficient in these other tools and languages. But more importantly, everyone has Excel and everyone can easily get started in Excel.

Think about a small nonprofit organization staffed by six, seven, or eight people. Maybe that organization has one person who is *the* data person—they are responsible for collecting and assembling the data, cleaning it, and making the graphs, slides, and reports.

Maybe that person showed an interest in data visualization or maybe they were thrust into the role because, well, there wasn't really anyone else who could (or wanted to) do it. That person may not have the interest—nor the time—to learn another tool. That person's organization might not be able to afford other tools or might not house a huge amount of data. Or maybe that person's needs are relatively simple—a good bar chart or line chart can go a long way—so creating interactive dashboards or websites is not what their organization needs.

I stick with Excel because for my purposes (and for many other data practitioners like me), Excel is all I need. Hopefully my approach to Excel in this book will demonstrate that you can create great, effective visualizations without having to lean on an entire suite of data visualization tools.

You can think of this book as the hands-on companion to my book on data visualization principles and practices, *Better Data Visualizations: A Guide for Scholars, Researchers, and Wonks*. In that book, I lay out the core principles for creating effective data visualizations and show that any of us can learn how to read different graphs and charts. I explore many different kinds of data visualizations, from static graphs to interactive dashboards, but the bulk of the book is dedicated to presenting more than 80 different graph types with examples from all over the world.

In this book, I show you how to build nearly 30 of the "non-standard" graphs in Excel, graphs that are sometimes more complex than those in the standard drop-down menus and that can sometimes show data in better or more engaging ways. I focus on how to extend and combine the basic graphs in the Excel charting engine; how to use Excel formulas to make your graphs and data more responsive and flexible; and how you can be more productive and efficient when working with the tool.

Learning the steps to create graphs in Excel is just one part of the process. Understanding the basic principles of data visualization design is central to visually communicating your message. I find three guiding principles especially useful to creating effective graphs, charts, and diagrams (each described in more detail in *Better Data Visualizations*):

- **Show the Data.** It's important to decide how much data to show and how to help our reader or user find the key argument, values, or trends. We don't need to show *all* of the data *all* of the time, but we do want to make the visualization as clear as possible.

In a default Excel chart, all elements are given the same weight and focus. The bars in a bar chart and the lines in a line chart, for example, have the same thickness and color weight. In many cases, this approach is fine, but in cases where we want to highlight the most important value or trend, it doesn't work as well. In those cases, we might need to thin some of the lines or lighten some of the colors. Notice in this example how the change from a default chart to one with thicker lines focuses our attention and ties directly to the title of the chart (Figures 1.4 and 1.5).

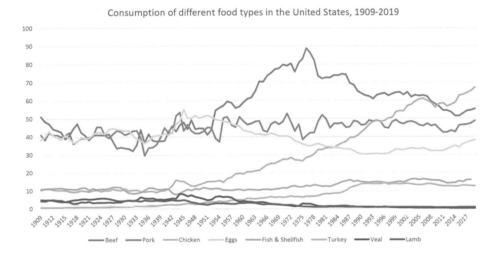

FIGURE 1.4

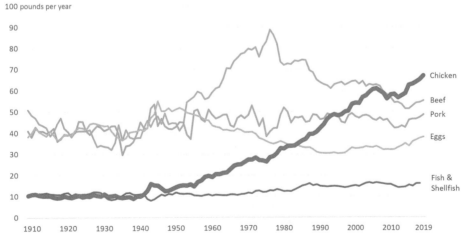

FIGURE 1.5

Setting

Making

Moving

- **Reduce the Clutter.** To help the reader get to the data as fast and as easily as possible, we should reduce or eliminate extraneous gridlines, tick marks, data labels, and data markers. Fortunately, newer versions of Excel are much better at keeping these non-data elements lighter and less emphatic. But as we consider how to add or change these elements, we need to keep in mind that the reader needs to process every additional element we add to a visual.

We could create this graph in Figure 1.6 and maybe, though probably not likely, have a good reason to do so. But all of the heavy gridlines, tick marks, and data markers make it difficult to understand what we are supposed to learn from the graph. By comparison, the graph in Figure 1.7 eliminates or lightens many of these non-data elements to make the point clear.

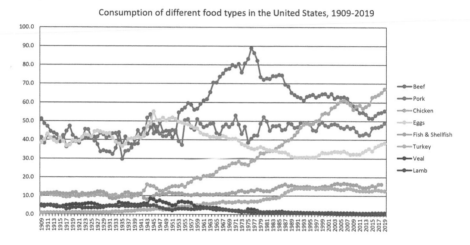

FIGURE 1.6

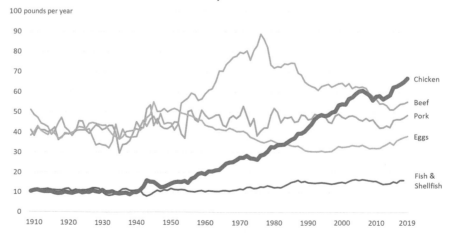

FIGURE 1.7

- **Integrate the Graphics and Text.** When possible, directly label the data in a chart—the bars, lines, and circles. We want to use concise, active titles that prime the reader for what they are supposed to take away from the graph rather than just describing what's in the graph. And we want to include explanatory labels and annotations in and around the graph to help people understand its content.

In Excel, we can add context by drawing lines and adding text boxes, but as you'll see in the chapters to come, I prefer to integrate labels and other annotations by attaching them to data. By inserting new data fields or series in our charts, we can be more certain we are placing these labels exactly where we want them and that they will look more consistent and better aligned. The graph in Figure 1.8 is a recreation of graphs I have seen in practice—with slanted lines and misaligned or inaccurately placed labels. It does not look as polished as the one in Figure 1.9, which has all of those non-data elements inserted by using data placed at the precise position.

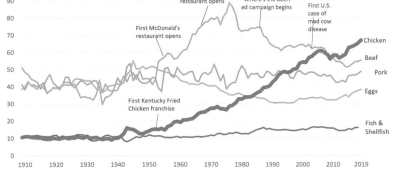

FIGURE 1.8

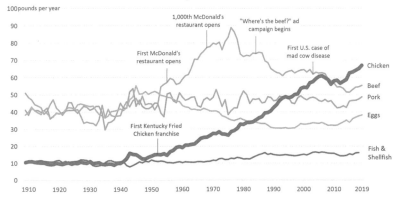

FIGURE 1.9

Setting

Making

Moving

Following these basic principles will help our graphs effectively communicate our data to our audience. Instead of simply handing our reader whatever graph the default Excel settings produce, we can take some active steps to make our data clearer so our readers can understand the point quickly and easily.

Setting

Making

Moving

Chapter **2**

How to Use This Book

Through this book, I intend to provide you with a step-by-step guide to creating better, different, and more effective data visualizations. The book is geared toward people who have at least some experience using Excel and making data visualizations, but Chapters 4 and 5 provide a basic overview of the tool and its charting capabilities. Even if you're an experienced Excel user, I hope you can find some valuable lessons in those chapters.

Before you begin the tutorials, I recommend you visit the website for this book (https://www.routledge.com/9781032343266) and download the tutorial Excel files. There are three files to download:

1. The first contains the data used in each graph but none of the formulas or the final visualization. You will need to work through each tutorial to insert the formulas before making the final graph.

2. The second file contains the data for each graph *and* the final graph shown in the tutorial, fully formatted.

3. The third includes the data and all of the completed formulas, but not the final visualization. This file is probably best used with the "Quick Instructions" tutorials that appear at the end of each chapter, which are discussed below.

DOI: 10.1201/9781003321552-3

All three files include the raw data with source information and website links. I recommend you use the first file to work through the tutorials. It's easy to open the final graphs and use them in your work, but it won't help you learn how to *build* those visualizations. If you don't want to bother with typing formulas, you can use the second or third file to copy the formulas to the first file.

You may already know how to create some of the graphs in this book, but I still recommend you read through the first few tutorials. In those chapters, I set up the primary menus that I use throughout the book. As you go further, you will find that I don't repeat the same basic steps about how to *Select Data, Change Chart* options, or navigate to the formatting menus. At some point, these steps will become second nature as you build, edit, and style your Excel graphs.

Over time, Microsoft has tried to bring the version of Excel on PCs and the version on Macs closer together. In general, the newest versions of Excel have relatively minor differences between the two operating systems. The two biggest differences are adding and editing data in a chart and combining charts. I explain how these differences affect data visualizations generally in the next chapter, and I highlight where those differences exist in each tutorial and how you can create the graph on your particular operating system.

In the tutorials, I use *italics* to refer to Excel menus, options, and buttons, and the `Courier` font to show Excel formulas. Most of the tutorials begin with the visualization in default Excel formats and ends with a version that I've formatted with different colors, fonts, and other layout changes. I don't discuss all of the formatting changes I make in the final graph, but hopefully you'll become familiar enough with the graphing options to make those changes on your own.

The tutorials are independent of one another, but the basic skills build from one to the next. In the first few tutorials, I'll remind you where to click and what button to select to add the data. But after a while, I'll assume you have that skill mastered and won't walk through each step in each menu. Sometimes, I'll use a shorthand like *A > B > C*, which simply means select option/menu A, then option B, then C. I also refrain from telling you to click the OK button on every single menu. It's worth noting that the menus and directions are based on the English (United States) version of the tool, and some tab names and button orders may differ for versions of Excel in other languages.

To help guide you through the tutorials, each chapter has a header table with four pieces of information:

- **Difficulty Level.** Beginner, Intermediate, or Advanced. This level is a rough classification based on the number of steps, how many different chart types are used, and how much data preparation is needed. Generally, the tutorials grow from the easiest to the hardest over the course of the book.

Setting | Making | Moving

- **Primary Data Type.** I cover five data types in this book and have included an entry for the *primary* data type typically used for each graph. It is possible, of course, that some graphs may be used to visualize multiple data types, so this categorization is just a guide.

  1. **Categorical**. Visualizations that are used to compare categories or different values—the classic case is a bar chart.

  2. **Distribution**. Visualizations that are used to show the spread of data, like a histogram or box-and-whisker plot.

  3. **Geospatial**. Visualizations that are used to show geographic patterns in the data or, in other words, maps.

  4. **Part-to-Whole**. Graphs that are used to show a value relative to the whole—think pie charts.

  5. **Time**. Graphs that are used to show changes over time, like a line chart.

- **Combine Charts.** This cell provides a Yes/No classification for whether the tutorial requires combining chart types. Although combining charts doesn't necessarily increase the difficulty of making the graph, it certainly adds an extra step. In Chapter 4, I describe how to combine chart types and how that process differs for PC users and Mac users.

- **Formulas.** To demonstrate how to prepare the data for graphing, some of the tutorials include formulas or other data manipulations. This field lists the formulas used in the tutorial. In Chapter 5, we explore how these Excel formulas work. If you don't want to bother with these steps, simply use the second or third Excel files, which have all of the data fields filled in.

Table 2.1 contains this information for every chapter.

The end of each chapter includes a "Quick Instructions" list, an abbreviated set instructions to build each graph. There is also a separate Appendix at the end of the book with a full collection of the Quick Instructions for every tutorial. These instructions don't always line up with the numbered steps in the full tutorials and tend to use more shorthand than a full description of each step. They also don't include the steps to set up and organize the data with formulas or how to style the colors, axes, text, and other aesthetic elements. Because the full details are not included in these bulleted lists, you may want to use the Excel file that includes the formulas and has the data preparation completed. If you feel you have mastered the steps or just need a quick refresher, these quick instructions may be what you need.

Setting

Making

Moving

Setting | Making | Moving

TABLE 2.1

Chapter Number	Chapter Title	Difficulty: Beginner/ Intermediate/ Advanced	Primary Data Type: Categorical/Time/ Geospatial/ Distribution/ Part-to-Whole	Combine Charts: Yes/No	Formulas: IF, SUMIF, AVERAGEIF, etc.
7	Sparklines	Beginner	Time	No	None
8	Heatmap	Beginner	Categorical	No	None
9	Stripe chart	Beginner	Categorical	No	None
10	Waffle chart	Beginner	Part-to-whole	No	IF, &
11	Gantt chart	Beginner	Time	No	IF, AND, &
12	Comparing values with two graph types	Intermediate	Categorical	Yes	None
13	Broken stacked bar chart	Intermediate	Categorical	No	MAX
14	Diverging bar chart	Intermediate	Categorical	No	SUM
15	Block shading (same frequency)	Beginner	Categorical	Yes	None
16	Block shading (different frequencies)	Intermediate	Categorical	Yes	None
17	Mark an event with a line	Intermediate	Time	Yes	IF, OR, VALUE, RIGHT
18	Dot plot	Intermediate	Categorical	No	IF, AVERAGE
19	Slope chart	Intermediate	Time	No	&
20	Overlaid gridlines	Intermediate	Categorical	Yes	None
21	Lollipop	Intermediate	Categorical	No	None
22	Bullet chart	Advanced	Categorical	No	MAX, AVERAGE, MATCH, TEXT, CHAR, &
23	Tile grid map	Advanced	Geospatial	No	VLOOKUP, MIN, MAX
24	Histogram	Advanced	Distribution	No	COUNTIFS, &
25	Marimekko	Advanced	Categorical	Yes	IF, INT, VLOOKUP, SUM
26	Cycle plot	Advanced	Time	Yes	IF, AVERAGEIF, TEXT
27	Strip chart	Intermediate	Distribution	No	None
28	Raincloud plot	Advanced	Distribution	Yes	WEEKNUM, AVERAGEIF, PERCENTILE, COUNTIF, IF

I maintain a separate webpage on my PolicyViz website (https://policyviz. com/pv_books/data-visualization-in-excel-a-guide-for-beginners-intermedia-tes-and-wonks/) with additional resources, files, and links to help you create better, more effective data visualizations in Excel. That page will expand over time with more Excel tutorials, tips, and answers to common questions from this book. If you run into trouble, check if the answers to your questions are available there.

Okay, we're now set up to go. Let's talk about data visualization in Excel.

Setting

Making

Moving

Chapter 3

The Philosophy of Data Visualization in Excel

Microsoft Excel, with its more than 750 million users worldwide (Wann, 2020), continues to be the standard for desktop data analysis. Excel's data visualization library has significantly expanded since it was introduced in 1985, but at its core, it's still a drag-and-drop tool. On the one hand, that simple functionality makes it more accessible because anyone can open it up, type in some data, and start making something. On the other hand, the tool is limited by what is in the drop-down menus and what is in the library of options.

I hope the tutorials in this book can move you beyond the standard graphs in the drop-down menu and show you how to create other data visualizations—even those that you think on the surface may not be something Excel can handle.

There are a lot of data analysis and visualization tools you can use to work with and display your data. But whatever tool you use, it's important to keep in mind that it's just that: a tool. As much as I am a fan of Excel and its capabilities, it clearly can't do everything. I wouldn't use Excel to create an interactive data visualization for the *Washington Post* website, and I wouldn't use it for a large dataset with millions of observations. But if I need to create a basic bar chart or line chart—or even some more complex charts like those found later in this book—Excel might be the perfect tool for the job.

Before diving into our Excel tutorials, it's worth understanding the world of data visualization tools. In the image below, I've organized almost 20 tools by their "barrier to entry," which we can think of as the difficulty of getting

DOI: 10.1201/9781003321552-4

started. On the left side of the axis, I've put tools that are primarily drag-and-drop or click-based—tools like Excel and Google Sheets, or browser-based tools like Datawrapper and Flourish. These tools are easy to use and anyone can open them up, paste in some data, and make a chart. On the right side of the axis, I've put tools that have a higher barrier to entry. These tools are primarily programming languages like JavaScript, Python, and R, which require some understanding of computer programming and its syntax (Figure 3.1). (See the Appendix 2 for a more detailed list of data visualization tools.)

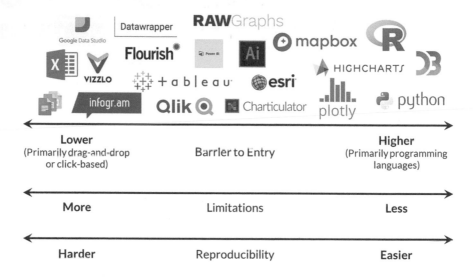

FIGURE 3.1   Source: Based on image from Jonathan Schwabish, Better Data Visualizations: A Guide for Scholars, Researchers, and Wonks.

There are two tradeoffs with this barrier to entry metric. The first is the *limitations* of these tools. The tools on the left, which everyone can use to create a graph, are more limited in what they can be used to create. What's included in the tool and in the drop-down menus dictates what we can make. For the tools on the right, we are only limited by our ability to write the correct code to make our preferred visualization.

The other tradeoff is how *reproducible* the visualizations are in each tool. To teach someone how to make a graph in Excel or Google Sheets, we need to show them each step in the process. And if the data changes in some way—say there are more values or an additional series—we might need to change the approach we used to create the graph. On the other side of the axis, however, we can share a snippet of code or script, and someone else can run it to create the same visualization with little additional work.

This book seeks to inch Excel to the right as much as possible—to make our data visualizations in Excel act like a coding language without requiring any actual code. By incorporating actual data into all elements of our charts—the labels, lines, shapes, and annotations—we can update the data or share it with someone else with fewer challenges of reproducing and extending it.

Using data in all facets of our Excel charts achieves two things. First, it makes the graphs easier to move from one tool to another. If we draw a line on top of a bar chart in Excel then try to copy it over to PowerPoint or Word, we need to select and copy both elements because Excel views them as two separate objects. But if we draw a line with data, Excel sees a single object, which makes moving it between programs easier and more consistent.

Second, this approach is more reproducible. We cannot avoid the fact that teaching someone how to create a complicated chart in Excel requires a step-by-step guide (ahem, this book?). But if we use formulas to subset and select our data and use data to add elements to our graphs, we can make that process easier and more reproducible.

Consider the annual unemployment rate in the US from 1950 through 2021 (Figure 3.2). We can insert a line chart of these data (in columns A and B) with just a few clicks. But what if we want to label the first year of each decade (e.g., 1950, 1960, 1970, and so on) and include its unemployment rate?

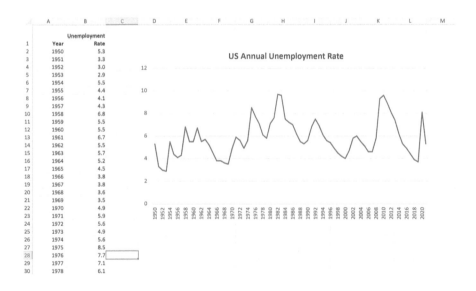

FIGURE 3.2

If we right-click on the line (CTRL+Click on Mac) and select the *Add Data Labels* option, Excel will add a label to every data point on the line. We could selectively delete the 64 labels we don't want, but this approach is tedious, isn't sensitive to adding more data, and really stinks if we make a mistake because we will have to start again (Figure 3.3).

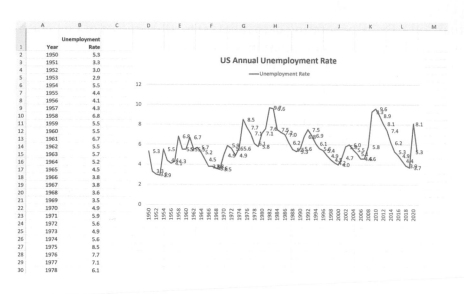

	Year	Unemployment Rate
1		
2	1950	5.3
3	1951	3.3
4	1952	3.0
5	1953	2.9
6	1954	5.5
7	1955	4.4
8	1956	4.1
9	1957	4.3
10	1958	6.8
11	1959	5.5
12	1960	5.5
13	1961	6.7
14	1962	5.5
15	1963	5.7
16	1964	5.2
17	1965	4.5
18	1966	3.8
19	1967	3.8
20	1968	3.6
21	1969	3.5
22	1970	4.9
23	1971	5.9
24	1972	5.6
25	1973	4.9
26	1974	5.6
27	1975	8.5
28	1976	7.7
29	1977	7.1
30	1978	6.1

FIGURE 3.3

What if we added another data series to the chart instead? For this new series, we include only the data for years we want to label (using a simple IF formula, which we'll cover later). Now, when we include both lines in the chart, we can select our second line (shown with the orange dots below) and right-click to add the data labels on just those eight points (Figure 3.4).

Using this strategy is faster, easier to extend, and easier to replicate with additional or other data. By incorporating formulas into the second series—which we will cover in Chapter 4—we can more easily paste in new data that automatically updates through the formulas and into the graphs.

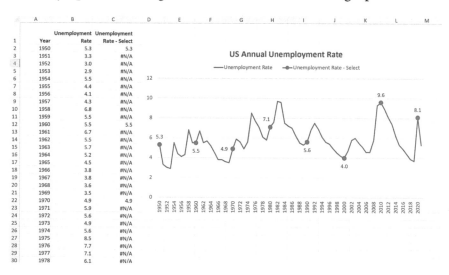

	Year	Unemployment Rate	Unemployment Rate - Select
1			
2	1950	5.3	5.3
3	1951	3.3	#N/A
4	1952	3.0	#N/A
5	1953	2.9	#N/A
6	1954	5.5	#N/A
7	1955	4.4	#N/A
8	1956	4.1	#N/A
9	1957	4.3	#N/A
10	1958	6.8	#N/A
11	1959	5.5	#N/A
12	1960	5.5	5.5
13	1961	6.7	#N/A
14	1962	5.5	#N/A
15	1963	5.7	#N/A
16	1964	5.2	#N/A
17	1965	4.5	#N/A
18	1966	3.8	#N/A
19	1967	3.8	#N/A
20	1968	3.6	#N/A
21	1969	3.5	#N/A
22	1970	4.9	4.9
23	1971	5.9	#N/A
24	1972	5.6	#N/A
25	1973	4.9	#N/A
26	1974	5.6	#N/A
27	1975	8.5	#N/A
28	1976	7.7	#N/A
29	1977	7.1	#N/A
30	1978	6.1	#N/A

FIGURE 3.4

To best create data visualizations in Excel, we need to recognize that Excel works within two main frameworks. First, it has three primary shapes (or encodings) to represent data: lines, bars, and circles. If the data visualization we want to create is made up of lines, bars, or circles, it's likely something that Excel can do. There is a small caveat here: the shapes need to be of a non-trivial size or length. Take a map—the coast of Florida, for example, has a lot of turns and curves. Excel is not going to be very good at drawing that coast because each turn and curve requires a new data point and line, ultimately necessitating a massive dataset.

Second, Excel works in a horizontal (X) and vertical (Y) space. Of course, this basic framework is how we plot data, but it's worth noting that Excel doesn't work in an X-Y-Z (3D) space, which many people use to create "cool-looking" graphs. Excel does have some 3D capability, but the 3D graphs in Excel are not truly 3D! Excel uses a perspective approach to rotate these graphs, so we don't need to wear the classic red-blue glasses to see them (Figure 3.5).

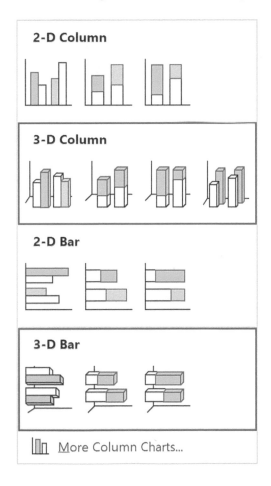

FIGURE 3.5

Setting

Making

Moving

Take a look at these two graphs. In the 2D representation in Figure 3.6, the value of each bar is clear—40, 30, 20, and 10. But in the 3D representation in Figure 3.7—using the exact same data—the tops of the bars don't touch the appropriate gridline. The "3D effect" in Excel distorts the data, and I recommend against using those graph types.

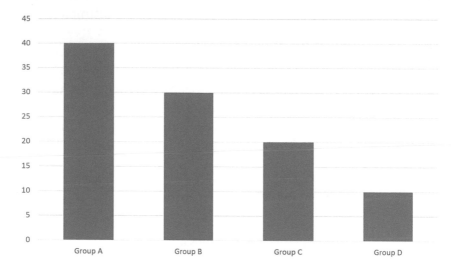

FIGURE 3.6

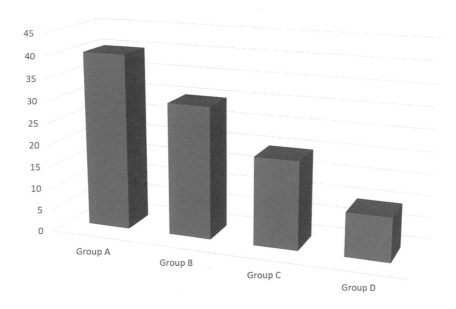

FIGURE 3.7

Excel certainly has its fair share of graphs that do not follow what many consider to be data visualization best practices. But it does have a core set of graphs that we can modify and combine to create even more data visualizations than the basic graphs in the drop-down menus. As you work your way through the tutorials in this book, keep in mind that Excel enables us to work in three basic shapes (lines, bars, and circles) and in a basic X-Y space. We will use a variety of formulas to analyze, clean, and organize our data to create graphs that are easy to manipulate and recreate with new data or data that changes.

Before we get to that point, let's cover some basics of how Excel works.

Setting

Making

Moving

Chapter 4

Introduction to Making Graphs in Excel

For a beginner Excel user, the program can seem daunting with its many available menus to clean, analyze, and visualize data. But once you have the lay of the land, you'll find the tool isn't as scary as it is at first glance. I find the tool is well-organized and enables users to gain familiarity by using the same menus time and again to make changes to the spreadsheet and graph elements. That means we don't need to learn new menus, views, or buttons for every task. And in my opinion, the newer versions of Excel—through the Office 365 subscription model—are a big improvement over the older versions.

Don't get me wrong: there are some things about Excel that drive me crazy, and many of the graphs in the basic drop-down menu are drop-down dreadful. But the tool is built in such a way that we can make more advanced visualizations simply by understanding what it can and cannot do.

In this chapter, I introduce some basic parts of Excel for users who may have never opened the tool or made a graph. I focus primarily on the sections of the tool that are most relevant to creating effective graphs. There are many terrific blogs, resources, and books available if you want to learn other aspects of Excel like Pivot Tables, PowerQuery, macros and the Visual Basic for Applications (VBA) language, and more advanced formulas (see Appendix 3 for a curated list).

This chapter also provides some valuable information for the more experienced user. Not every Excel user knows about the *Plot Area* and the *Chart Area* or how to modify the properties of Excel charts. I've inserted this icon (🗿)

DOI: 10.1201/9781003321552-5

before the sections that I think everyone can benefit from learning, not just the first-time users. If you are experienced with Excel, you can jump to those icons to see if there are some nuggets of wisdom here to help you become a better Excel user.

The Excel View

Before we begin to explore using Excel, we must understand how the program is organized. The main area at the top of the Excel window is called the *ribbon* and each section of the ribbon (e.g., *Home*, *Insert*, etc.) are called *Tabs*. Within each Tab are a variety of options, menus, and buttons. Additional Tabs will appear when we are working within a specific element of Excel, like a graph or Pivot table. Below the ribbon is the *Formula Bar* where we can begin to type in a formula for our spreadsheet and Excel will prompt us with formula options (see next chapter) (Figure 4.1).

FIGURE 4.1

🌐 The narrow area above the ribbon is called the *Quick Access Toolbar* or *QAT*. When opening Excel for the first time, there will be two or three icons, likely for *Save* (⊟), *Undo* (⤺), and *Redo* (⤻). We can customize the QAT by selecting the down arrow on the far right side and choosing *Customize the Ribbon*. Once the dialog box opens up, we can add commands to the QAT or even create a new Tab. Adding a variety of commands to the QAT can help us be more productive by reducing the number of clicks we have to make.

🦎 Alternatively, instead of customizing the QAT, you can familiarize yourself with keyboard shortcuts. You're most likely familiar with common shortcuts like CTRL+C for *Copy*, CTRL+V for *Paste*, and CTRL+S for *Save*. There are hundreds of other shortcuts that my memory isn't strong enough to remember all of the time (and they differ between PCs and Macs). But one other incredibly useful shortcut is CTRL+1 (CMD+1 on Macs), which will bring you to the *Format > Current Selection* menu (the drop-down menu in the far left part of the *Format* tab) of whatever you have selected. Want to format the horizontal (x-) axis in your chart? Select it and hit CTRL+1. Want to format the cells in the spreadsheet? Select them and hit CTRL+1. For me, CTRL+1 is as important as all of the other standard shortcuts we have come to know and love.

The spreadsheet itself—called "worksheets" in Excel parlance—takes up the main area of the view and consists of rows (horizontal) and columns (vertical), with the intersections called cells. Rows are numbered in Excel, and their default height depends on the computer's monitor and resolution—rows on my Windows Surface Pro have a default height of 38 pixels, while rows on my MacBook Pro have a default height of 16 pixels. Columns are labeled with letters, and their size will also depend on the screen—columns on my Surface Pro have a default width of 136 pixels and columns on my MacBook Pro have a default width of 65 pixels. Both dimensions can be adjusted by selecting the column/row and right-clicking or by dragging the column/row edge. The spreadsheet gridlines can also be modified or turned off by using the *Show* menu in the *View* tab.

You may notice that Excel shows two numbers for row heights and column widths. A column width unit in Excel is equal to the width of one character, with the default on my Surface Pro equal to 47 characters or 136 pixels. Row height is measured in pixels *and* points, which can make it a little annoying to compare the dimensions of rows and columns. Fortunately, if we stick to pixels and don't worry about converting to characters or points, it's not such a big deal. Excel determines the width of columns by the character width of the font, which can vary between monitors, screen resolutions, operating systems (e.g., Windows and Mac), and font families. As a result, some of the column widths or row heights in the tutorials might not look perfect on every machine, but we can adjust them to fit our preferences.

At the bottom of the Excel window are some basic controls of the worksheet. Each worksheet has a default name and number (e.g., Sheet1, Sheet2), but the name and color of the tabs can be controlled by right- or double-clicking. We can toggle between sheets by clicking on the desired sheet or by using the left/right triangles/arrows. We can also control the view (*Normal, Page Layout, Page Break*) with the buttons on the right side and the zoom level with the slider next to that.

Setting

Making

Moving

A few other keyboard combinations can come in handy when selecting data and navigating through the various menus.

1. CTRL+Arrow keys (CMD+Arrow on Macs) will bring us to the last used cell in the current data region. If there is data in cells A1 to A100, place the cursor in cell A1 and press CTRL+Down Arrow. The cursor will go all the way down to cell A100.

2. SHIFT+CTRL+Arrow (SHIFT+CMD+Arrow on Macs) will let us *select* all of the data in the cells going in the direction of the arrow. In the previous example, if we pressed SHIFT+CTRL+Down Arrow, we would select all of the data in cells A1 to A100.

3. ALT+. Many of the buttons in the ribbon have a dedicated keyboard shortcut assigned to them. With any cell selected, if we press the ALT key plus a letter, number, or function key, we can shortcut right to that tab or command. Personally, I'm a mouse-first user, so I don't rely on the ALT+ commands (plus, they don't work on Macs), but ALT+ commands can help you work faster. Table 4.1 contains a curated list of the most important shortcuts.

TABLE 4.1 Selected Useful Excel Keyboard Shortcuts

Shortcut	PC	Mac
Copy	CTRL+C	CMD+C
Cut	CTRL+X	CMD+X
Paste	CTRL+V	CMD+V
Undo last action	CTRL+Z	CMD+Z
Redo last action	CTRL+Y	CMD+Y
Find	CTRL+F	CMD+F
Save	CTRL+S	CMD+S
Save as	CTRL+SHIFT+S	CMD+SHIFT+S
Add hyperlink	CTRL+K	CMD+K
Format (almost) anything	CTRL+1	CMD+1
Go to next worksheet	CTRL+PgDn	Option+Right Arrow
Go to previous worksheet	CTRL+PgUp	Option+Left Arrow
Select entire row	SHIFT+SPACE	SHIFT+SPACE
Select entire column	CTRL+SPACE	CTRL+SPACE
Select entire worksheet	CTRL+A	CMD+A
Move active cell/menu right in a selection	TAB	TAB
Move active cell/menu left in a selection	SHIFT+TAB	SHIFT+TAB

Excel Graph Types

To insert a chart in Excel, we must navigate to the *Insert* tab. There are about eight main chart types listed in the default *Charts* tab of the ribbon (again, the layout looks a little different between PCs and Macs) (Figure 4.2).

FIGURE 4.2

Inserting a chart is easy—select the data in the worksheet and select one of the charts from the *Insert* menu. Excel will place the graph closest to your cursor, but you can always move it to wherever you want it in the worksheet. Once these steps are done, a few things will happen.

1. A new *Chart Design* tab appears in the ribbon. This tab enables us to add different elements to the chart, select data, and change the chart type (Figure 4.3).

   The *Chart Design* menu contains some especially important parts:

   a. On the far-left area of the menu is the *Add Chart Element* button. Clicking on this button will reveal a number of ways we can add,

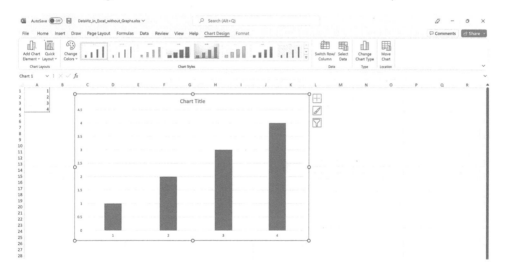

FIGURE 4.3

   subtract, or edit elements in the chart, including axis titles, gridlines, data labels, and more (Figure 4.4). We will use this menu extensively in the tutorials. As you gain more experience using the various menus and creating visualizations, I will assume you can find the menu on your own and won't describe it each time.

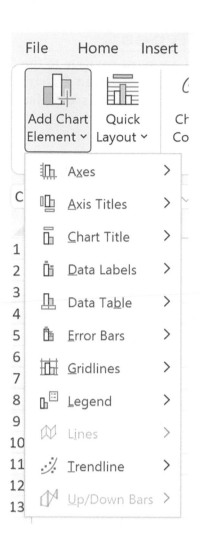

FIGURE 4.4

b. Toward the right side of the tab is the *Switch Row/Column* button. Excel orients the selected data based on the program's default behavior, so if our data stretch across columns, Excel might plot it along the rows and vice versa. We can easily switch the orientation of our data by selecting this button rather than changing the layout of the data (Figure 4.5).

c. Next to that button is the *Select Data* button, which we can use to add, subtract, and edit the data in the chart. We can also access this button by right-clicking in the chart and choosing the *Select Data* option in the menu. We will add and edit data in our charts throughout the book, so it's important to know how to use this menu as we will use it over and over again (Figures 4.6–4.8).

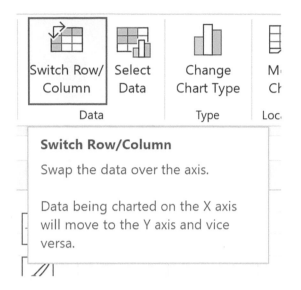

Switch Row/Column

Swap the data over the axis.

Data being charted on the X axis will move to the Y axis and vice versa.

FIGURE 4.5

FIGURE 4.6

Setting

Making

Moving

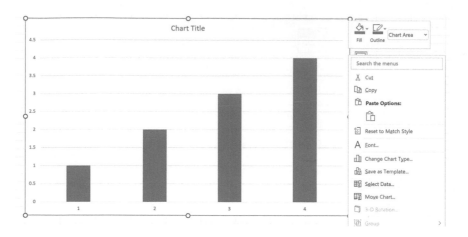

FIGURE 4.7

FIGURE 4.8

Sometimes when we add or edit a new series, Excel will insert a placeholder in the selection box. That text will be a "={1}" character, and we will need to overwrite or delete it before inserting our data series. If we don't overwrite it, we will end up with a data entry like "={1}=Sheet1!$A$1:$A$10" and Excel will show an error message. To fix our data, we will need to correct the formula or re-insert the reference.

d. Finally, the *Change Chart Type* button (found by right-clicking on the chart or by using the button in the *Chart Design* tab) enables us to change the chart type directly without having to delete what we have (Figure 4.9). We can also use this menu to combine chart types, something we will do a lot in this book. On PCs, there is a *Combo* chart option at the bottom of this menu, which allows us to select a chart type for one data series and a different chart type for another data series. Be careful to note that if we select an entire chart and use the *Combo* chart option, Excel will change every series to the *Clustered Column* chart (which is apparently the default chart option). 🙄 Although it's not specified, every time you use the *Combo* chart option, it's best practice to select the chart series you want to change first before navigating to the *Combo* chart option (Figure 4.10).

On Macs, select the series in the chart you want to change, then select the new chart type in the *Change Chart Type* menu (Figure 4.11). There is no *Combo* chart option on Macs, so you need to have the series selected to change it.

Not all charts can be combined, and with few exceptions, we can only combine two chart types at a time.

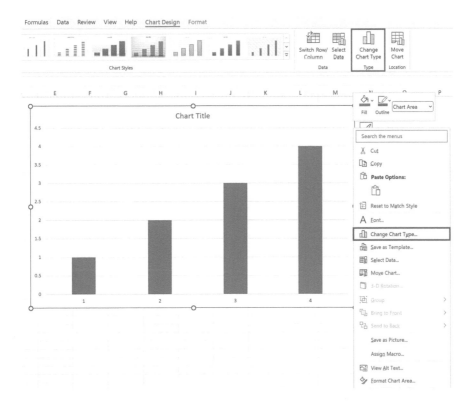

FIGURE 4.9 *Change chart type menu on PCs.*

Setting

Making

Moving

FIGURE 4.10 Combo chart option menu on PCs.

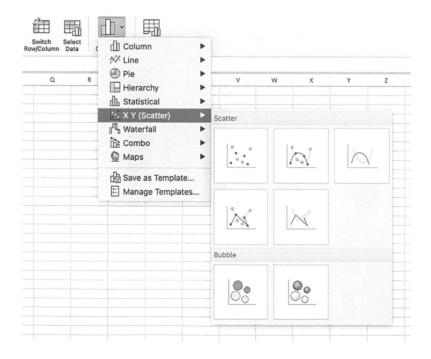

FIGURE 4.11 Change chart type menu on Macs.

2. When we select a chart, a new *Format* tab will appear. This tab houses various formatting options including colors, text options, and chart dimensions (Figure 4.12).

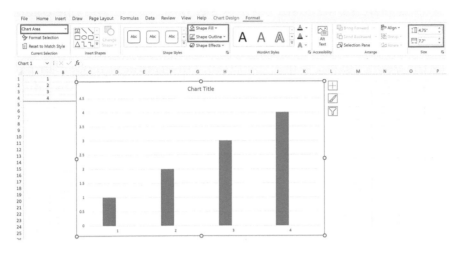

FIGURE 4.12

A few buttons and menus are particularly important here:

a. 🕷 The drop-down menu on the far left in the *Current Selection* area ("Chart Area" in the image) lists all of the elements in our chart, including axes, gridlines, and the data. If we have a chart with a lot of data or other elements in it, we can use this drop-down menu to select an element.

b. The *Shape Fill* and *Shape Outline* buttons near the center of the menu enable us to control the "fill" colors and "outline" colors of the elements in our chart.

c. On the far right of the tab are two fields that control the size of the chart. The default size for a chart is 3×5 inches. If we want to change the size and keep this ratio the same, we can check the box next to these fields and change the values by using the up/down arrows or typing new numbers.

3. The chart will appear near the center of the window and will have a series of default aspects, including a horizontal (x-) and vertical (y-) axis, default colors, a "Chart Title" box, and a default size of 3×5 inches.

4. When the chart is selected, the data included in the chart will be highlighted in the worksheet.

Setting

Making

Moving

Office 365, which launched in 2013, introduced better and more current security features and allowed Microsoft to add features or fix bugs. One feature that Microsoft added to Excel was a new set of graphs. Some of these graphs—such as treemaps, sunburst diagrams, and box-and-whisker plots—require different data layouts than the standard one row per observation and one column per variable. 🕶 If you'd like to explore these graph types but don't know how to set up the data, you can insert the chart in PowerPoint (using the standard *Chart* area of the *Insert* menu). When you do so, PowerPoint will open an Excel file with placeholder data, which you can use as a template for your own data entry and graph creation.

Chart Parts and Properties

Many new data practitioners assume that a chart is nothing more than a horizontal axis, a vertical axis, and plotted data. But it's worth recognizing that a graph consists of many different parts that we can control and change.

Take this basic line chart, which shows the monthly unemployment rate in the US from 1960 to 2021 (Figure 4.13). At first glance, you may think, "Okay, the line goes up and down, up and down." You may also notice that there is a horizontal (x-) axis, a vertical (y-) axis, a title at the top, and so on.

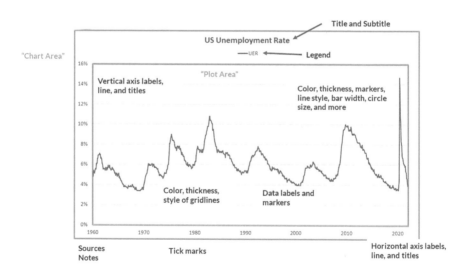

FIGURE 4.13

But there is a *lot* more going on in this graph than the basic line and title, and we can control and style all of it. We can set the font type, size, and orientation of the title, subtitle, sources, and notes. We can show or hide the vertical and horizontal axes, and style their color and thickness. We can turn tick marks on or off; change the style, thickness, color, and frequency of the gridlines; and, of course, style the actual data shown in the graph, be it bars, lines, or circles.

In the example, I annotated (and added a line around) what Excel calls the *Plot Area* and the *Chart Area*. The styles, sizes, and arrangement of these areas can be adjusted—the *Plot Area* can be made smaller, for example, to make room for labels or other text—and is something that we will encounter in a few of the tutorials.

There are a few ways to modify the different chart elements. First, we can select the chart and use the *Add Chart Element* button in the *Chart Design* menu (which will often appear as *Chart Design > Add Chart Element* in the tutorials). Second, we can select the *plus* button that appears next to a selected chart (PCs only). Third, we can right-click on any element of the chart and select the appropriate *Format* menu, such as *Format Axis* or *Format Data Series*. Finally, we can use the CTRL+1 keyboard shortcut (CMD+1 on Macs) to modify the selected object.

Using any of these options will bring you to the *Format* menu. This menu has numerous options, but the top-line icons are as follows (Figure 4.14):

- The *paint can* icon lets us change the fill and outline colors of chart elements as well as change or style markers in the chart.

- The *pentagon* icon allows us to add styling options like a shadow or a glow around chart elements.

- The *arrow/square* icon contains options to control different text alignment features such as direction and margins.

- The *bar chart* icon differs for each part of the chart, but can include axis ranges, bar widths, and number formats.

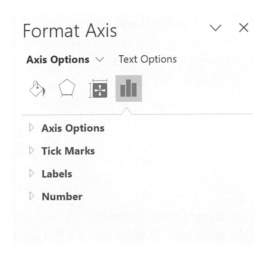

FIGURE 4.14

🦎 All of these options are available for the chart as a whole as well, so we can change the border or background color of the entire chart. The *Format Chart Area* menu also includes a *Chart Options* area, which you can see in Figure 4.15. Here, we can control the dimensions of the entire chart using the fields under *Size* (though there are no direct controls for the *Plot Area*). We can also set whether the chart can be moved and/or sized with the cells in the *Properties* area of the menu. If we create a chart and insert or delete a row or column, the default option (*Move and size with cells*) in the *Properties* area dictates that the size of the chart will also change. But if we want to change things in the spreadsheet without changing the size of our chart, we can select the other options.

FIGURE 4.15

Excel is sensitive to using actual numbers in our charts, which means it won't know what to do with text or with spaces. Although it can be infuriating when we get an error and can't figure out why, it can also be used to our advantage. We can (and we will!) insert an "=NA()" formula in our worksheet cells when making graphs because Excel will ignore those values. Let's say we want to add a data series to a chart in order to add labels (again, something we will do a lot!), we can insert NAs in the data series instead of 0s because Excel will ignore the NAs but will plot the 0s.

Recognizing the Defaults

Throughout all of these options and menus, we must recognize Excel's defaults and when we need to change them. Excel simply plots the data how we specify—it's not doing anything right or wrong, so being aware of its default behaviors and how to change them is crucial.

There are six main default behaviors in Excel that are worth keeping in mind because they will come up again and again in the tutorials.

1. **Adjusting the Vertical Axis Range and Units.** As a default, Excel will not let you plot data to the top of the vertical axis. If you need to change the vertical axis limits, you can do so in the *Format Axis* menu.

   The scatterplot in Figure 4.16 shows per capita gross domestic product (GDP) on the x-axis and life expectancy on the y-axis. The default range for the vertical axis is 0 to 100, but we should adjust that minimum for two reasons. First, 0 is (fortunately) not an average life expectancy for any country. Second, unlike in a bar chart where a baseline of 0 is important and necessary, in a scatterplot, we can use a nonzero axis. In this case, we can type "50" in the *Minimum* box to manually fix the starting point. If you add more data, the *Maximum* value might change, but the *Minimum* will stay at 50 until you reset it.

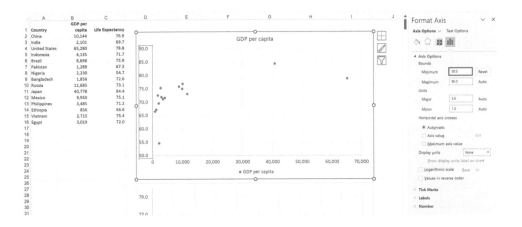

FIGURE 4.16

2. **Length of Error Bars.** Error bars are useful for our graphs because they allow us not only to denote uncertainty or ranges but also to add annotations or pointers to specific data points. Excel has preset defaults when we insert error bars into our charts. 🦠 For scatterplots, Excel will insert two error bars: one along the vertical dimension and one along the horizontal dimensions. For line charts and bar charts, Excel will only insert an error bar along one dimension.

We can also adjust the length and appearance of the error bars, but it's worth noting that the default value of all error bars is set at a *Fixed Value* equal to one. If I zoom into the GDP-life expectancy scatterplot and add error bars, the vertical error bars are visible but the horizontal error bars are not (Figure 4.17). The horizontal bars exist, but because they have a length of 1, they cannot be seen because the range on the x-axis (0–5,000) is much, much larger than that of the y-axis (65–80).

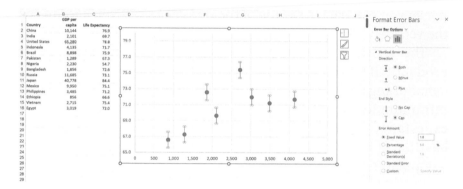

FIGURE 4.17

3. **Creating the graph.** There are some basic defaults that apply when we insert a chart in Excel. Take a scatterplot—when we select two data series and insert a scatterplot (or what Excel calls a *Scatter*), Excel will, by default, place the first series in the X (horizontal) position and the second series in the Y (vertical) position. We can always change the organization of the data in the worksheet or in the chart by using the options in the *Select Data Source* menu (Figure 4.18).

4. **Color transparency.** We will sometimes have bars, lines, or dots that overlap one another. In some cases, we might need to winnow down our data to show a smaller number of series, but in other cases, we can change the transparency of the colors to help show the data behind the object. In the *Format Data Series* menu, we can change the transparency of the fill and border colors by selecting a color and adjusting the *Transparency* slider (Figure 4.19).

Setting

Making

Moving

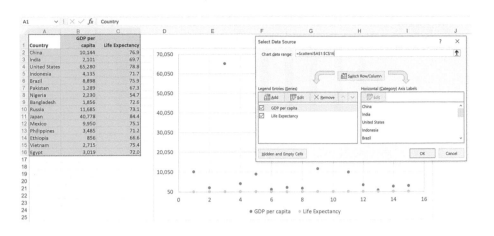

FIGURE 4.18

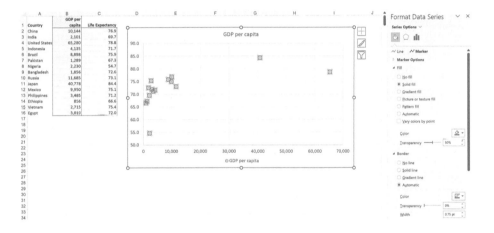

FIGURE 4.19

5. **Bars and gap width.** For bar charts, Excel sets the default widths of the bars and the gaps between bars to −27% and 219%, respectively. We can adjust these widths by right-clicking on the bars and selecting the *Format Data Series* menu. Here, we can use the *Series Overlap* and *Gap Width* options to adjust. *Series Overlap* refers to having bars sit on top of each other instead of next to each other. *Gap Width* refers to the space between the bars, so adjusting the width of the gap changes the width of the bars. The chart on the left of Figure 4.20 uses the default settings for these options, while the chart on the right uses edited values of 0% and 100%. Personally, I prefer the 0% and 100% combination because the ratio of bar width to white space looks better to me, but neither setting is objectively better than the other.

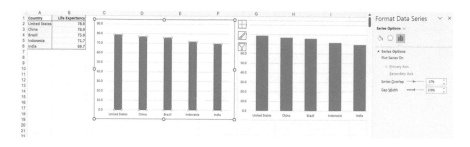

FIGURE 4.20

6. **Primary and Secondary Axes.** The final styling Excel default to be aware of is the ability to place data on secondary axes. When we insert a column chart, for example, Excel places the data along a horizontal (x-) axis at the bottom of the chart and a vertical (y-) axis along the left side of the chart. We could add more data and apply them to the "secondary" axes—a horizontal axis at the top of the chart and a vertical axis along the right side of the chart. 🐢 In most cases, Excel will not show the *secondary horizontal axis* by default. Instead, we need to make that axis visible by using the *Chart Options* menus. If we add a data series to a chart on the secondary axis but it doesn't look quite right, we may need to turn on and adjust those axis values (Figure 4.21).

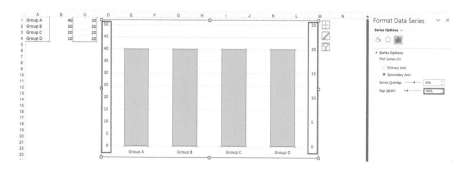

FIGURE 4.21

Worksheet Formatting

Although this book focuses on data visualization, the formatting options in worksheets, which are generally used for text elements, can still be useful for us. As you'll see, there are lots of charts we can make directly in the worksheet by using the formatting options.

The primary formatting tools in Excel are located in the *Home* tab of the ribbon, and we'll discuss each area, delineated by vertical lines, from left to right along the first half of the tab (Figure 4.22).

FIGURE 4.22

Copying and Pasting

You probably know the basic keyboard shortcuts for copying and pasting (CTRL+C and CTRL+V), but the *Paste* drop-down menu is important because it can allow us to paste data or calculations as formulas with or without the cell formatting, as values (just the numbers, no formulas), or as a variety of other options. In addition to the *Paste* menu options and the well-known keyboard shortcuts, Excel also lets you can drag the contents of a cell—values or formulas—across rows or columns by grabbing the green square in the bottom-right part of the selected cell. You can double-click on that part of the square and the cell contents (including formulas) will fill up to the next blank cell (Figure 4.23).

FIGURE 4.23

In the tutorials, when you see something like, "Copy-and-paste the formula down the column," I am referring to three steps: select the cell with the original formula and copy (CTRL+C), select the cells where you want to add the formula, and paste (CTRL+V). Alternatively, you can select the cell with the original formula and drag it down the length of the column using the green square in the bottom-right part of the cell.

Text Formatting

In the text formatting area, we can control the font type and size by using the two drop-down menus, and we can add boldface, italics, or underline.

The button with the grid is the *Borders* area of the tab, which allows us to add borders around cells. The color and thickness of the border can be controlled at the bottom of that menu. The default is a black border, but we might have cells filled with color and want to use a white border so changing the color of the border can be helpful. Finally, we can change the color fill of a cell in the menu with the paint can icon and the color of the text in the menu with the capital letter *A* icon.

Cell Alignment

Here, we can control the vertical alignment of the cells using the top three icons and the horizontal alignment using the bottom three icons. We can also rotate the text by using the icon with the letters "ab" on top of an arrow. Finally, we can indent text with the two icons that show arrows and three lines, a tool that can be useful when we want to align numbers in tables (see Chapter 29).

Although a vertical line separates the indent icons from the next area of the tab, that area is also part of the alignment section. The *Wrap Text* tool lets us expand a cell so text appears on multiple lines instead of overlapping with other cells. The *Merge & Center* tool merges selected cells together and offers a few formatting options. These tools can be used together to save time when creating data visualizations by merging cells and wrapping the text so the text isn't entered separately in multiple cells.

🔲 One last thing worth knowing: we can force a carriage return in our cells by placing the cursor where we would like the return and using the ALT+ENTER keyboard combination (Option+ENTER on Macs). If we want to insert a carriage return in a formula, we can use the CHAR(10) formula (with the *Wrap Text* option turned on)—see Chapter 22 to see how this function works in practice.

Data Sorting

Another aspect of formatting data in your worksheet is understanding how to arrange and sort your data. The menu to sort your data is not located in the *Home* tab of the ribbon but in the *Data* tab. There are four primary buttons in this area of the ribbon:

1. The *A → Z shortcut* automatically sorts the data from smallest to largest.

2. The *Z → A shortcut* automatically sorts the data from largest to smallest.

3. The *Sort* button lets us specify the direction to sort the data, which variable (or variables) to sort by, and whether to sort the data from left-to-right rather than up-to-down.

Setting
Making
Moving

4. The *Filter* button lets us add sorting and filter options to the cells at the top of our data columns. This button can be especially useful if we want to make some quick sorting and filtering changes to our data (Figure 4.24).

FIGURE 4.24

Number Formats

The last part of this section of the *Home* tab is the number formatting area. The drop-down menu with the word "General" in it has default formatting options included. The buttons below ($, %, and ,) format the numbers in your cells. The buttons to the right with the zeros add or subtract decimals from the data.

We can access more number formatting options by using the formal *Number Format* menu. Right-click on a cell and select the *Format Cells* option. In the first area of the menu (under *Number*), a list of formatting options, including "Number," "Currency," "Percentage," and "Scientific," appears. Each area lets us apply various formatting options to include different symbols, decimal places, commas, and so on.

The *Custom* area of the *Format Cells* menu is particularly powerful. Here, we can add custom formats to the entries in the spreadsheet cells or graphs. With this tool, we can change how the number looks without changing any data. Custom number formats have a specific structure with four arguments, separated by semi-colons:

a. Positive values

b. Negative values

c. Zero values

d. Text values

We don't need to include all four arguments for every formula, and we can skip a format by simply adding another semi-colon. (Where we enter the custom number format will be called different things depending on the operating system and use case: on PCs, it will be a box called *Type* when working in a spreadsheet but *Format Code* when working in a graph; on Macs, the box is always called *Type*.)

I'll demonstrate how a custom number format works with the highlighted example in Figure 4.25.

$$\#, \#\#0\_);[Red](\#, \#\#0)$$

This format will style positive and negative values. The pound sign (#) is a place-holder for optional digits. The "#, ##0" format tells Excel to use a comma in the number and not to include decimals. The underscore tells Excel to add a space the width of whatever character comes next, so the "_)" character tells Excel to add a space the width of a closed parenthesis. The format for negative numbers is included after the semicolon and will color the numbers red ("[Red]") and wrap them in parentheses.

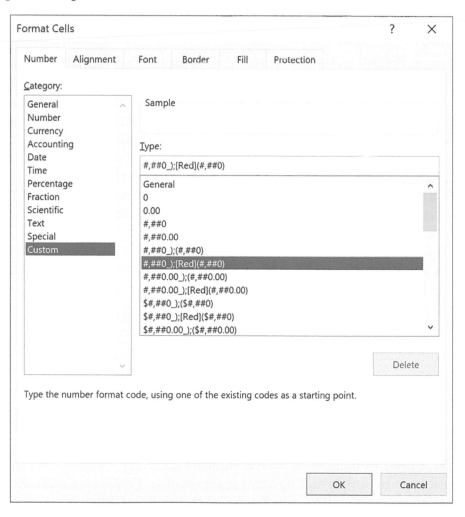

FIGURE 4.25

You can see a variety of formatting results in the image below. A much longer list as well as excellent details about how to create custom number formats can be found on the ExcelJet website (https://exceljet.net/custom-number-formats) (Table 4.2).

TABLE 4.2

Value	Code	Result	Notes
123456	#,##0_)	123,456	Positive number format
-123456	;[Red](#,##0)	(123,456)	Negative number format
18-Jan-21	yyyy	2021	Year only
18-Jan-21	mmmm-yyyy	January-2021	Month and year
15.5	##.#" years old"	15.5 years old	Text for units
155	#,##0	155	Positive number format
1550	#,##0	1,550	Positive number format
15500	#,##0	15,500	Positive number format
12000	0,"K"	12K	Number in thousands
65	;;;		Hide the content
100	\VA	VA	Escape character
125	[Blue][>100]#,##0	125	Conditional format

Pulling It All Together

Now that we've gone over all of these menus, let's create a basic column chart. We're not going to add fancy formatting or complex parts, but we'll walk through a few of the basic chart formatting options so you can become familiar with how the more advanced tutorials will look.

For this example, we'll use data from the World Bank to make a paired column chart of gross domestic product (GDP) measured in thousands of dollars for seven countries in 2010 and 2020.

First, we select the data in cells A1:E8 and use the *Insert* tab to create a *Clustered Column Chart*, which is the first column chart in the top-left menu and is labeled as *2-D Column* (Figure 4.26).

Notice the space between the columns? There's nothing objectively wrong with that space, but personally, I'm not a fan. So let's tighten it up. Select the bars, right-click, select the *Format Data Series* option in the drop-down menu, and change the *Series Overlap* to 0% and the *Gap Width* in to 100% in the menu. In the tutorial chapters, these directions will look something like: right-click on the bars > *Format Data Series* > *Series Overlap* to 0% and *Gap Width* to 100% (Figure 4.27).

Setting

Making

Moving

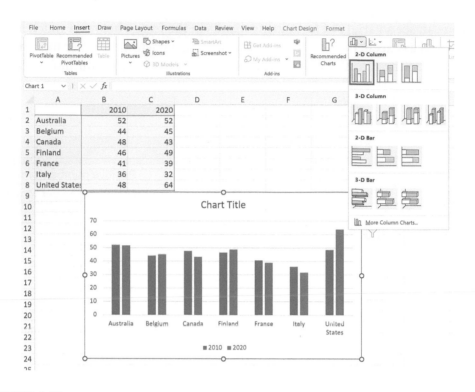

FIGURE 4.26

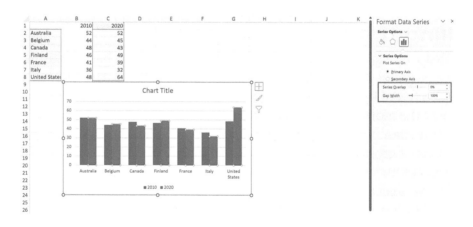

FIGURE 4.27

Let's adjust the formatting of the numbers on the y-axis. Select the y-axis labels and right click: *Format Axis* > *Number* > *Currency*. Again, this notation is intended to lead us from one step to the next. In the *Currency* menu, select the dollar sign ($) in the drop-down menu (if it wasn't automatically selected) (Figure 4.28).

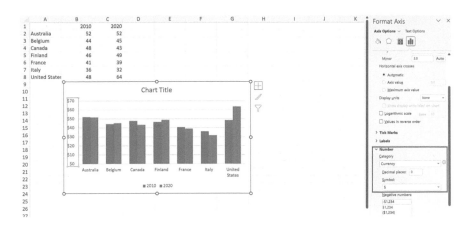

FIGURE 4.28

Just for fun, let's add some labels to each set of bars: right-click on the bars and select the *Add Data Labels* option in the menu. Because the numbers in the worksheet cells are shown as whole numbers, the data labels will appear as whole numbers. Let's modify the format in the chart by selecting the data labels, right-clicking, and *Format Data Labels > Number*. Now, set the number of decimal places to 1 in the box (Figure 4.29).

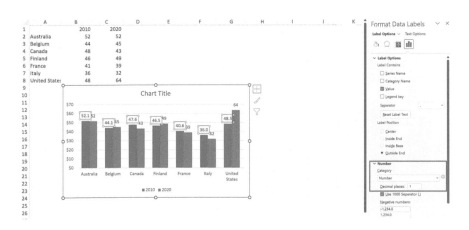

FIGURE 4.29

Let's move the legend to the top: select the legend, right-click, and in the *Legend Options* menu, select the *Top* option (Figure 4.30).

Sorting the bars based on the data values is usually better than the default alphabetical sorting. We can make this change in the worksheet by selecting the data (cells C1:C8), navigating to *Data > Sort*, and sorting on the 2020 per capita GDP values in column C (Figure 4.31).

Setting

Making

Moving

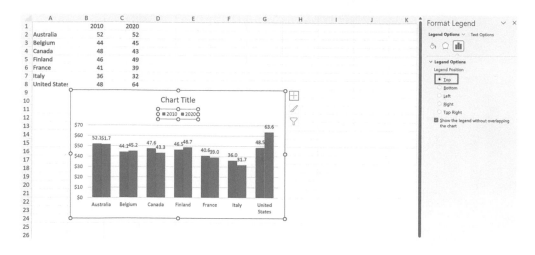

FIGURE 4.30

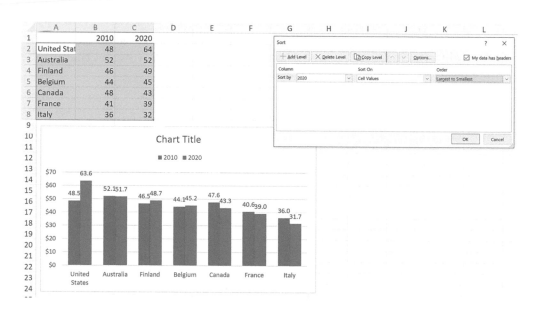

FIGURE 4.31

Finally, we can make a few finishing changes to the chart. I might change the size of the chart (3x5 inches is pretty small) and insert a title by editing the default *Chart title* area. Personally, I would also change the colors of the bars and use a different font to get away from the default settings. If I were including labels above each bar, I would delete the y-axis labels and the horizontal gridlines (by simply selecting and deleting) because they are redundant with the visible data labels (Figure 4.32).

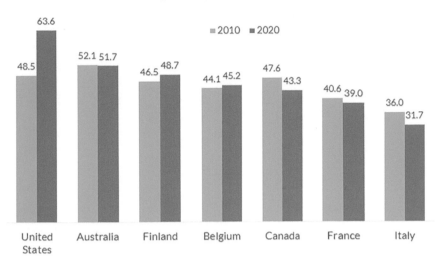

Per capita GDP in the United States is more than double per capita GDP in Italy in 2020

FIGURE 4.32

Going Forward

We've only just scratched the surface of what Excel can do. If you're new to Excel, this chapter has hopefully given you a peek into the power of how you can use the tool to analyze, organize, format, and visualize your data. If you've been using Excel for a while, you've likely seen a few techniques and strategies that can make your work in Excel more productive and efficient. Of course, no single chapter—or even a single book—can teach you everything there is to learn about Excel. A lot of Excel knowledge comes with time and practice (and patience). I've included a list of some of my favorite data visualization websites in Appendix 3 at the end of the book to help you continue your learning journey.

Setting

Making

Moving

Chapter **5**

Fundamental Formulas Used in Building Your Graphs

Throughout the tutorials in this book, you'll see the heavy use of formulas to arrange and organize the data for your graphs. I will often read in my full dataset to Excel before pulling the specific data points or series I need for the graph, but the full dataset remains for me to update, reference later on, pull additional data points or series, or make other changes.

In this section, I define and show examples for 17 Excel formulas that I use regularly in my work and that you will see throughout the tutorials. There is no way to show every Excel formula here—nor is it really necessary—but these formulas should serve you well when using the tool.

For each formula, I demonstrate how it works using a simple dataset of population estimates for 14 countries around the world (Table 5.1).

Before we get into specific formulas, it's worth understanding how formulas are copied and pasted within an Excel spreadsheet. To insert a formula in a cell, start by typing an equal sign (=). From there, Excel will prompt different formula options as we type. In the pop-up that appears, we can click on the linked (blue) text and a separate window will open with an Excel help window (Figure 5.1).

We can edit the formulas in the "formula bar," which is the white text box above the worksheet. Excel has a number of built-in reference tools to help us find the right formula for our purposes.

DOI: 10.1201/9781003321552-6

TABLE 5.1

Region	Country	Population, 2020
Africa	Ethiopia	114,963,583
Asia	Vietnam	97,338,583
Asia	Turkey	84,339,067
Asia	Thailand	69,799,978
Africa	South Africa	59,308,690
Europe	Spain	47,351,567
South America	Argentina	45,376,763
South America	Peru	32,971,846
Asia	Nepal	29,136,808
Africa	Chad	16,425,859
Europe	Belarus	9,379,952
Europe	Denmark	5,831,404
Asia	Singapore	5,685,807
Asia	Mongolia	3,278,292

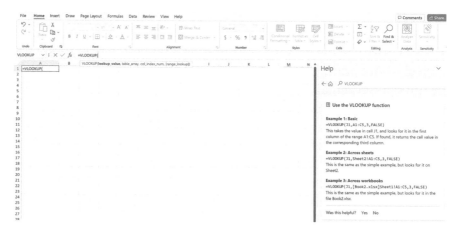

FIGURE 5.1

Absolute and Relative References

Once we have inserted a formula, we can copy and paste it anywhere in our Excel workbook (or even another workbook). The elements of the formula "follow" their position to the next location. Take a simple example: type a number in cell B1 and another cell C1. In cell A1, insert a simple formula that multiplies the values in those cells: =B1*C1.

If we copy the formula in cell A1 (CTRL+C) and paste it in cell A2 (CTRL+V), the formula updates automatically to the following: =B2*C2. In other words,

Excel is "looking" at the inputs to the formula relative to its position, so we call these inputs *relative references.*

This functionality can be problematic if we want to reference the input in a formula elsewhere in a worksheet. Say we want to multiply a whole bunch of numbers by the value in cell C1. Copying our original formula won't reference that cell unless we convert it to an *absolute reference.* To do so, we can "lock" the cell reference by inserting a dollar sign ($) before the row reference (number), column reference (letter), or both. (We can also use a keyboard shortcut to insert the absolute reference rather than typing it in—F4 or FN+F4 on PCs and CMD+T on Macs.)

Let's demonstrate with our population data. We have the region of the world in column A, the country name in column B, and the 2020 population in column C. We can convert the numbers to millions by dividing each number in column C by 1,000,000. To do so, we type 1,000,000 in cell E2. In cell D2, we type =C2/E2, which converts the population of Ethiopia to 115.0. If we copy and paste that formula, we get an error because the formula in cell D3 for Vietnam is =C3/E3, and cell E3 is empty. Again, the formula inputs are always relative to their initial position (Figure 5.2 and Table 5.2).

FIGURE 5.2

TABLE 5.2

	A	B	C	D	E	F
1	Region	Country	Population, 2020	Millions		Millions
2	Africa	Ethiopia	114,963,583	115.0	1,000,000	115.0
3	Asia	Vietnam	97,338,583	#DIV/0!		97.3
4	Asia	Turkey	84,339,067	#DIV/0!		84.3
5	Asia	Thailand	69,799,978	#DIV/0!		69.8
6	Africa	South Africa	59,308,690	#DIV/0!		59.3
7	Europe	Spain	47,351,567	#DIV/0!		47.4
8	South America	Argentina	45,376,763	#DIV/0!		45.4
9	South America	Peru	32,971,846	#DIV/0!		33.0
10	Asia	Nepal	29,136,808	#DIV/0!		29.1
11	Africa	Chad	16,425,859	#DIV/0!		16.4
12	Europe	Belarus	9,379,952	#DIV/0!		9.4
13	Europe	Denmark	5,831,404	#DIV/0!		5.8
14	Asia	Singapore	5,685,807	#DIV/0!		5.7
15	Asia	Mongolia	3,278,292	#DIV/0!		3.3

Setting

Making

Moving

If we change the formula to =C3/$E$3, we "lock" that cell reference. Now, when we copy the formula down the column, we still reference cell E3 in the denominator. For Thailand (in row 5), the formula is =C5/$E$3. We could have also typed =C3/E$3 because we are not copying across columns, so the column reference does not change.

You will see these *relative* and *absolute references* throughout the tutorials. I use them liberally to copy-and-paste formulas without worrying about making manual changes.

IF Formulas

```
=IF(Evaluation, if TRUE, if FALSE)
```

We start with one of the easiest formulas in Excel, the IF formula. The IF formula has three arguments: what we are going to evaluate, what happens if the evaluation is true, and what happens if the evaluation is false. As an example, let's create a binary variable that tells us whether a country has more than or fewer than 50 million people.

```
=IF(C2>50000000,1,0)
```

When we copy and paste this formula down column D, we'll get 1s for countries with more than 50 million people and 0s for countries with fewer than 50 million people.

We can also use this formula with text by placing what we want to come out of the formula in quotation marks. For example:

```
=IF(C2>50000000,"More than 50 million","Fewer than
                50 million")
```

When we copy and paste this formula down column E, we get the relevant text in each cell (Figure 5.3 and Table 5.3).

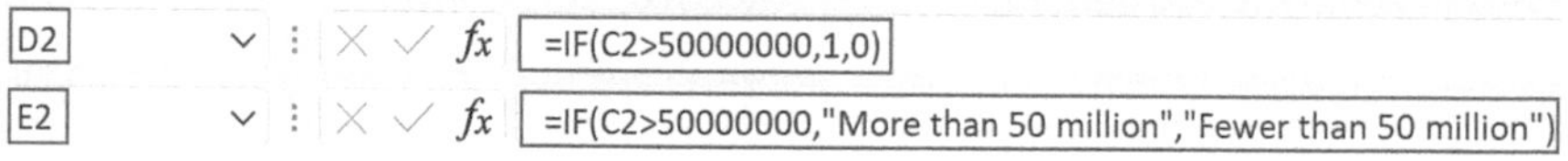

| D2 | ∨ : × ✓ *fx* | =IF(C2>50000000,1,0) |
| E2 | ∨ : × ✓ *fx* | =IF(C2>50000000,"More than 50 million","Fewer than 50 million") |

FIGURE 5.3

TABLE 5.3

	A	B	C	D	E
1	Region	Country	Population, 2020	IF-Number	IF-Text
2	Africa	Ethiopia	114,963,583	1	More than 50 million
3	Asia	Vietnam	97,338,583	1	More than 50 million
4	Asia	Turkey	84,339,067	1	More than 50 million
5	Asia	Thailand	69,799,978	1	More than 50 million
6	Africa	South Africa	59,308,690	1	More than 50 million
7	Europe	Spain	47,351,567	0	Fewer than 50 million
8	South America	Argentina	45,376,763	0	Fewer than 50 million
9	South America	Peru	32,971,846	0	Fewer than 50 million
10	Asia	Nepal	29,136,808	0	Fewer than 50 million
11	Africa	Chad	16,425,859	0	Fewer than 50 million
12	Europe	Belarus	9,379,952	0	Fewer than 50 million
13	Europe	Denmark	5,831,404	0	Fewer than 50 million
14	Asia	Singapore	5,685,807	0	Fewer than 50 million
15	Asia	Mongolia	3,278,292	0	Fewer than 50 million

```
=AND(argument 1, argument 2,…)
```

Another simple formula: when using the AND function, Excel returns the word "TRUE" if every argument in the formula is true. For example, =AND(C2>50000000,A2="Asia") will return the word "TRUE" for Vietnam, Turkey, and Thailand as each country has more than 50 million people and is located in Asia, but "FALSE" for all other countries (Figure 5.4 and Table 5.4).

D2   ∨ ⋮ ✕ ✓ *fx*   =AND(C2>50000000,A2="Asia")

FIGURE 5.4

```
=OR(argument 1, argument 2,…)
```

Similar to the AND function, the OR function returns TRUE if *any* of its arguments are true and returns FALSE if *all* of its arguments are false. Here, we can insert =OR(C2>50000000,A2="Asia") and see TRUE for countries that have more than 50 million people OR are located in Asia (Figure 5.5 and Table 5.5).

```
SUMIF(range, criteria, sum_range)
```

The SUMIF formula lets us sum a series of data values if it satisfies a certain condition. The three arguments in the SUMIF formula are:

TABLE 5.4

	A	B	C	D
1	Region	Country	Population, 2020	AND
2	Africa	Ethiopia	114,963,583	FALSE
3	Asia	Vietnam	97,338,583	TRUE
4	Asia	Turkey	84,339,067	TRUE
5	Asia	Thailand	69,799,978	TRUE
6	Africa	South Africa	59,308,690	FALSE
7	Europe	Spain	47,351,567	FALSE
8	South America	Argentina	45,376,763	FALSE
9	South America	Peru	32,971,846	FALSE
10	Asia	Nepal	29,136,808	FALSE
11	Africa	Chad	16,425,859	FALSE
12	Europe	Belarus	9,379,952	FALSE
13	Europe	Denmark	5,831,404	FALSE
14	Asia	Singapore	5,685,807	FALSE
15	Asia	Mongolia	3,278,292	FALSE

| D2 | ⌄ | : | ✕ ✓ | f_x | =OR(C2>50000000,A2="Asia") |

FIGURE 5.5

TABLE 5.5

	A	B	C	D
1	Region	Country	Population, 2020	OR
2	Africa	Ethiopia	114,963,583	TRUE
3	Asia	Vietnam	97,338,583	TRUE
4	Asia	Turkey	84,339,067	TRUE
5	Asia	Thailand	69,799,978	TRUE
6	Africa	South Africa	59,308,690	TRUE
7	Europe	Spain	47,351,567	FALSE
8	South America	Argentina	45,376,763	FALSE
9	South America	Peru	32,971,846	FALSE
10	Asia	Nepal	29,136,808	TRUE
11	Africa	Chad	16,425,859	FALSE
12	Europe	Belarus	9,379,952	FALSE
13	Europe	Denmark	5,831,404	FALSE
14	Asia	Singapore	5,685,807	TRUE
15	Asia	Mongolia	3,278,292	TRUE

Setting — Making — Moving

- *range*, which refers to the list of values that reference the condition;

- *criteria*, which is the value we set a condition on; and

- *sum_range*, which is the range of values across which we want to sum.

For this example, let's sum the population across the six Asian countries. We insert this formula in cell C2:

```
=SUMIF(A2:A15,"Asia",C2:C15)
```

The first argument is the *range*, which points us to the *Region* column. The second argument, the *criteria*, is what we are looking for in the range ("Asia"). And the final argument, *sum_range*, is the column of data we want to add up (C2:C15). I typed "Asia" in the formula for this example, but I could have typed it in a cell somewhere and referenced that cell in the formula (Figure 5.6 and Table 5.6).

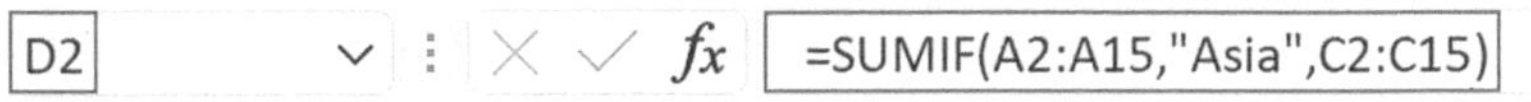

| D2 | ∨ ⋮ ✕ ✓ *fx* | =SUMIF(A2:A15,"Asia",C2:C15) |

FIGURE 5.6

TABLE 5.6

	A	B	C	D
1	Region	Country	Population, 2020	SUMIF
2	Africa	Ethiopia	114,963,583	289,578,535
3	Asia	Vietnam	97,338,583	
4	Asia	Turkey	84,339,067	
5	Asia	Thailand	69,799,978	
6	Africa	South Africa	59,308,690	
7	Europe	Spain	47,351,567	
8	South America	Argentina	45,376,763	
9	South America	Peru	32,971,846	
10	Asia	Nepal	29,136,808	
11	Africa	Chad	16,425,859	
12	Europe	Belarus	9,379,952	
13	Europe	Denmark	5,831,404	
14	Asia	Singapore	5,685,807	
15	Asia	Mongolia	3,278,292	

Setting

Making

Moving

The SUMIF formula is valuable for adding data values automatically, especially if you might update or sort your data in different ways.

```
SUMIFS(sum_range, criteria_range1, criteria1,
[criteria_range2, criteria2], ...)
```

Unlike the SUMIF formula, which only lets us apply one condition, the SUMIFS formula lets us apply multiple conditions. Let's expand our dataset to include 2 years of data and see what happens when we apply a revised formula:

```
=SUMIFS(D2:D15,A2:A15,"Asia",C2:C15,"2020")
```

Here, we are going to sum the population estimates in column D for countries in Asia *and* in 2020. Notice that the order of the arguments is slightly different than in SUMIF—we start with the column that we are going to sum, then the condition range, then the actual condition (Figure 5.7 and Table 5.7).

E2   ∨ ⋮ × ✓ *fx*   =SUMIFS(D2:D15,A2:A15,"Asia",C2:C15,"2020")

FIGURE 5.7

TABLE 5.7

	A	B	C	D	E
1	Region	Country	Year	Population	SUMIFS
2	Asia	Nepal	1960	10,105,060	280,614,436
3	Asia	Nepal	2020	29,136,808	
4	Asia	Vietnam	1960	32,670,048	
5	Asia	Vietnam	2020	97,338,583	
6	South America	Argentina	1960	20,481,781	
7	South America	Argentina	2020	45,376,763	
8	Asia	Thailand	1960	27,397,208	
9	Asia	Thailand	2020	69,799,978	
10	Asia	Turkey	1960	27,472,339	
11	Asia	Turkey	2020	84,339,067	
12	South America	Peru	1960	10,155,011	
13	South America	Peru	2020	32,971,846	
14	Europe	Spain	1960	30,455,000	
15	Europe	Spain	2020	47,351,567	

Setting

Making

Moving

You can see these arguments more clearly if I highlight the three parts of the formula:

```
=SUMIFS(D2:D15,A2:A15,"Asia",C2:C15,"2020")
```

The first part of the formula in green is the series we want to add up; the second section in blue defines that we want to search for "Asia" in cells A2:A15; and the third section in pink defines that we want to look for "2020" in cells C2:C15.

Using SUMIF rather than a simple SUM formula is valuable because it makes the task less prone to error (i.e., selecting the wrong cells) and is more flexible to the format of our data. If we were to sort these data by population, the result of the SUMIFS formula will remain the same, but the results of a regular SUM formula would be incorrect.

- AVERAGEIF(range, criteria, average_range)
- AVERAGEIFS(average_range, criteria_range1, criteria1, [criteria_range2, criteria2], ...)

AVERAGEIF and AVERAGEIFS work the same way as SUMIF and SUMIFS. In this example, we calculate the average population for all Asian countries in both 1960 and 2020 and for all Asian countries in 2020 only (Figure 5.8 and Table 5.8).

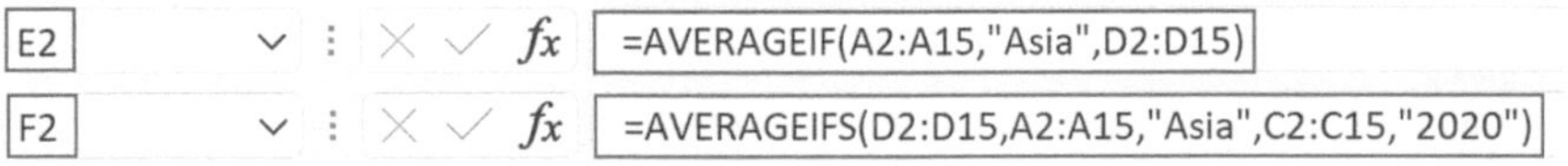

| E2 | ∨ ⋮ ✕ ✓ *fx* | =AVERAGEIF(A2:A15,"Asia",D2:D15) |
| F2 | ∨ ⋮ ✕ ✓ *fx* | =AVERAGEIFS(D2:D15,A2:A15,"Asia",C2:C15,"2020") |

FIGURE 5.8

Cell E2: =AVERAGEIF(A2:A15,"Asia",D2:D15)

Cell F2: =AVERAGEIFS(D2:D15,A2:A15,"Asia",C2:C15,"2020")

- COUNTIF(criteria_range, criteria1)
- COUNTIFS(criteria_range1, criteria1, [criteria_range2, criteria2]...)

TABLE 5.8

	A	B	C	D	E	F
1	**Region**	**Country**	**Year**	**Population**	**AVERAGEIF**	**AVERAGEIFS**
2	Asia	Nepal	1960	10,105,060	47,282,386	70,153,609
3	Asia	Nepal	2020	29,136,808		
4	Asia	Vietnam	1960	32,670,048		
5	Asia	Vietnam	2020	97,338,583		
6	South America	Argentina	1960	20,481,781		
7	South America	Argentina	2020	45,376,763		
8	Asia	Thailand	1960	27,397,208		
9	Asia	Thailand	2020	69,799,978		
10	Asia	Turkey	1960	27,472,339		
11	Asia	Turkey	2020	84,339,067		
12	South America	Peru	1960	10,155,011		
13	South America	Peru	2020	32971846		
14	Europe	Spain	1960	30455000		
15	Europe	Spain	2020	47351567		

The COUNTIF and COUNTIFS formulas are slightly different than SUMIF and AVERAGEIF because we only need to look at one condition and not the sum or average of the values in another column (Figure 5.9 and Table 5.9):

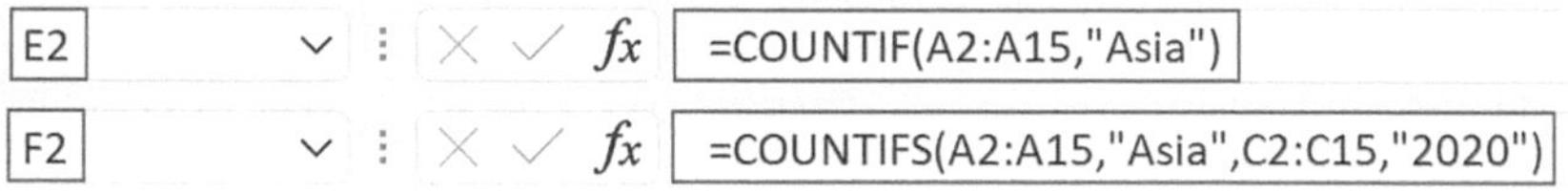

E2	⌄ ⋮ ✕ ✓ *fx*	=COUNTIF(A2:A15,"Asia")
F2	⌄ ⋮ ✕ ✓ *fx*	=COUNTIFS(A2:A15,"Asia",C2:C15,"2020")

FIGURE 5.9

Cell E2: =COUNTIF(A2:A15,"Asia")

Cell F2: =COUNTIFS(A2:A15,"Asia",C2:C15,"2020")

TABLE 5.9

	A	B	C	D	E	F
1	Region	Country	Year	Population	COUNTIF	COUNTIFS
2	Asia	Nepal	1960	10,105,060	8	4
3	Asia	Nepal	2020	29,136,808		
4	Asia	Vietnam	1960	32,670,048		
5	Asia	Vietnam	2020	97,338,583		
6	South America	Argentina	1960	20,481,781		
7	South America	Argentina	2020	45,376,763		
8	Asia	Thailand	1960	27,397,208		
9	Asia	Thailand	2020	69,799,978		
10	Asia	Turkey	1960	27,472,339		
11	Asia	Turkey	2020	84,339,067		
12	South America	Peru	1960	10,155,011		
13	South America	Peru	2020	32,971,846		
14	Europe	Spain	1960	30,455,000		
15	Europe	Spain	2020	47,351,567		

Find the Top and Bottom

- MIN(number1, [number2], ...)
- MAX(number1, [number2], ...)

The MIN (minimum) and MAX (maximum) formulas let us pull out the largest and smallest values in a data series (Figure 5.10 and Table 5.10).

Cell E2: =MIN(D2:D15)

Cell F2: =MAX(D2:D15)

FIGURE 5.10

TABLE 5.10

	A	B	C	D	E	F
1	Region	Country	Year	Population	MIN	MAX
2	Asia	Nepal	1960	10,105,060	10,105,060	97,338,583
3	Asia	Nepal	2020	29,136,808		
4	Asia	Vietnam	1960	32,670,048		
5	Asia	Vietnam	2020	97,338,583		
6	South America	Argentina	1960	20,481,781		
7	South America	Argentina	2020	45,376,763		
8	Asia	Thailand	1960	27,397,208		
9	Asia	Thailand	2020	69,799,978		
10	Asia	Turkey	1960	27,472,339		
11	Asia	Turkey	2020	84,339,067		
12	South America	Peru	1960	10,155,011		
13	South America	Peru	2020	32,971,846		
14	Europe	Spain	1960	30,455,000		
15	Europe	Spain	2020	47,351,567		

Combine Pieces of Information

- CONCATENATE(text1, [text2],…)
- CONCAT(text1, [text2],…)
- Ampersand (&) symbol

We can combine (concatenate) data fields in Excel using a few methods. The CONCATENATE formula was the original way to combine data fields but has been replaced with the CONCAT function. Both work in the same way—the arguments inside the formula are joined together. A faster and a slightly easier way is to use the ampersand (&) symbol.

Using these techniques, we can combine data fields to create data labels or to use in another formula. With our country population dataset, we can create a label for each country in "country name, year" format by using:

```
Cell E2: =B2&", "&C2
```

This formula joins the value in cell B2 ("Nepal") with a comma and space (", ") and the value in cell C2 (1960). I often use this approach to create custom labels or specific search identifiers for a data value (Figure 5.11 and Table 5.11).

| E2 | | ∨ | ⋮ | × | ✓ | *fx* | =B2&", "&C2 |

FIGURE 5.11

TABLE 5.11

	A	B	C	D	E
1	Region	Country	Year	Population	Label
2	Asia	Nepal	1960	10,105,060	Nepal, 1960
3	Asia	Nepal	2020	29,136,808	Nepal, 2020
4	Asia	Vietnam	1960	32,670,048	Vietnam, 1960
5	Asia	Vietnam	2020	97,338,583	Vietnam, 2020
6	South America	Argentina	1960	20,481,781	Argentina, 1960
7	South America	Argentina	2020	45,376,763	Argentina, 2020
8	Asia	Thailand	1960	27,397,208	Thailand, 1960
9	Asia	Thailand	2020	69,799,978	Thailand, 2020
10	Asia	Turkey	1960	27,472,339	Turkey, 1960
11	Asia	Turkey	2020	84,339,067	Turkey, 2020
12	South America	Peru	1960	10,155,011	Peru, 1960
13	South America	Peru	2020	32,971,846	Peru, 2020
14	Europe	Spain	1960	30,455,000	Spain, 1960
15	Europe	Spain	2020	47,351,567	Spain, 2020

LOOKUP Functions

- VLOOKUP(lookup _ value, table _ array, col _ index _ num, [range _ lookup])

- HLOOKUP(lookup _ value, table _ array, row _ index _ num, [range _ lookup])

- XLOOKUP(lookup _ value,lookup _ array,return _ array,[if _ not _ found], [match _ mode], [search _ mode])

We now get into the LOOKUP formulas, which are extremely helpful for simplifying or organizing our data. There are three primary LOOKUP formulas in Excel:

- VLOOKUP is a vertical lookup function that looks up and down columns.

- HLOOKUP is a horizontal lookup function that looks across rows.

- XLOOKUP is a newer function that looks across rows and columns.

The formulas all work similarly, and the VLOOKUP formula appears throughout the tutorials, so we'll focus on it here. There are four arguments in VLOOKUP:

- The *lookup_value* is what we are looking for in our dataset, such as a country name.

- The *table_array* is the table or set of columns where we are looking to find the data value or values we want. The thing we are looking for (e.g., country name) must exist in the first column of the table.

- The *col_index_num* is the column number we want to look through in our table. The column in which we are looking for the *lookup_value* counts as the first column.

- The *range_lookup* has two options:

  - Exact match (0 or FALSE) searches for the exact value in the first column.

  - Approximate match (1 or TRUE) assumes the first column in the table is sorted and searches for the closest value. This option is the default in Excel, but we don't always want to find an approximate match so it's always worth specifying.

Admittedly, there are a lot of parts to the VLOOKUP formula, so let's break it down:

```
=VLOOKUP("Peru",A2:B15,2,0)
```

We've got our four pieces:

- The first argument is the thing we are looking for: the word "Peru".

- The second argument is the data table range *where* we are looking (A2:B15). The thing we are looking for ("Peru") must appear in the first column of this range.

- The third argument is the column number from which we want to pull our result—the first column contains the list of things we are looking for (country names) and extends to the right. In this case, we want to get the population value for Peru, so we want to pull the data from the second column in the range (column B).

- The last argument is the *exact* or *approximate* match identifier. In this case, we want to find the value for Peru *exactly*, so we insert the number 0 (or the word FALSE if you like) (Figure 5.12 and Table 5.12).

FIGURE 5.12

TABLE 5.12

	A	B	C
1	Country	Population, 2020	VLOOKUP
2	Ethiopia	114,963,583	32,971,846
3	Vietnam	97,338,583	
4	Turkey	84,339,067	
5	Thailand	69,799,978	
6	South Africa	59,308,690	
7	Spain	47,351,567	
8	Argentina	45,376,763	
9	Peru	32,971,846	
10	Nepal	29,136,808	
11	Chad	16,425,859	
12	Belarus	9,379,952	
13	Denmark	5,831,404	
14	Singapore	5,685,807	
15	Mongolia	3,278,292	

Setting

Making

Moving

What about using the *approximate* match? Let's say we want to add an indicator to our dataset that classifies countries as "small," "middle," or "large." We can accomplish this task by using a VLOOKUP formula.

First, we must set up a smaller "lookup" table to the side, which defines our conditions for what constitutes a "small," "medium," or "large" country. Then, in column C (starting in cell C2), we insert this formula:

```
=VLOOKUP(B2,$E$2:$F$4,2,1)
```

Our formula starts by looking at cell B2, the population of Ethiopia. With the second argument (i.e., $E$2:$F$4), we instruct our formula to compare that population number in cell B2 to the thresholds we created in the blue-shaded lookup table in columns D and E (Figure 5.13 and Table 5.13). (Remember, the thing we are looking for must be in the first column.) Here, we use *absolute references* (the dollar signs) so the reference to the lookup table doesn't change when we copy the formula down column C. The third argument, 2, specifies that we are going to extract the word in the second column from our lookup table) using an *approximate match* (the 1 in the last argument).

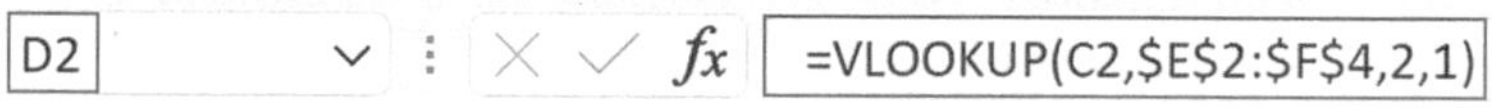

| D2 | ⌄ | ⋮ | ✕ ✓ | *fx* | =VLOOKUP(C2,$E$2:$F$4,2,1) |

FIGURE 5.13

But what does the *approximate match* do? In short, it takes the data (here in column E) and builds ranges with it. Countries with populations between 0 and 50 million people are considered "small," countries with 50–100 million people are considered "middle," and countries with 100 million or more people are classified as "large." When the formula looks in the table for the population of Ethiopia (cell C2), it compares the 115 million data point to each of those thresholds: to 0 million—greater than that; to 50 million—greater than that; and finally 100 million or more. The formula sees that Ethiopia's population exceeds the 100 million threshold, so it inserts the text value in the second column ("Large") into the cell.

TABLE 5.13

	A	B	C	D	E	F
1	**Region**	**Country**	**Population, 2020**	**VLOOKUP**		
2	Africa	Ethiopia	114,963,583	Large	0	Small
3	Asia	Vietnam	97,338,583	Middle	50,000,000	Middle
4	Asia	Turkey	84,339,067	Middle	100,000,000	Large
5	Asia	Thailand	69,799,978	Middle		
6	Africa	South Africa	59,308,690	Middle		
7	Europe	Spain	47,351,567	Small		
8	South America	Argentina	45,376,763	Small		
9	South America	Peru	32,971,846	Small		
10	Asia	Nepal	29,136,808	Small		
11	Africa	Chad	16,425,859	Small		
12	Europe	Belarus	9,379,952	Small		
13	Europe	Denmark	5,831,404	Small		
14	Asia	Singapore	5,685,807	Small		
15	Asia	Mongolia	3,278,292	Small		

I use the VLOOKUP formula a lot in this book, so it's worth familiarizing yourself with how it works. Absolute references can be added to any of its arguments, and we can embed many of the formulas shown above—IF, AND, OR, and the ampersand symbol—inside the VLOOKUP. To demonstrate, let's extend our previous example with the following formula in cell F2:

```
=VLOOKUP(G2&" "&G3,A2:E15,5,0)
```

Here, we have a table with a new *Label* column that combines the country name and the year of data. Our new formula combines the values in cells G2 and G3 and separates them with a space (e.g., "Vietnam 2020"). It then looks through our *Label* column for the same combined value and pulls out the data point from the fifth column of the designated range for the specific country-year combination specified in cells G2 and G3 (Figure 5.14 and Table 5.14).

F2	∨ : × ✓ *fx*	=VLOOKUP(G2&" "&G3,A2:E15,5,0)

FIGURE 5.14

TABLE 5.14

	A	B	C	D	E	F	G
1	Label	Region	Country	Year	Population	VLOOKUP	
2	Nepal 1960	Asia	Nepal	1960	10,105,060	97,338,583	Vietnam
3	Nepal 2020	Asia	Nepal	2020	29,136,808		2020
4	Vietnam 1960	Asia	Vietnam	1960	32,670,048		
5	Vietnam 2020	Asia	Vietnam	2020	97,338,583		
6	Argentina 1960	South America	Argentina	1960	20,481,781		
7	Argentina 2020	South America	Argentina	2020	45,376,763		
8	Thailand 1960	Asia	Thailand	1960	27,397,208		
9	Thailand 2020	Asia	Thailand	2020	69,799,978		
10	Turkey 1960	Asia	Turkey	1960	27,472,339		
11	Turkey 2020	Asia	Turkey	2020	84,339,067		
12	Peru 1960	South America	Peru	1960	10,155,011		
13	Peru 2020	South America	Peru	2020	32,971,846		
14	Spain 1960	Europe	Spain	1960	30,455,000		
15	Spain 2020	Europe	Spain	2020	47,351,567		

```
XLOOKUP(lookup _ value,lookup _ array,return _
array,[if _ not _ found], [match _ mode], [search _ mode])
```

XLOOKUP works similarly to VLOOKUP, but it's worth defining because I expect it to become the go-to formula in the coming years. XLOOKUP is more flexible than VLOOKUP for two main reasons. First, the value you are looking for does not need to appear in the first column of the data table. Second, XLOOKUP can return an *array* with multiple items, so one formula can return multiple fields.

Let's say our data table is rearranged so the country names are in the far-right column. With XLOOKUP, we can conduct a simple lookup:

```
=XLOOKUP(B2,D8:D14,B8:B14)
```

The formula looks for the value in cell B2 (Turkey) in the moved country column, cells D8:D14. It then looks for the value in cells B8:B14 that corresponds to our lookup value, Turkey.

In row 5, we have another XLOOKUP formula, which pulls both population estimates into new cells. That formula is:

=XLOOKUP(B5,D8:D14,B8:C14)

By setting the last argument as cells B8:C14, Excel returns the corresponding values from each column when we click the Enter or Return key. VLOOKUP, by comparison, would require us to add a separate column reference that would need to change from column to column (Figure 5.15 and Table 5.15).

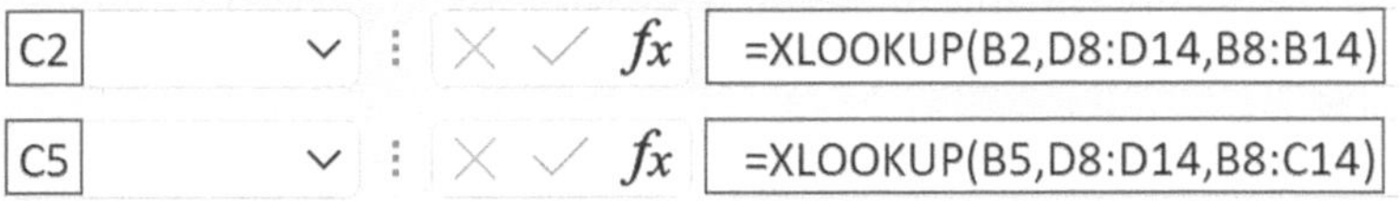

| C2 | ∨ : ✕ ✓ *fx* | =XLOOKUP(B2,D8:D14,B8:B14) |
| C5 | ∨ : ✕ ✓ *fx* | =XLOOKUP(B5,D8:D14,B8:C14) |

FIGURE 5.15

TABLE 5.15

	A	B	C	D
1		Country	Population, 1960	
2		Turkey	27,472,339	
3				
4		Country	Population, 1960	Population, 2020
5		Peru	10,155,011	32,971,846
6				
7	Region	Population, 1960	Population, 2020	Country
8	South America	20,481,781	45,376,763	Argentina
9	Asia	10,105,060	29,136,808	Nepal
10	South America	10,155,011	32,971,846	Peru
11	Europe	30,455,000	47,351,567	Spain
12	Asia	27,397,208	69,799,978	Thailand
13	Asia	27,472,339	84,339,067	Turkey
14	Asia	32,670,048	97,338,583	Vietnam

Wrap-Up

There are two other lookup formulas that many people like to use in Excel: INDEX and MATCH. Both formulas work similarly to the LOOKUP formulas but are faster (in terms of computer processing speed) and more flexible in terms of how the data table can be organized. But they also have more arguments, which can make them difficult to build and understand. I consider myself a "LOOKUP" person, so I don't present these formulas here.

Excel has a myriad of formula types and a variety of ways to construct and combine formulas. Some formulas can pull data directly from the web (e.g., STOCKHISTORY), and others are *arrays* that can hold a collection of values, not just in a single cell. The Microsoft Office suite also houses the Visual Basic for Applications (VBA) programming language, which can be used to automate certain tasks or expand Excel's general capabilities. In short, the formulas and approaches that I use in this book may not be the right formulas or even what the most experienced Excel users would choose to use. But I have used these formulas for many years, and they have served me well to analyze, extract, organize, and visualize my data.

Setting

Making

Moving

Chapter 6

Building a Custom Color Palette in Excel

Choosing and implementing color palettes is a challenging task when visualizing data. Color can highlight and draw attention, but it can also make a graphic look confusing or ugly. As computer scientist Maureen Stone once wrote, "Color used poorly will obscure, muddle, and confuse" (Stone, 2006).

Using the default color palettes in Excel will yield visualizations that look like everything else you can make in Excel. For me, using the default colors suggests a level of laziness—the creator couldn't bother to consider alternatives to better display the data or convey their argument (Figure 6.1).

We can create our own custom color palettes and add them to Excel, allowing us to easily switch between the default palette and our own. Even better, once we've created our palettes, we can share them with others to create consistent graphs and charts across an entire team or organization. We can load the palettes into all of the other Microsoft tools as well to create visually cohesive Word documents and PowerPoint slides.

A Primer on Choosing Colors

Building a custom color palette is no easy task and demands an understanding of design, contrast, accessibility, and how different color models work. Going in depth on how to choose the colors for your palette is beyond the scope of this book, but I would point to four general considerations when generating custom colors.

DOI: 10.1201/9781003321552-7

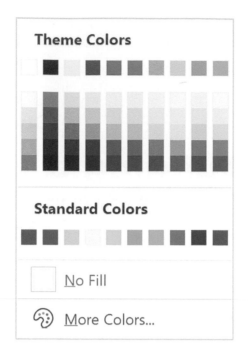

FIGURE 6.1

First, leave it to the experts. As someone who does not have a background in graphic design, I leave building custom color palettes to the experts. With so many considerations around color theory and how we perceive color, you are probably best served by letting an expert construct the palette for you. But keep in mind that data visualizations have different color needs than traditional branding purposes. Some colors may work well in a logo or on a website, but not necessarily in a bar or line chart. Thus, when you work with an expert in color, *you* may need to be the expert in data visualization to create a palette that will work in charts, graphs, and diagrams.

Second, keep accessibility in mind (see Box 6.1). There are many forms of vision impairments that can make differentiating between colors difficult. Other kinds of vision impairments can lead to light sensitivity or blurred vision, which makes color choices important.

Third, use good tools. There are *lots* of color-picking and color-testing tools available on the web, many of which are free to use. Some of these tools also have libraries or collections of existing palettes you can use in your work. I have included a list of some of the tools I use regularly in Appendix 2.

Fourth, test your colors. Once you have a palette, do some testing. Create a variety of visualizations and see if the colors work well together—and be sure to try multiple visualizations with different numbers of series and values. Ask others to read your charts and provide feedback on the color palette. This process is the easiest kind of user testing you can do and will pay off in the long run.

> **Box 6.1: Accessibility Considerations**
>
> A full exploration of how to make your graphs and other visual content accessible to people with vision, physical, intellectual, or other impairments is beyond the scope of this book. But there are two things we can all do to make our data visualizations as accessible as possible.
>
> First, carefully consider the colors you use. About 300 million around the world have some form of color vision deficiency, the most common of which (deuteranopia) makes it difficult for people to distinguish between similar shades of reds and greens. But this isn't the only vision impairment that some of our readers might have—some people might have sensitivity to light or contrast and others might have low visual acuity, which refers to the clarity or sharpness of vision (World Wide Web Consortium, 2019). A number of tools listed in Appendix 1 offer useful guides to picking and creating color palettes that address many of these vision impairments.
>
> Second, be sure to write alternative text (known as "alt text") for all your graphs. Alt text provides a description of the visual content. Assistive tools like screen readers read the alt text out loud so users with vision impairments can hear the content. Without alt text attached to your images, screen readers will either skip over the image or read the filename.
>
> To write usable alt text for graphs, consider including these three components (Cesal, 2020):
>
> 1. **The Chart Type**. Tell the user if the graph is a line chart, bar chart, or pie chart.
> 2. **Type of Data**. Explain what the x- and y-axes show.
> 3. **A Bottom Line**. Tell the reader what they should learn from the chart. If you've written an active title for your chart, start with that.
>
> In Excel (and other Microsoft Office products), you can use the *Alt Text* option in the *Format* menu or right-click on the graph to type in your alt text.
>
> There is a growing body of work around best practices and ways to make your data and data visualization accessible to a wider audience. Utilizing the resources available at the Web Content Accessibility Guidelines (WCAG)—an international consortium focused on making the web accessible to everyone—is a great starting point (https://www.w3.org/WAI/standards-guidelines/wcag/). Chartability (https://chartability.fizz.studio/) also offers a set of testable questions we can apply to our data visualizations to help ensure accessible visuals. And the *Do No Harm Guide* from me and others (Schwabish, Feng, and Popkin, 2022) brings together some of the current best practices in this area.

Creating Your Own Color Palette

Modern versions of Excel contain about 25 alternative color palettes. On the left side of the *Page Layout* tab, there is a *Themes* group, in which there is a *Colors* drop-down menu, among other options (Figure 6.2).

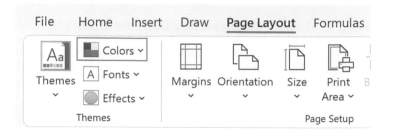

FIGURE 6.2

Selecting any of the alternatives in the drop-down menu changes the default colors applied across the entire Excel workbook. So with one click, we can go from the blue-orange-gray default color palette to shades of blue in the "Blue Warm" palette (Figure 6.3; we're coming to the custom colors).

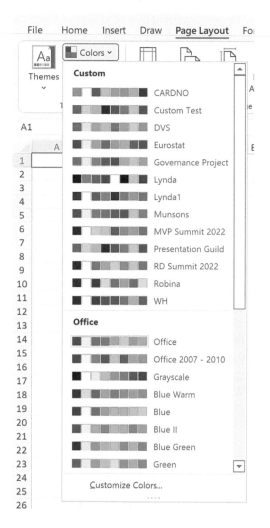

FIGURE 6.3

At the bottom of this drop-down menu, there is a *Customize Colors* option. Selecting this option allows us to manually change each of the colors in the Excel palette and save our new palette in an XML file format. (This process only works on PCs, but you can still create custom palettes on Macs by following the same steps in PowerPoint in the *Design > Variants > Colors* menu. You can also create custom color palettes in PowerPoint on PCs if you'd prefer to work there.)

As you can see in Figure 6.4, there are two text/background combination options, six "accent" colors, and options for the hyperlinks and followed hyperlinks in the default palette. The "Sample" area on the right part of the menu provides a preview of how the colors will work in practice. Note that the order matters here. If we create a bar chart with one series using the default color palette, the bars will be the blue color in the *Accent 1* box. If we add a second series, those bars will be colored in orange, shown in the *Accent 2* box.

To add your own colors, select the drop-down menu next to each color/text option and type in the "Red Green Blue" (RGB) code (three numbers ranging from 0 to 255) or the hexadecimal (HEX) code (a six-character combination of letters and numbers; Figure 6.5). If you are on a Mac computer or using PowerPoint on a Windows computer, you can use the eyedropper tool to select the color from an image directly.

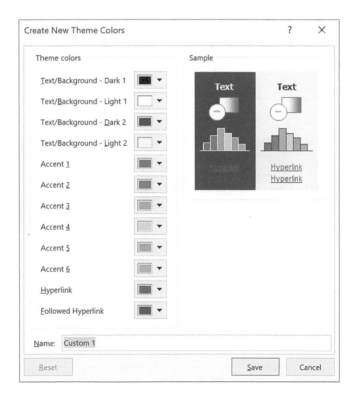

FIGURE 6.4

Setting

Making

Moving

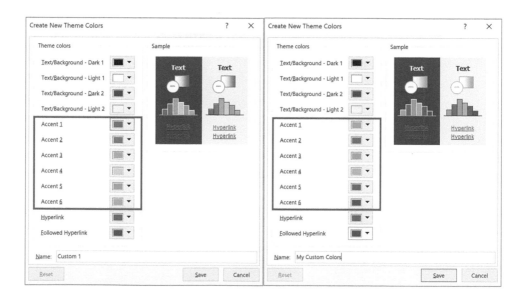

FIGURE 6.5

When you've changed all of your colors, name the palette and click the *Save* button (Figure 6.6). Excel (or PowerPoint, depending on where you built the palette) will generate a full color palette XML file for you.

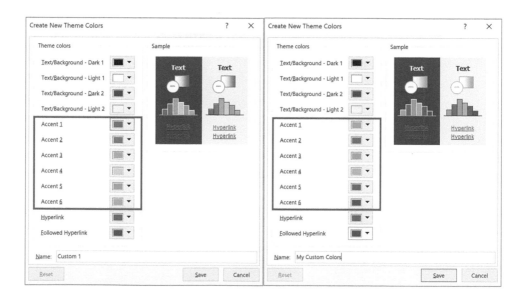

FIGURE 6.6

Microsoft automatically generates the tints and shades of your colors to fill in the entire color palette menu (Figure 6.7). Now, when you open the *Colors* drop-down menu in any of your Office tools (you may need to restart the application, but you shouldn't need to restart your computer), your new color palette will appear and you can start using it. Even if you created the palette in Excel, it will be available to you in PowerPoint and Word (Figure 6.8).

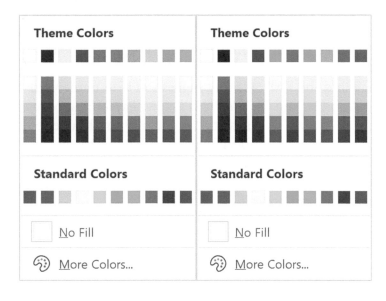

FIGURE 6.7

FIGURE 6.8

Setting

Making

Moving

Where Is the XML File?

Now that we've created the new color palette, where does Microsoft save the XML file for us to share it with our team or organization? It's not the same on all computers and all versions of Windows, but on my PC running Windows 11, the Microsoft Colors folder can be found here: **C:\Users\USERNAME\ AppData\Roaming\Microsoft\Templates\Document Themes\Theme Colors.**

You will need to replace the USERNAME section with your username on your computer. If you can't find the "AppData" folder, it's probably hidden. Open File Explorer/Windows Explorer and type %AppData% in the address bar and hit enter.

If you can't find the XML file, my suggestion is to name your color palette something outlandish and use the PC *Windows Explorer* or Mac *Finder* tool to find the file. Remember, it's just a regular file like anything else on your computer, so if you name it "Schwabish," chances are it will be the only file that will come up in a search. (Of course, that strategy doesn't work for me!) Once you locate the folder, you'll see your color palette(s) in individual XML files, which you can share with your colleagues (Figure 6.9).

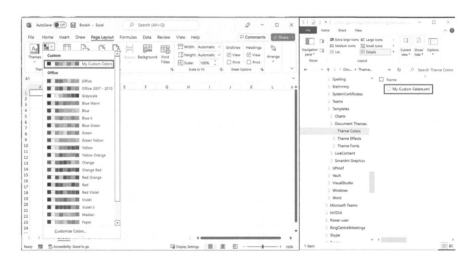

FIGURE 6.9

One last thing: we can do this task another way, which works if we have multiple color palettes that we want to load into Excel quickly. With this method, we can write our own XML file and place it in the appropriate folder.

The XML file follows a basic template, elements of which we can modify for our own needs. To create the file, open a text editor and write the code shown on the next page. We just need to edit the name of the palette shown in blue and the HEX color codes shown in green (Figure 6.10).

```
<?xml version="1.0" encoding="UTF-8" standalone="yes"?>
<a:clrScheme xmlns:a="http://schemas.openxmlformats.org/
drawingml/2006/main" name="Viridis">
<a:dk1><a:srgbClr val="000000"/>
</a:dk1><a:lt1><a:srgbClr val="FFFFFF"/>
</a:lt1><a:dk2><a:srgbClr val="44546A"/>
</a:dk2><a:lt2><a:srgbClr val="E7E6E6"/>
</a:lt2><a:accent1><a:srgbClr val="430C54"/>
</a:accent1><a:accent2><a:srgbClr val="404486"/>
</a:accent2><a:accent3><a:srgbClr val="29778E"/>
</a:accent3><a:accent4><a:srgbClr val="20A784"/>
</a:accent4><a:accent5><a:srgbClr val="7AD051"/>
</a:accent5><a:accent6><a:srgbClr val="FCE625"/>
</a:accent6><a:hlink><a:srgbClr val="0563C1"/>
</a:hlink><a:folHlink><a:srgbClr val="954F72"/>
</a:folHlink></a:clrScheme>
```

The name of the palette appears in quotation marks on line three and the text/colors in quotation marks on the other lines. To change any of the colors, replace their HEX codes. The first accent color in this palette is "430C54," which is a rich purple. (With this approach, we have to use HEX color codes,

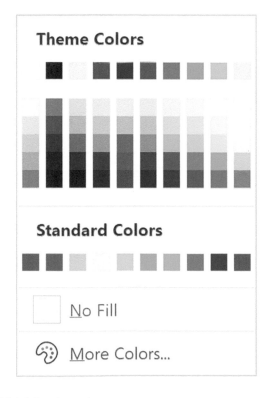

FIGURE 6.10   *The "Viridis" color palette.*

so we will need to convert any RGB codes to HEX codes. There are tools available online to make these conversions, like this one at the COLORRRS website at *https://www.webfx.com/web-design/hex-to-rgb/*. A curated list of my favorite color tools can be found in Appendix 1.) Once you've finished entering your color palettes, save the file with a .xml file extension to the *Theme Colors* folder as described above and Excel will generate the tints and shades, as in the standard palette (Figure 6.10).

Now we have a series of separate color palettes we can use in any of our Microsoft tools and share with our colleagues to create visually cohesive graphs in Excel, slides in PowerPoint, and objects in Word.

Setting

Making

Moving

Part 2

Making Graphs in Excel

Chapter 7

Sparklines

Sparklines	
Level: **Beginner**	
Data Type: **Time**	
Combine Charts: **No**	
Formulas Used: **None**	

Sparklines are small line charts intended to be embedded within a table. With sparklines, instead of needing a huge, unwieldy table with a large number of rows or columns, we can simplify the data and make it more visual.

Here, we have the stock market trading volume for 10 large technology firms (Figure 7.1). We have each company's stock symbol in column A, the company's full name in column B, the trading volume at the beginning of January 2022 in column C, the trading volume at the end of January 2022 in column D, and the percent change from the start to the end of January in column E. We'll place the sparklines in column F, which will reference the daily data shown in columns H to AA.

1. In the *Insert* tab, select the *Line* option in the *Sparklines* drop-down menu, which is located to the right of the standard *Charts* area on the ribbon (Figure 7.2).

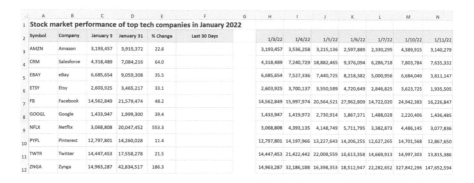

Symbol	Company	January 3	January 31	% Change	Last 30 Days		1/3/22	1/4/22	1/5/22	1/6/22	1/7/22	1/10/22	1/11/22
AMZN	Amazon	3,193,457	3,915,372	22.6			3,193,457	3,536,258	3,215,136	2,597,889	2,330,295	4,389,915	3,140,279
CRM	Salesforce	4,318,489	7,084,216	64.0			4,318,489	7,240,729	18,882,465	9,376,094	6,286,718	7,803,784	7,635,332
EBAY	eBay	6,685,654	9,059,308	35.5			6,685,654	7,527,336	7,440,725	8,218,382	5,000,956	6,684,049	3,811,147
ETSY	Etsy	2,603,925	3,465,217	33.1			2,603,925	3,700,137	3,550,589	4,720,649	2,846,825	3,623,725	1,935,505
FB	Facebook	14,562,849	21,579,474	48.2			14,562,849	15,997,974	20,564,521	27,962,809	14,722,020	24,942,383	16,226,847
GOOGL	Google	1,433,947	1,999,300	39.4			1,433,947	1,419,972	2,730,914	1,867,371	1,488,028	2,220,406	1,436,485
NFLX	Netflix	3,068,808	20,047,452	553.3			3,068,808	4,393,135	4,148,749	5,711,795	3,382,873	4,486,145	3,077,836
PYPL	Pinterest	12,797,801	14,260,028	11.4			12,797,801	14,197,966	13,227,643	14,206,255	12,627,265	14,701,568	12,867,650
TWTR	Twitter	14,447,453	17,558,278	21.5			14,447,453	21,422,442	22,008,559	16,613,358	14,669,913	14,997,303	13,815,386
ZNGA	Zynga	14,963,287	42,834,517	186.3			14,963,287	32,186,188	16,398,353	18,512,947	22,282,652	327,842,296	147,652,594

FIGURE 7.1

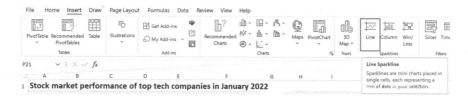

FIGURE 7.2

2. To create our sparklines, we only need to insert two references: the data we want to graph and the location of the sparklines. In the first box, we'll enter the data reference (cells H3:AA12), and in the second box, we'll enter the location of the sparklines (cells F3:F12). Once we hit OK, the sparklines will automatically generate (Figure 7.3).

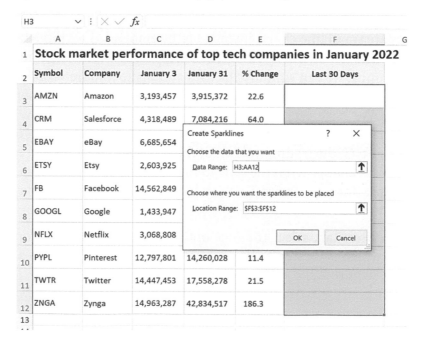

FIGURE 7.3

3. If we select any of the sparklines in column F, a new *Sparkline* tab will appear on the ribbon, which is where we can do all of our styling. We can format the color of the sparklines in the *Sparkline Color* drop-down menu, add markers in the *Show* tab, or even change the chart type to columns in the *Type* tab (Figure 7.4).

As a default, the vertical axis for each sparkline will be different because sparklines are intended to show users general patterns, not specific values. If we want to enable users to see more specific comparisons by using the same vertical axis for each row, we can standardize the range in the *Axis* area of the Sparkline menu.

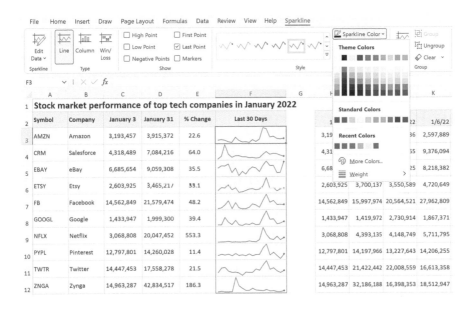

FIGURE 7.4

By using sparklines, we can present our data to the user in one small visual table instead of showing the exact values across 30-plus columns. The sparklines show the overall trend during January, with the data marker showing the trading volume at the end of the month (Figure 7.5).

Stock Market Performance of Top Tech Companies in January 2022

Symbol	Company	January 3	January 31	% Change	Last 30 Days
AMZN	Amazon	3,193,457	3,915,372	22.6	
CRM	Salesforce	4,318,489	7,084,216	64.0	
EBAY	eBay	6,685,654	9,059,308	35.5	
ETSY	Etsy	2,603,925	3,465,217	33.1	
FB	Facebook	14,562,849	21,579,474	48.2	
GOOGL	Google	1,433,947	1,999,300	39.4	
NFLX	Netflix	3,068,808	20,047,452	553.3	
PYPL	Pinterest	12,797,801	14,260,028	11.4	
TWTR	Twitter	14,447,453	17,558,278	21.5	
ZNGA	Zynga	14,963,287	42,834,517	186.3	

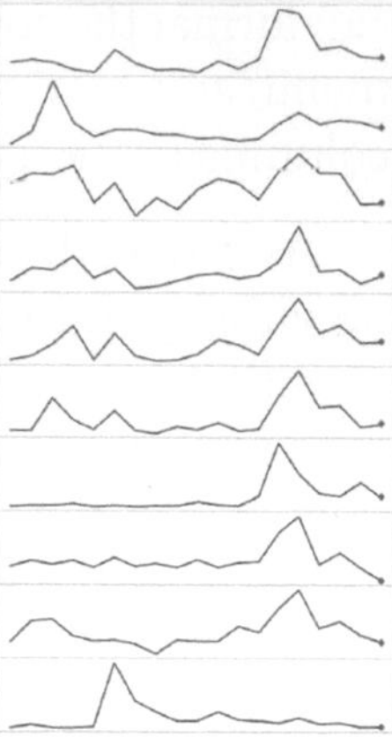

FIGURE 7.5

Quick Instructions

1. *Insert > Sparklines > Line*
2. Enter the data range (H3:AA12) in the top box and the placement range (F3:F12) in the bottom box

Setting

Making

Moving

Chapter 8

Heatmap

Heatmap	
Level: **Beginner**	
Data Type: **Categorical**	
Combine Charts: **No**	
Formulas Used: **None**	

Heatmaps are similar to a table, but instead of showing the actual numbers, the heatmap shows colors. They are typically used to show high-frequency data in a compact format.

Creating heatmaps is relatively easy to do using Excel's *Conditional Formatting* menu, combined with a little trick to hide the numbers. We'll use the power of *Conditional Formatting* several times in this book, so this tutorial serves as a good introduction to how the menu works.

The basic data for this example consists of the total number of singles, doubles, triples, and home runs hit by every Major League Baseball team during the 2021 baseball season. We want to show the totals for each category, and a basic table, while not a terrible option, is not particularly useful for easily picking out patterns or trends in the data (Figure 8.1).

DOI: 10.1201/9781003321552-10

	A	B	C	D	E	F
1	Team	1B	2B	3B	HR	Total
2	Arizona Diamondbacks	814	308	31	144	1,297
3	Atlanta Braves	779	269	20	239	1,307
4	Baltimore Orioles	820	266	15	195	1,296
5	Boston Red Sox	862	330	23	219	1,434
6	Chicago Cubs	794	225	26	210	1,255
7	Chicago White Sox	886	275	22	190	1,373
8	Cincinnati Reds	822	295	13	222	1,352
9	Cleveland Indians	796	248	22	203	1,269
10	Colorado Rockies	847	275	34	182	1,338
11	Detroit Tigers	847	236	37	179	1,299
12	Houston Astros	962	299	14	221	1,496
13	Kansas City Royals	906	251	29	163	1,349
14	Los Angeles Angels	853	265	23	190	1,331
15	Los Angeles Dodgers	822	247	24	237	1,330
16	Miami Marlins	837	226	23	158	1,244
17	Milwaukee Brewers	784	255	18	194	1,251
18	Minnesota Twins	795	271	17	228	1,311
19	New York Mets	821	228	18	176	1,243
20	New York Yankees	819	213	12	222	1,266
21	Oakland Athletics	795	271	19	199	1,284
22	Philadelphia Phillies	804	262	24	198	1,288
23	Pittsburgh Pirates	862	240	35	124	1,261
24	San Diego Padres	831	273	21	180	1,305
25	San Francisco Giants	823	271	25	241	1,360
26	Seattle Mariners	766	233	11	199	1,209
27	St. Louis Cardinals	822	261	22	198	1,303
28	Tampa Bay Rays	790	288	36	222	1,336
29	Texas Rangers	838	225	24	167	1,254
30	Toronto Blue Jays	895	285	13	262	1,455
31	Washington Nationals	914	272	20	182	1,388

FIGURE 8.1

1. First, we need to add color to the cells using *Conditional Formatting*, which we can do by selecting the first category (cells B2:B31) and going to the *Home tab > Conditional Formatting > Color Scales > More Rules* (Figure 8.2).

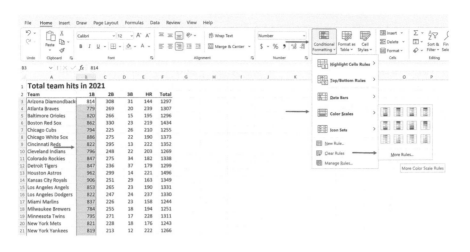

FIGURE 8.2

2. In the resulting menu, we can select the colors we want to use. The standard "sequential color palette" uses lighter colors for smaller values and darker colors for larger values. We can select other options in the *Minimum* and *Maximum* drop-down menus, but the default options, *Lowest Value* and *Highest Value*, are sufficient for our purposes. Select the colors in the "Color:" drop-down menu and click OK (Figure 8.3).

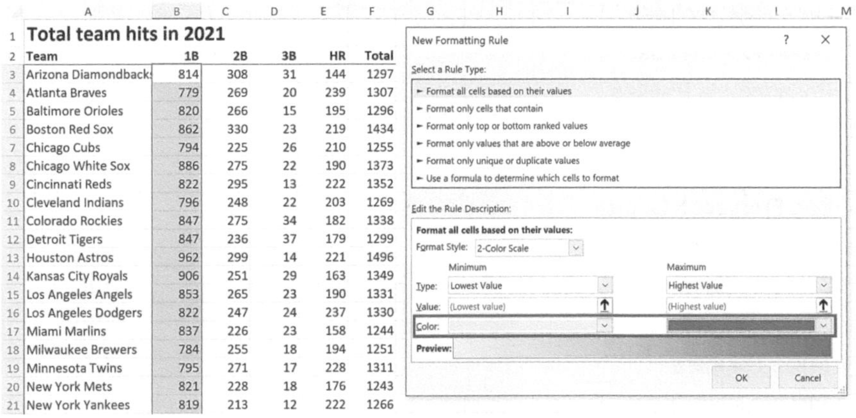

FIGURE 8.3

The column will now display the colors selected (Figure 8.4).

3. Repeat the process with new colors for the remaining columns. Keep in mind that there may be cases where we want to use shades and tints of a single color for the entire table. In those cases, we will follow the same process—select the entire table and apply the color palette. If we apply a single color palette to the entire table, we'll get a different perspective of

	A	B	C	D	E	F
1	**Team**	**1B**	**2B**	**3B**	**HR**	**Total**
2	Arizona Diamondbacks	814	308	31	144	1,297
3	Atlanta Braves	779	269	20	239	1,307
4	Baltimore Orioles	820	266	15	195	1,296
5	Boston Red Sox	862	330	23	219	1,434
6	Chicago Cubs	794	225	26	210	1,255
7	Chicago White Sox	886	275	22	190	1,373
8	Cincinnati Reds	822	295	13	222	1,352
9	Cleveland Indians	796	248	22	203	1,269
10	Colorado Rockies	847	275	34	182	1,338
11	Detroit Tigers	847	236	37	179	1,299
12	Houston Astros	962	299	14	221	1,496
13	Kansas City Royals	906	251	29	163	1,349
14	Los Angeles Angels	853	265	23	190	1,331
15	Los Angeles Dodgers	822	247	24	237	1,330
16	Miami Marlins	837	226	23	158	1,244
17	Milwaukee Brewers	784	255	18	194	1,251
18	Minnesota Twins	795	271	17	228	1,311
19	New York Mets	821	228	18	176	1,243
20	New York Yankees	819	213	12	222	1,266
21	Oakland Athletics	795	271	19	199	1,284
22	Philadelphia Phillies	804	262	24	198	1,288
23	Pittsburgh Pirates	862	240	35	124	1,261
24	San Diego Padres	831	273	21	180	1,305
25	San Francisco Giants	823	271	25	241	1,360
26	Seattle Mariners	766	233	11	199	1,209
27	St. Louis Cardinals	822	261	22	198	1,303
28	Tampa Bay Rays	790	288	36	222	1,336
29	Texas Rangers	838	225	24	167	1,254
30	Toronto Blue Jays	895	285	13	262	1,455
31	Washington Nationals	914	272	20	182	1,388

FIGURE 8.4

the data. In the version on the left of Figure 8.5, we can see which teams had the most hits of each type. Arizona and Boston hit a lot of doubles (2B), and Toronto hit a lot of home runs (HR). But in the version on the right, we can see that singles (1B) were by far the most common type of hit for every team.

Team	1B	2B	3B	HR	Total
Arizona Diamondbacks	814	308	31	144	1,297
Atlanta Braves	779	269	20	239	1,307
Baltimore Orioles	820	266	15	195	1,296
Boston Red Sox	862	330	23	219	1,434
Chicago Cubs	794	225	26	210	1,255
Chicago White Sox	886	275	22	190	1,373
Cincinnati Reds	822	295	13	222	1,352
Cleveland Indians	796	248	22	203	1,269
Colorado Rockies	847	275	34	182	1,338
Detroit Tigers	847	236	37	179	1,299
Houston Astros	962	299	14	221	1,496
Kansas City Royals	906	251	29	163	1,349
Los Angeles Angels	853	265	23	190	1,331
Los Angeles Dodgers	822	247	24	237	1,330
Miami Marlins	837	226	23	158	1,244
Milwaukee Brewers	784	255	18	194	1,251
Minnesota Twins	795	271	17	228	1,311
New York Mets	821	228	18	176	1,243
New York Yankees	819	213	12	222	1,266
Oakland Athletics	795	271	19	199	1,284
Philadelphia Phillies	804	262	24	198	1,288
Pittsburgh Pirates	862	240	35	124	1,261
San Diego Padres	831	273	21	180	1,305
San Francisco Giants	823	271	25	241	1,360
Seattle Mariners	766	233	11	199	1,209
St. Louis Cardinals	822	261	22	198	1,303
Tampa Bay Rays	790	288	36	222	1,336
Texas Rangers	838	225	24	167	1,254
Toronto Blue Jays	895	285	13	262	1,455
Washington Nationals	914	272	20	182	1,388

FIGURE 8.5

Moving | Making | Setting

4. If we want, we can hide the numbers. We can't delete them entirely because the shading would disappear, and we can't change the letter coloring to white to match the background because the numbers would show through the colors (though there are cases where you might want to do this). Instead, we can use a small formatting trick to hide the numbers. Select all of the numbers in the table, right-click (or use the CTRL+1/CMD+1 keyboard shortcut), and select *Format Cells* (Figure 8.6).

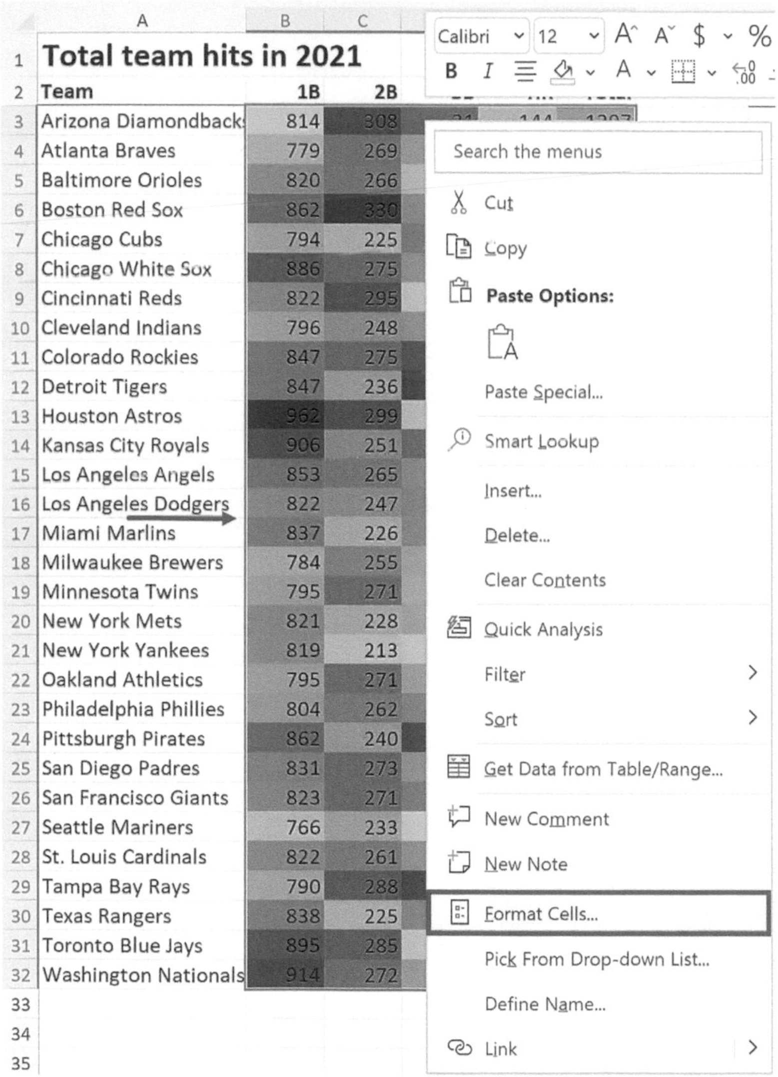

FIGURE 8.6

5. Select the *Custom* option at the bottom of the *Category:* menu. Type three semicolons (;;;) in the *Type* box and press OK (Figure 8.7).

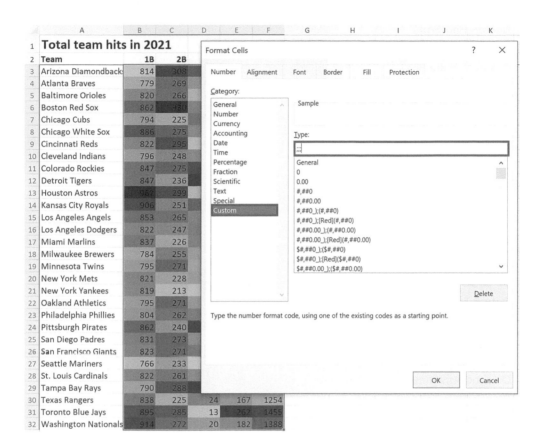

FIGURE 8.7

6. This format hides the numbers. They are still in the cells and can be used or manipulated, but the colors remain. Personally, when possible, I like to add a few more styling pieces to the heatmap.

   a. I sort the data by value rather than alphabetically, unless alphabetically makes the most sense. In Figure 8.8, I sorted the data by the total number of hits.

   b. I add a border, usually white, to the cells using the standard border options in the *Home* tab.

   c. I turn off the worksheet gridlines using the *Show* drop-down menu in the *View* tab before exporting the chart (Figure 8.8).

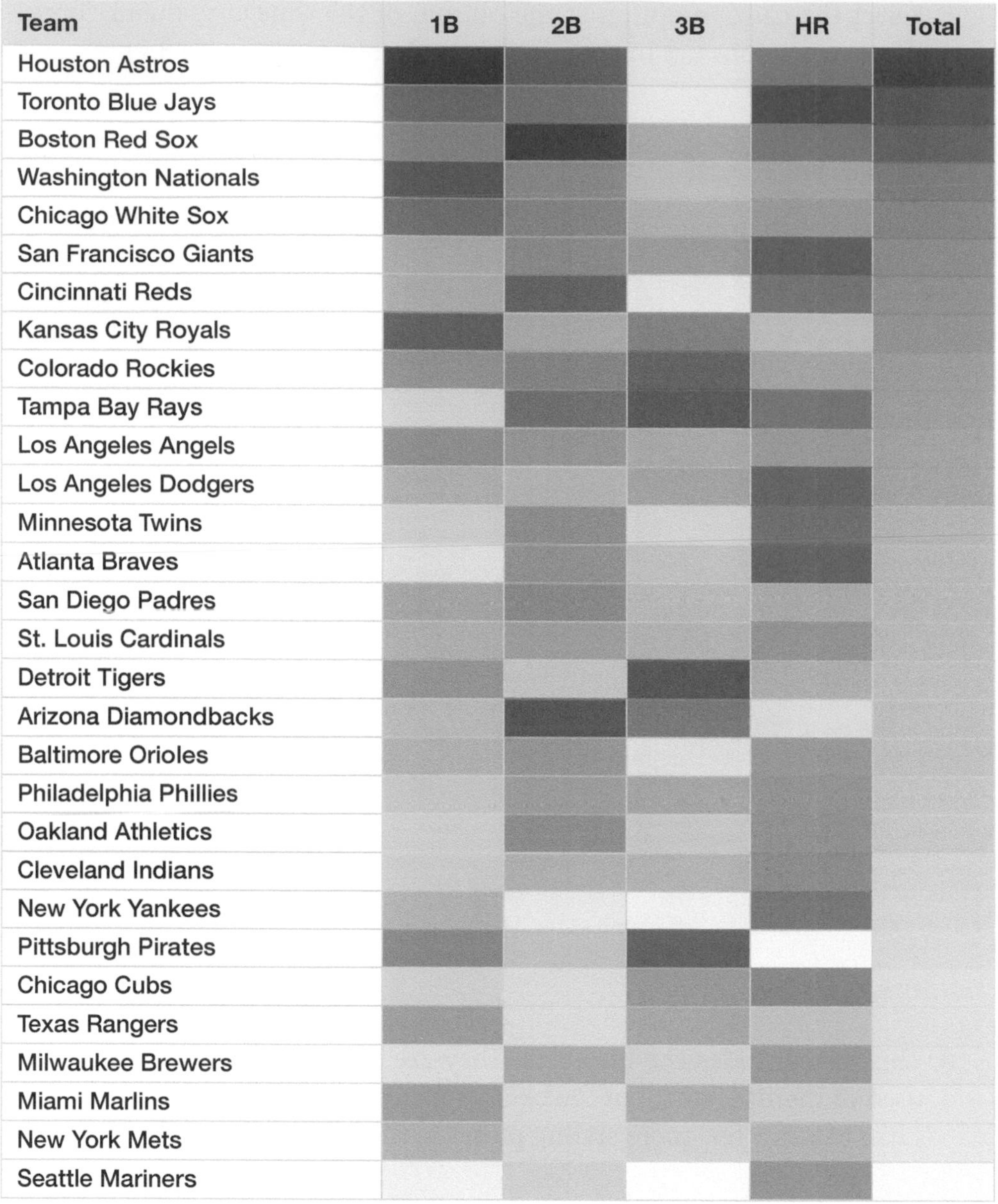

Setting

Making

Moving

Team	1B	2B	3B	HR	Total
Houston Astros					
Toronto Blue Jays					
Boston Red Sox					
Washington Nationals					
Chicago White Sox					
San Francisco Giants					
Cincinnati Reds					
Kansas City Royals					
Colorado Rockies					
Tampa Bay Rays					
Los Angeles Angels					
Los Angeles Dodgers					
Minnesota Twins					
Atlanta Braves					
San Diego Padres					
St. Louis Cardinals					
Detroit Tigers					
Arizona Diamondbacks					
Baltimore Orioles					
Philadelphia Phillies					
Oakland Athletics					
Cleveland Indians					
New York Yankees					
Pittsburgh Pirates					
Chicago Cubs					
Texas Rangers					
Milwaukee Brewers					
Miami Marlins					
New York Mets					
Seattle Mariners					

FIGURE 8.8 Total team hits in 2021

Quick Instructions

1. Select data (either entire data table or each column individually)

2. *Home > Conditional Formatting > Color Scales > More Rules*

3. Set *Minimum* and *Maximum* colors

4. Hide numbers: right-click > *Format Cells > Number > Custom* > type three semicolons (;;;) into the *Type* box

Chapter 9

Stripe Chart

Stripe Chart		
Level: **Beginner**		
Data Type: **Categorical**		
Combine Charts: **No**		
Formulas Used: **None**		

I'm a big fan of stripe charts, which are lines or dots that show individual elements in the data and are often used to show how data are distributed. Making a stripe chart in Excel is not that difficult—it just requires smart conditional formatting and some resizing of the columns or rows.

For this example, we are going to remake the "climate stripes" visualizations popularized by Ed Hawkins in 2018. The data measure the difference between the average temperature in each year and the overall average in degrees Celsius, and can be used to show the average rise in the planet's temperature. Our data run from 1850 to 2021, with labels for the years in the first row and the data in the second row (Figure 9.1).

1. Creating a stripe chart is primarily an exercise in using the *Conditional Formatting* menu. For our stripe chart, we are going to arrange the data horizontally. First, select all of the data in the third row, cells A3:FP3

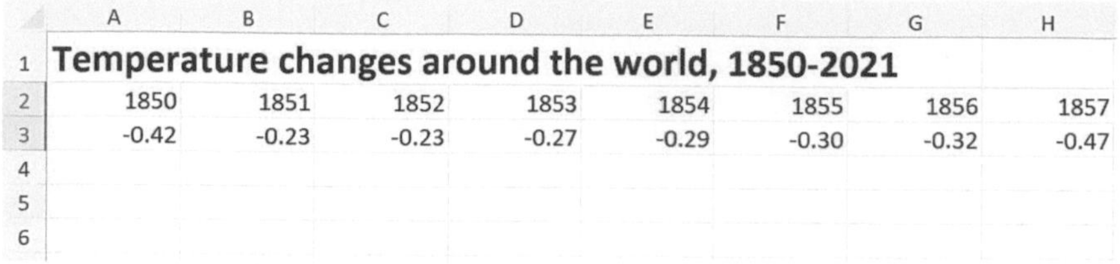

	A	B	C	D	E	F	G	H
1	**Temperature changes around the world, 1850-2021**							
2	1850	1851	1852	1853	1854	1855	1856	1857
3	-0.42	-0.23	-0.23	-0.27	-0.29	-0.30	-0.32	-0.47
4								
5								
6								

FIGURE 9.1

(we can use the CTRL+SHIFT+Right Arrow keyboard combination), and navigate to *Home > Conditional Formatting > Color Scales > More Rules*.

For this particular chart, we want to use a "diverging color palette," which will start at dark blue for the coolest temperatures and continue to red for the hottest temperatures. We will also add a midpoint of white for 0° by changing the "Midpoint" option to *Number*. To implement the color palette, we need to select the *3-Color Scale* option in the drop-down menu and select our colors (blue, white, red) for each of the three options. We can change the hues of blue and red by using the *More Colors* option, or we can select the built-in colors. Once the colors are set, press OK (Figure 9.2).

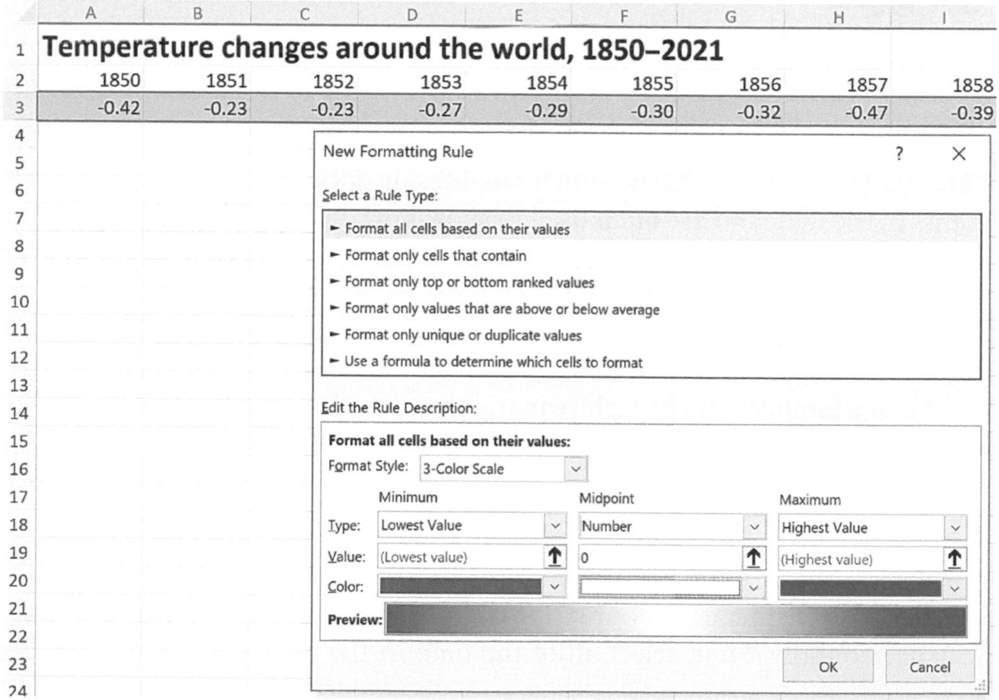

FIGURE 9.2

2. We are going to make the columns much thinner to make the final chart, but before we do so, let's format the year labels along the top of the chart. Insert a new row below the year labels to add labels for each decade: 1850, 1860, 1870, and so on. We could use a formula here to reference the years, but it might be easier to type "1850" in cell A3, merge it with cells A3 through J3, and then left-align the text. Use the "Merge & Center" button in the *Home* tab to merge the cells and the standard alignment menu (also in the *Home* tab) to left-align the text within the merged cells.

   With that first-year label set up, we can copy-and-paste the merged cell across the entire row to fill in the rest. This process is manual, but it's not all that tedious. For the last year—which only has two columns of data (2020 and 2021)—follow the same procedure to merge and resize these last two data columns with eight blank columns (Figure 9.3).

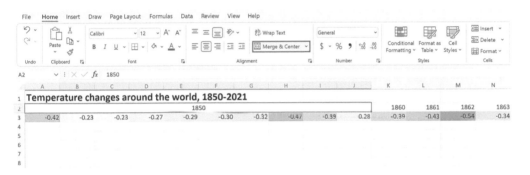

FIGURE 9.3

3. Now we need to set the column width. For this chart that includes 172 years, I use a width of eight pixels on my computer. There are two ways to adjust column widths. Select all of the columns that we want to change and either move the cursor over one of the column breaks to manually make it narrower, or right-click and select the *Column Width* option to manually insert the value. We can also make the rows taller using the same process. Here, I use a row height of 225 pixels, but you may need a different height (or column width) depending on your monitor and operating system (Figure 9.4).

4. Finally, if we want to further delineate the years, we can add a left border to those particular cells (with this much data, I'm not sure it's necessary). In either case, we can hide the spreadsheet gridlines (*View > Show*) to create a blank white background for the chart (Figures 9.5 and 9.6).

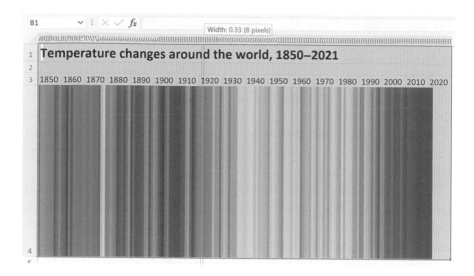

FIGURE 9.4

FIGURE 9.5

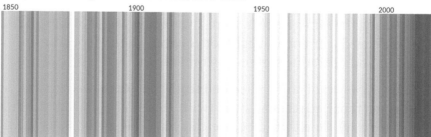

FIGURE 9.6

Quick Instructions

1. Select cells A3:FP3

2. *Home > Conditional Formatting > Color Scales > More Rules > Format Style > 3-Color Scale*

3. Set *Minimum* color to blue and *Maximum* color to red

4. Change *Midpoint* value to *Number,* type zero (0) in the box, and change color to white

5. Hide numbers: right-click *> Format Cells > Number > Custom >* type three semicolons (;;;) into the *Type* box

6. Select columns A to FP and change column width

7. Select row number 3 and make it taller

8. To add or adjust year labels, see full tutorial

Setting

Making

Moving

Chapter **10**

Waffle Chart

Waffle Chart	
Level: **Beginner**	
Data Type: **Part-to-whole**	
Combine Charts: **No**	
Formulas Used: **IF, &**	

Although pie charts are generally the go-to visualization for showing part-to-whole relationships, a waffle chart can provide a good alternative. I define a waffle chart as a 10x10 grid with each square representing a single percentage point, so the sum of all the squares is 100 percent. The waffle chart can be extended to create a *unit chart*, which is a set of shapes that can sum to any amount or show other data types. For a waffle/unit chart, the plotted data should consist of whole numbers because each shape represents a value (though I'm going to cheat a bit in this example and round my data to whole numbers).

Here, we use Vermont's voting results in the 2020 Presidential election. There are four categories—the share of people voting for Republicans, the share of people voting for Democrats, the share of people who voted for another party, and the share of people who didn't vote.

DOI: 10.1201/9781003321552-12

1. First, we need to convert our part-to-whole data to cumulative values. Here, we have 47% for the first group and 22% for the second group, so the first cumulative value is 47 (not 47%) and the second cumulative value is 69. Because we're working with percentages, the last cumulative value should equal 100 (Table 10.1).

TABLE 10.1

	A	B	C	D
1		Group	Share	Cumulative
2	1	Democrat	47	47
3	2	Republican	22	69
4	3	Other	3	72
5	4	Did not vote	28	100

2. We now set up the "map" for the waffle chart, which will be a 10×10 grid starting from 1 in the bottom-left corner to 100 in the top-right corner (Table 10.2). I number the header columns and rows (gray-shaded cells) for my own organizational purposes. Because the waffle chart uses squares, I'll set the row and column widths to be the same. Select the columns by clicking on the column letter and holding the SHIFT key to select multiple columns. We can right-click and choose the *Column Width* option to manually enter the width of the column. Alternatively, we can click on the right edge of the column, hold it, and slide to the left to make the column thinner. We can adjust the height of the row or rows similarly. The "##" symbol appears in the top-right square where 100 should be because the column isn't wide enough for three digits.

TABLE 10.2

E	F	G	H	I	J	K	L	M	N	O	P
2		1	2	3	4	5	6	7	8	9	10
3	1	91	92	93	94	95	96	97	98	99	##
4	2	81	82	83	84	85	86	87	88	89	90
5	3	71	72	73	74	75	76	77	78	79	80
6	4	61	62	63	64	65	66	67	68	69	70
7	5	51	52	53	54	55	56	57	58	59	60
8	6	41	42	43	44	45	46	47	48	49	50
9	7	31	32	33	34	35	36	37	38	39	40
10	8	21	22	23	24	25	26	27	28	29	30
11	9	11	12	13	14	15	16	17	18	19	20
12	10	1	2	3	4	5	6	7	8	9	10

Setting

Making

Moving

3. In the waffle chart itself, which starts in column R, we are going to reference the "map" and our cumulative data using an IF formula, which looks complicated but isn't really so bad. Here's the full formula in cell R12, the bottom-right cell of the chart:

=IF(G12<=$D$2,1,IF(G12<=$D$3,2,IF(G12<=$D$4,3,IF(G1 2<=$D$5,4,0))))

Although the formula looks like a lot, it's just four-layered IF statements. Let me show it to you again, but with added color:

=IF(G12<=$D$2,1,IF(G12<=$D$3,2,IF(G12<=$D$4,3,IF(G12< =$D$5,4,0))))

All we are doing here is comparing the values in each cell of the "map" to the cumulative shares. The first IF statement says if the value in the first cell of the waffle chart (1 in the "map") is less than or equal to the share of the first group, enter a 1 in the cell. But if that's not true, the formula introduces a new IF statement to test against the cumulative share for the second group, and so on. Using the absolute references to the raw data ($D$2, $D$3, $D$4, and $D$5) allows us to simply copy and paste the formula, so it updates correctly (Table 10.3).

TABLE 10.3

		Q	R	S	T	U	V	W	X	Y	Z	AA
2			1	2	3	4	5	6	7	8	9	10
3	1		4	4	4	4	4	4	4	4	4	4
4	2		4	4	4	4	4	4	4	4	4	4
5	3		3	3	4	4	4	4	4	4	4	4
6	4		2	2	2	2	2	2	2	2	2	3
7	5		2	2	2	2	2	2	2	2	2	2
8	6		1	1	1	1	1	1	1	2	2	2
9	7		1	1	1	1	1	1	1	1	1	1
10	8		1	1	1	1	1	1	1	1	1	1
11	9		1	1	1	1	1	1	1	1	1	1
12	10		1	1	1	1	1	1	1	1	1	1

To illustrate, look at the first value in the waffle chart, the bottom-left cell. The value in the "map" is 1, which is less than the 47 value, so the IF statement enters a 1 in the cell. Now let's look at the top row of the waffle chart, in the top-left cell. Here, the value in the "map" is 91, which is greater than all of the values in our cumulative data except for 100, so the formula enters a 4 in the cell.

4. With the dataset in the waffle chart, we can go to the *Home > Conditional Formatting* and set separate colors for each number. In this case, instead of using the *Color Scales* option like we did in the heatmap, we select *Conditional Formatting > Highlight Cells Rules > Equal To*, which brings us to a menu where we should enter a "1" in the box. We can use the default styling options or, even better, select the *Custom Format* option at the bottom of the drop-down menu to change the cell fill, font color, outline, and more. When we're done selecting our formatting options, press OK, then OK again in the main menu. We repeat the process for each number in the waffle chart (2, 3, and 4) (Figure 10.1).

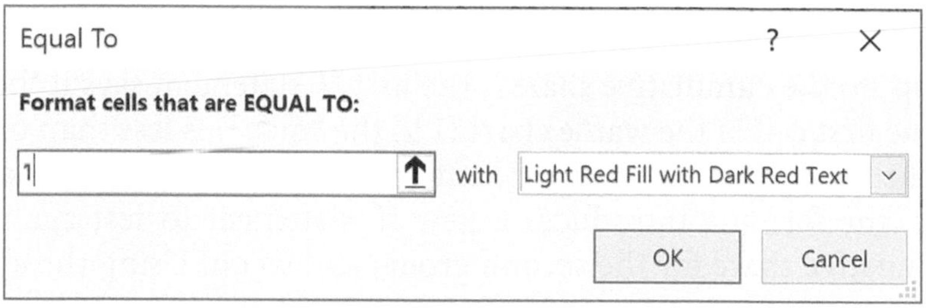

FIGURE 10.1

5. As with the heatmap, I like to add a white border to each cell using the standard *Borders* menu in the *Home* tab. Select the entire table, then select the downward triangle next to the borders icon in the *Font* menu of the *Home* tab. Toward the bottom of that menu, we can change the color of the line. Once that's done, we automatically exit the menu and can draw the borders manually with a little pencil. I'm personally not a fan of trying to do it manually, so I go back to the *Border* menu and select the option (e.g., *Bottom Border, Top Border*, etc.) that I need (Figure 10.2). Finally, to hide the numbers, we can use our three semi-colons ";;;" number formatting trick in the *Type* area of the *Number Formatting* menu (right-click on the cells or use the CTRL+1 or CMD+1 keyboard shortcut).

We can handle the labels in a few ways. I usually just type them, but we could use a simple concatenate formula to make it slightly easier. Here, the formula for the "Did not vote 28%" label is =B5&" "&C5&"%", which takes the value in cell B5 ("Did not vote"), puts a space after it (" "), adds the value in C5 ("28"), then adds a percentage sign ("%"). We could also place our labels on the right side of the waffle chart or align them vertically for each series by merging cells

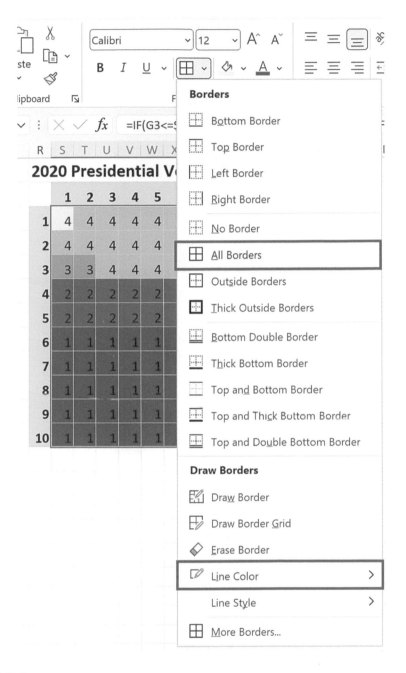

FIGURE 10.2

and changing the vertical alignment in the *Alignment* section of the *Home* tab (Figure 10.3).

In either case, turn off the worksheet gridlines and you have yourself a waffle chart: a decent alternative to the standard pie chart (Figure 10.4 and 10.5).

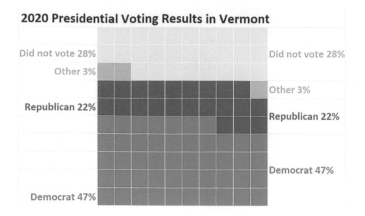

FIGURE 10.3

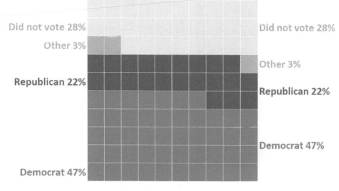

FIGURE 10.4

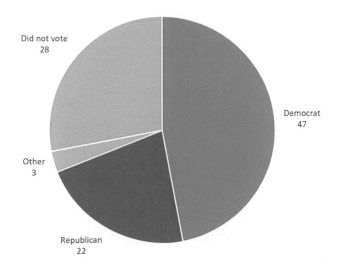

FIGURE 10.5

This approach can be extended for multiple waffle charts or to set up a unit chart. I once created a tile grid map of the US where each state was a waffle chart showing the distribution of ages. It takes a lot of organization to get this to work, but in the end, it's no different than the process we used for this tutorial (Figure 10.6).

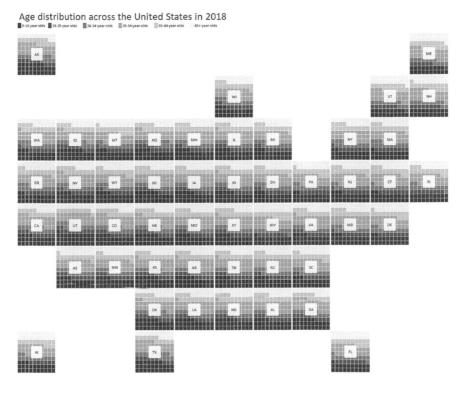

FIGURE 10.6

Quick Instructions

1. Arrange data and formulas

2. Select cells R3:AA12

3. *Home > Conditional Formatting > Highlight Cells Rules > Equal To*

4. Type one (1) in the box and set fill color in the drop-down menu: *Custom Format > Fill*

5. Repeat for each number (1, 2, 3, and 4)

6. Hide numbers: right-click *> Format Cells > Number > Custom >* type three semicolons (;;;) into the *Type* box

7. Add borders: *Home > Borders* (in *Font* area) *> All Borders*

Setting

Making

Moving

Chapter **11**

Gantt Chart

Gantt Chart
Level: **Beginner**
Data Type: **Time**
Combine Charts: **No**
Formulas Used: **IF, AND, &**

Typically used as a schedule-tracking device, the Gantt chart consists of horizontal lines or bars that show the duration of different values or actions. There are a couple of ways to create a Gantt chart in Excel. One uses the *Conditional Formatting* menu in the spreadsheet itself, and another uses the standard charting engine.

In this example, we use the top 10 career scoring leaders in the National Hockey League. At the end of the 2021–2022 season, the Washington Capitals' Alexander Ovechkin had 780 goals, on his way toward breaking the all-time record held by the great Wayne Gretzky. These Gantt charts show the time span of each players' career.

Conditional Formatting Approach

First, we will create a Gantt chart by using the *Conditional Formatting* menu and making the chart directly in the spreadsheet. This approach allows us to embed the chart within a table, making it a stripe chart with a few tweaks.

1. To create this chart, we are going to enter a series of 1s and 0s in the cells to denote when the player was playing and when they were not. The chart will extend from 1945 to 2021, so there will be a couple of columns of 0s until Gordie Howe enters the league in 1947. We could type the numbers, but a formula is a better, more accurate, and more reproducible approach (Figure 11.1).

	SUM	⌄ ⋮ ✕ ✓ *fx*	=IF(AND($D3<=F$2,$E3>=F$2),1,0)					
	A	B	C	D	E	F	G	H
1	**NHL All-Time Goals Leaders**							
2	**Rank Player Name**		**Career**	**First Year**	**Last Year**	**1945**	**1946**	**1947**
3	1 Wayne Gretzky		1979-1999	1979	1999	),1,0)		
4	2 Gordie Howe		1947-1980	1947	1980			
5	3 Alex Ovechkin		2006-present	2006	2030			
6	4 Jaromir Jagr		1991-2018	1991	2018			
7	5 Brett Hull		1987-2006	1987	2006			
8	6 Marcel Dionne		1972-1989	1972	1989			
9	7 Phil Esposito		1964-1981	1964	1981			
10	8 Mike Gartner		1979-1998	1979	1998			
11	9 Mark Messier		1980-2004	1980	2004			
12	10 Steve Yzerman		1984-2006	1984	2006			

FIGURE 11.1

In cell F3, we enter this formula:

`=IF(AND($D3<=F$2,$E3>=F$2),1,0)`

Press *Enter*, and copy and paste to all of the cells in the table: F3:CD12.

Our formula is a simple IF statement with three arguments:

a. The first argument is the evaluation, which is wrapped within an AND statement so we can evaluate two things at once. In this case, the evaluation is true if the first year ($D3) is less than or equal to the current year we are looking at (F$2) AND the last year ($E3) is greater than or equal to the current year (F$2). Notice we strategically use the absolute reference dollar sign symbol so our formula will still be correct when we copy and paste to the rest of the table.

b. If the evaluation is true, enter a 1 in the cell.

c. If the evaluation is false, enter a 0 in the cell.

Let's look at two cells then:

i. In 1947, Wayne Gretzky (row 3) had not yet started playing. His first year, 1979, is not less than or equal to 1947. As such, the evaluation in cell H3 is false, and 0 is entered in the cell.

ii. In 1947, Gordie Howe (row 4) had started his career, so his first year (1947) is equal to 1947 *and* his last year (1980) is *greater* than 1947. Both conditions are true, so a 1 is entered in cell H4.

2. With the cells of 1s and 0s selected, we can use the *Home > Conditional Formatting > Highlight Cells Rules > Equal To* option to add color, just like for waffle chart. Use the *Custom Format* option to format the cells and press OK when done (Figure 11.2).

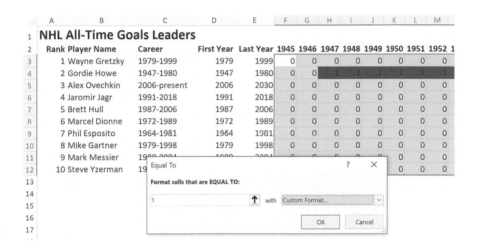

FIGURE 11.2

3. For the final graph, we are going to make the columns much thinner. Before we do so, let's add some year labels to the top of the graph, using the same strategy as the stripe chart in Chapter 9. Labels for every 10 years should suffice. To do so, make a duplicate of the header row by inserting a new row then copy and pasting the original row. Next, merge the cells for every 10 years starting in 1945 and left-align the text. We can't delete the original header row because the formula in the table is tied to that row, so we can just hide it by right-clicking and selecting *Hide* in the menu (Figure 11.3).

4. We can hide the numbers in the chart by changing the number format to three semicolons (;;;) just like we did for the heatmap (select cells >

	A	B	C	D	E	F	G	H	I	J	K	L	M	N	O	P	Q	R	S
1	**NHL All-Time Goals Leaders**																		
2	Rank	Player Name	Career	First Year	Last Year	1945	1946	1947	1948	1949	1950	1951	1952	1953	1954	1955	1956	1957	1958	1
3	Rank	Player Name	Career	First Year	Last Year	1945										1955			
4	1	Wayne Gretzky	1979-1999	1979	1999	0	0	0	0	0	0	0	0	0	0	0	0	0	0
5	2	Gordie Howe	1947-1980	1947	1980	0	0	1	1	1	1	1	1	1	1	1	1	1	1
6	3	Alex Ovechkin	2006-present	2006	2030	0	0	0	0	0	0	0	0	0	0	0	0	0	0
7	4	Jaromir Jagr	1991-2018	1991	2018	0	0	0	0	0	0	0	0	0	0	0	0	0	0
8	5	Brett Hull	1987-2006	1987	2006	0	0	0	0	0	0	0	0	0	0	0	0	0	0
9	6	Marcel Dionne	1972-1989	1972	1989	0	0	0	0	0	0	0	0	0	0	0	0	0	0
10	7	Phil Esposito	1964-1981	1964	1981	0	0	0	0	0	0	0	0	0	0	0	0	0	0
11	8	Mike Gartner	1979-1998	1979	1998	0	0	0	0	0	0	0	0	0	0	0	0	0	0
12	9	Mark Messier	1980-2004	1980	2004	0	0	0	0	0	0	0	0	0	0	0	0	0	0
13	10	Steve Yzerman	1984-2006	1984	2006	0	0	0	0	0	0	0	0	0	0	0	0	0	0
14																			
15																			
16																			

FIGURE 11.3

right-click > *Format Cells > Custom > Type*). And we can change the width of the columns to 0.5 (or whatever width works on your computer) like we did for the waffle chart. Remember to select the columns here, not just the cells. (See how it all builds?) (Figure 11.4)

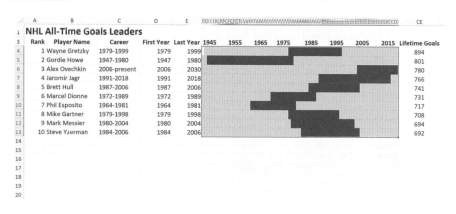

FIGURE 11.4

5. There are a few additional formatting things we can do:

a. Hide the gridlines by going to the *View* tab and unchecking the box next to *Gridlines.*

b. Add a line below the header row in the *Border* menu. If you want to add a little space between the header row and the first bar for Wayne Gretzky, you can add another row and change the height to something like 7 pixels.

c. Add white borders to the bottom of each row in the chart, which will help give the bars a bit of breathing room. This work is manual, and we need to select each row individually to add a bottom or top border (Figure 11.5).

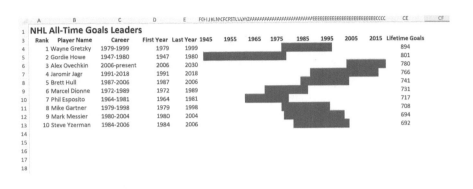

FIGURE 11.5

d. We can also move the *First Year* and *Last Year* columns somewhere off the table by hiding them or cutting (CTRL+X) and pasting (CTRL+V). Don't delete them—remember, the formulas are tied to those cells.

e. Finally, if we want to more precisely mark the year labels, we can add a vertical border to the left side of each column (Figure 11.6).

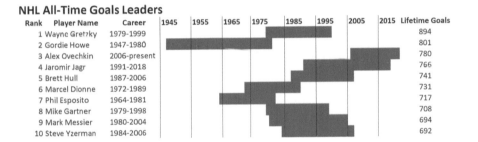

FIGURE 11.6

5. By making the chart in the spreadsheet, we can add another data value by resizing the row height (Figure 11.7). Let's say we want to adjust the height of each row to correspond to the number of lifetime goals. We can decide on a row height for Gretzky—say, 35 pixels—and scale the other rows to that value. (This process requires a little bit of math. Divide Gretzky's lifetime goals by the row height, so 894/35=25.5. Now, divide everyone else's goals by that number to determine the correct row height. For Gordie Howe, we get a row height of 801/25.5=31, and for Steve Yzerman, 692/25.5=27.) These calculations can be automated using VBA code, but that is beyond what we are going to cover in this book.

Setting

Making

Moving

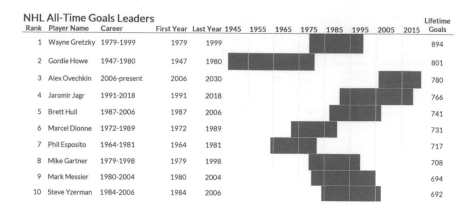

FIGURE 11.7

Graphing Approach

We can also create a Gantt chart by using the standard Excel graphing engine, which requires creating a "filler" series and, if preferred, some tweaks to get the styling in order.

1. We start by creating a *Stacked Bar* chart with cells A1:C11. (The second data series, *Length*, is the difference between each player's last and first year in the league.) Select the data and insert a *Stacked Bar* chart in the *Charts* area of the *Insert* tab (Figure 11.8).

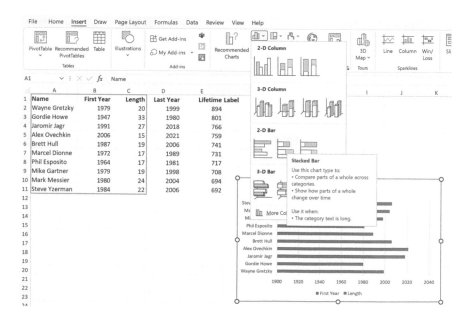

FIGURE 11.8

2. We've created the plot, but Excel puts the last entry (Steve Yzerman) at the top of the chart and the first entry (Wayne Gretzky) at the bottom. I don't know about you, but I want the data in my chart to match how the data are set up in the worksheet. So we need to make a change. To do so, format the y-axis (select the axis and right-click or hit CTRL+1), and in that menu, make two changes:

a. In the *Axis Options* tab, check the box next to *Categories in reverse order*, which will reverse the order of the bars.

b. Change the *Horizontal axis crosses* option to *At maximum category*, which moves the x-axis labels back to the bottom of the chart (Figure 11.9).

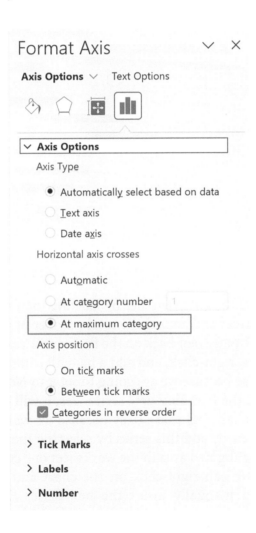

FIGURE 11.9

Setting

Making

Moving

3. If we want to stop here, we can make a few simple changes to the chart and be done:

   a. Hide the *First Year* series by setting its fill color to none: right-click > *Format Data Series* > *Fill* > *No Fill*.

   b. Change the x-axis to range from 1940 to 2021: right-click on the axis and in the *Format Axis* menu set the *Minimum* and *Maximum* bounds to those 2 years.

   c. Make the bars a little wider: right-click on the bars > *Format Data Series* > *Gap Width* > change to 100% in the box (Figure 11.10).

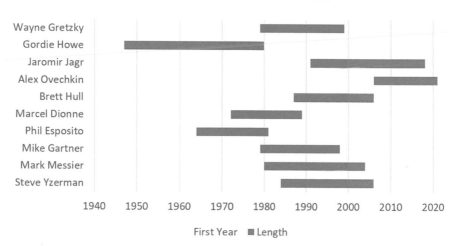

FIGURE 11.10

4. Let's take this chart a step further by labeling the first and last year of each player's career and adding the total number of goals scored.

   First, put the blue color back on the first series. Select the bars for the *First Year* series, right-click, and add a blue fill color—it doesn't matter what blue we use because we are going to set it to *No Fill* in just a bit.

   Second, add the *Last Year* data series. Yes, it will extend beyond the bounds of the chart, but that's okay because we want to use it for our labels. We can easily add this series by selecting the chart and extending the blue-highlighted area in the worksheet one column to the right. Alternatively, we can right-click on the chart and choose the *Select Data* option to manually insert the new series (Right-click > *Select Data* > *Add*). Because we changed the bounds on the x-axis to 1940 and 2021 in the previous step, the last series looks a little weird extending beyond the bounds of the chart, but don't worry, we are only going to use the bars for the labels (Figure 11.11).

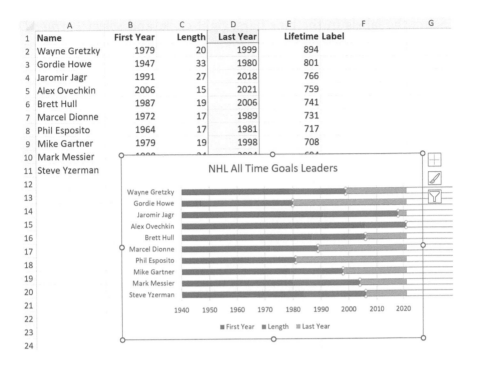

FIGURE 11.11

5. To add the labels, select the blue series, right-click, and select the *Add Data Labels* option. Then do the same thing for the gray series. We can see the labels in the blue series but not in the gray series. That's because, by default, Excel places the label in the middle of the bar, which is off the edge of the graph for the gray bars (Figure 11.12).

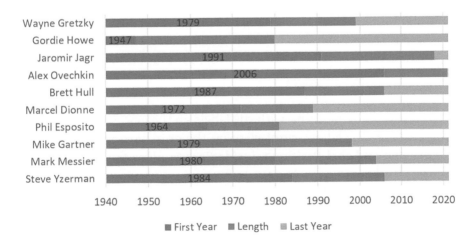

FIGURE 11.12

6. Select the labels in the blue bars, right-click, and select *Format Data Labels > Label Position > Inside End.* This step moves the label to the right end of the bars (Figure 11.13).

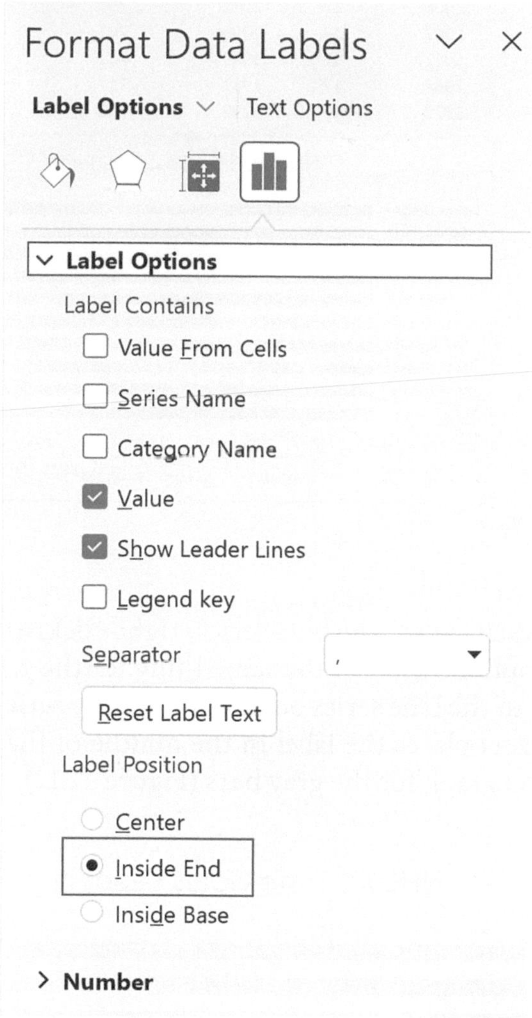

Format Data Labels ⌄ ✕

Label Options ⌄   Text Options

⌄ **Label Options**

Label Contains

☐ Value From Cells

☐ Series Name

☐ Category Name

☑ Value

☑ Show Leader Lines

☐ Legend key

Separator   [, ▾]

[Reset Label Text]

Label Position

○ Center

⦿ Inside End

○ Inside Base

> **Number**

FIGURE 11.13

7. We can do the same thing with the labels on the gray bars. Even though you can't see the labels, right-click on the gray bars and select *Format Data Labels > Label Position > Inside Base* to place the labels at the left edge of the bars (Figure 11.14).

8. Let's do some styling. Set the fill color on the blue and gray bars to *No Fill.* If the label for 2021 (for Alexander Ovechkin) overlaps the bar, grab the right edge of the *Plot Area* (recall the Chart Parts and Properties section in Chapter 4) and move it to the left slightly (Figure 11.15).

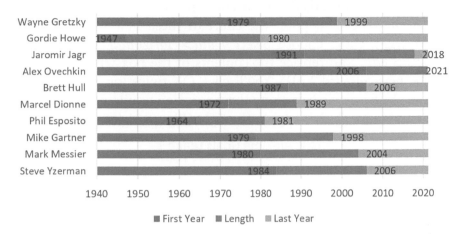

FIGURE 11.14

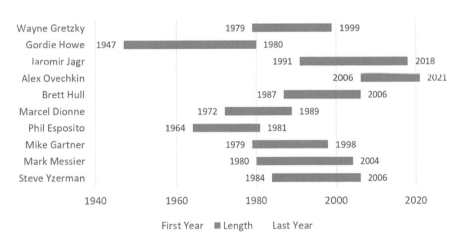

FIGURE 11.15

9. Finally, we can add the number of lifetime goals in parentheses next to each name on the y-axis. All we need to do is create new labels and reference them in the chart. We could just type these, but as you might suspect by now, a formula will make our chart easier to update and replicate. In cell F2 for Wayne Gretzky, we can use this formula:

=A2&" ("&E2&")"

This formula pulls the values in cell A2 (the player's name), then a space with an open parenthesis (" ("), then the values in column E (the number of lifetime goals), and finally a closed parenthesis (")"). Copy and paste that formula down the column.

We now need to point the chart to these new labels. Select the chart, right-click, choose *Select Data > Horizontal (Category) Axis Labels: > Edit*, and replace the contents of the box with the reference to the new cells (=F2:F11). You'll click OK twice (on PCs) to exit the menus. If the new labels along the y-axis don't quite fit, select the *Plot Area* and move the left edge to the right (Figure 11.16).

FIGURE 11.16

Quick Instructions

Method #1: Conditional Formatting

1. Arrange data and formulas

2. Select cells F3:CD12

3. *Home > Conditional Formatting > Highlight Cells Rules > Equal To*

4. Type one (1) in menu box

5. Set the style (e.g., fill color) for the cells: *Custom Format > Fill*

6. Hide numbers: right-click > *Format Cells > Number > Custom >* type three semicolons (;;;) into the *Type* box

7. Select columns F to CD and change column width

8. Resize rows to correspond to the number of *Lifetime Goals* (see cells CG17:CH27)

9. To add or adjust year labels, see full tutorial

Method #2: Stacked Bar Chart

1. Arrange data and formulas

2. Select cells A1:D11 and insert a *Stacked Bar Chart*

3. Format vertical axis:

   - Right-click > *Format Axis* > *Axis Options* > *Categories in reverse order*

   - Right-click > *Format Axis* > *Axis Options* > *Horizontal axis crosses* > *At maximum category*

4. Add labels:

   - Right-click on the *First Year* series > *Add Data Labels*

   - Right-click on the *Last Year* series > *Add Data Labels*

5. Format labels:

   - Right-click on labels for *First Year* series > *Format Data Labels* > *Label Position* > *Inside End*

   - Right-click on labels for *Last Year* series > *Format Data Labels* > *Label Position* > *Inside Base*

6. Edit range of horizontal axis: right-click > *Format Axis* > *Bounds* > 1940 for *Minimum* and 2021 for *Maximum*

7. Remove fill color of *First Year* series and *Last Year* series: right-click > *Format Data Series* > *Fill* > *No Fill*

8. Delete legend and adjust *Plot Area* to fit all labels by dragging the right edge of the *Plot Area* to the left

Setting

Making

Moving

Chapter 12

Comparing Values with Two Graph Types

Comparing Values with Two Graph Types
Level: **Intermediate**
Data Type: **Categorical**
Combine Charts: **Yes**
Formulas Used: **None**

If we want the reader to compare two different data values or metrics for multiple observations, combining two graph types could be the way to go. In this example, we are going to use the official poverty rate in the US compared with an experimental measure created by the US Census Bureau called the Supplemental Poverty Rate (SPM).

We'll create our graph in two ways: first using a vertical layout, which is really easy, and second using a horizontal layout, which requires a bit more trickery.

Vertical layout

1. Create a *Clustered Column* chart using the poverty rate data in cells A1:C11 (Figure 12.1).

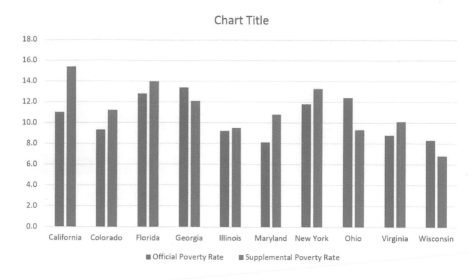

FIGURE 12.1

2. Select the SPM series (the orange bars) and go to *Chart Design > Change Chart Type > Combo* to change the chart type for that series to a *Line with Markers*. (On Macs, we select the series and use the *Change Chart Type* menu to select the *Line with Markers* series directly.) This change gives us a marked line on top of the column chart (Figure 12.2).

3. To get rid of the line but keep the markers, select the line, right-click (or CTRL+1), and *Format Data Series > Line > No line*. We can also change the size of the markers (in the *Marker* tab) to make them stand out more. I increased them to a size of ten units in Figure 12.3.

4. For the labels, we can use the legend or we could add a data label to one or more of the elements. In this case, I think the legend is sufficient (Figure 12.4). Depending on the size of the graph, we might need to rotate the x-axis labels to make them easier to read or, if they are really long, try a horizontal layout.

Horizontal layout

1. Unfortunately, we can't take the same approach with the horizontal bar chart version of this data visualization. For a horizontal layout, we combine a bar chart and scatterplot, but we need to do a little extra data preparation before building the chart. By definition, a scatterplot needs two dimensions. The values for the Supplemental Poverty Rate (SPM) will serve as our x-values, but we need to create a new series (*Height* in

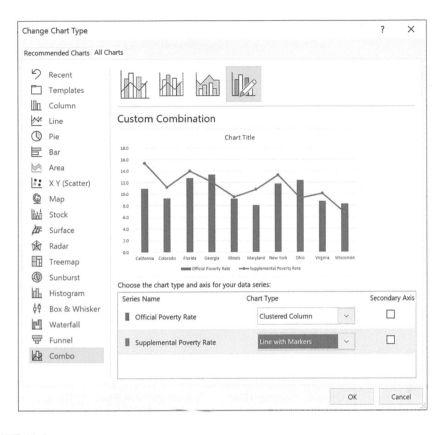

FIGURE 12.2

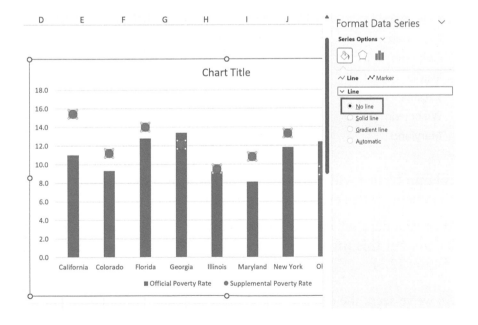

FIGURE 12.3

Setting

Making

Moving

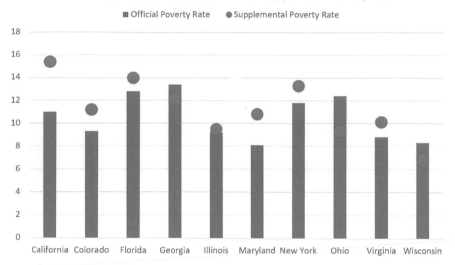

FIGURE 12.4

TABLE 12.1

	A	B	C	D
1		**Official Poverty Rate**	**Supplemental Poverty Rate**	**Height**
2	Georgia	13.4	12.1	9.5
3	Florida	12.8	14.0	8.5
4	Ohio	12.4	9.3	7.5
5	New York	11.8	13.3	6.5
6	California	11.0	15.4	5.5
7	Colorado	9.3	11.2	4.5
8	Illinois	9.2	9.5	3.5
9	Virginia	8.8	10.1	2.5
10	Wisconsin	8.3	6.8	1.5
11	Maryland	8.1	10.8	0.5

column D) that will serve as the y-values. This series consists of an arbitrary counter that runs from 0.5 in cell D11 to 9.5 in cell D2 (Table 12.1).

2. With the data set up, we'll start building the chart the same way as before, but this time creating a *Clustered Bar* chart with cells A1:C11 (Figure 12.5).

3. As we've seen, the order of the data in the chart differs from the order in the spreadsheet. We want the two to match, especially for this chart, because the order will matter. Select the y-axis and right-click (or use

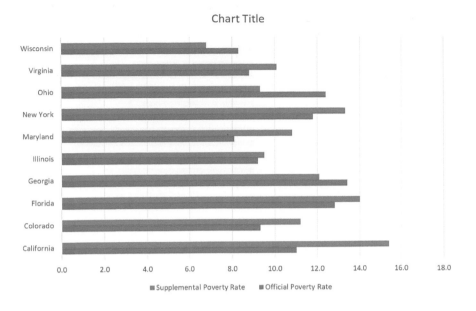

FIGURE 12.5

the CTRL+1 keyboard shortcut): *Format Axis > Axis Options > At maximum category* and *Format Axis > Axis Options > Categories in reverse order* (Figure 12.6).

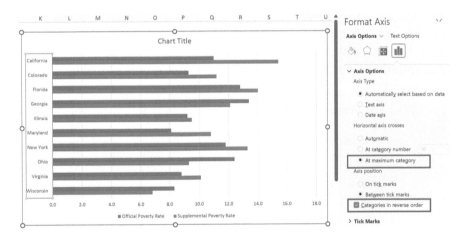

FIGURE 12.6

4. Now, we are going to change the SPM (orange) series to a scatterplot. With the SPM series selected, click *Change Chart Type > Combo* and change to a *Scatter* chart. (Make sure the *Official Poverty Rate* series is a *Clustered Bar* chart.) Click OK. The resulting graph is going to look very weird because Excel puts the state names (cells A2:A11) in the x-values box and the SPM values (cells C2:C11) in the y-values box of the *Supplemental Poverty Rate* series (Figure 12.7).

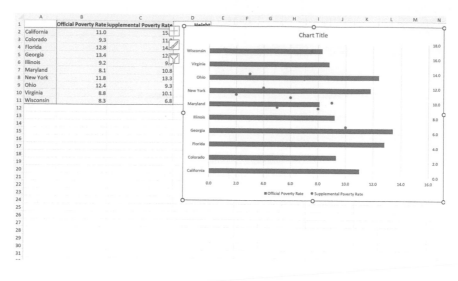

FIGURE 12.7

5. We need to change both the x- and y-dimensions: right-click on the chart and choose the *Select Data* option. Select the SPM series and click *Edit*. Reference the actual data for the *Series X Values*: (cells C2:C11) and the *Height* series for the *Series Y Values*: (cells D2:D11) and press OK (Figure 12.8). The arbitrary numbers we typed in earlier should now make a little more sense—when the limits of the right ("secondary") y-axis are set to 0 and 10, the dots line up with the center of the bars. (If the y-axis range doesn't automatically change to 0–10, change it manually using the *Format Axis* menu options.)

Edit Series	? ✕
Series name:	
='Comparison-Horizontal'!$C$1 ⬆	= Supplemental P...
Series X values:	
='Comparison-Horizontal'!$C$2:$C$11 ⬆	= 15.4, 11.2, 14...
Series Y values:	
='Comparison-Horizontal'!$D$2:$D$11 ⬆	= 9.5, 8.5, 7.5,...
	OK Cancel

FIGURE 12.8

Notice how important it was for us to switch the order of the bars. If we kept the original graph with Wisconsin at the top and California at the bottom, the two poverty rate estimates would not line up.

6. From here, we can do a little styling:

   a. **Make the Dots Bigger**: select the dots>*Format Data Series*>*Marker*>*Marker Options*>*Built-In.*

   b. **Widen the Bars**: select the bars>*Format Data Series*>*Gap Width* to 100%.

   c. **Delete the right (secondary) y-axis.**

   d. **Change the Format of the Numbers on the x-Axis to No Decimals**: right-click>*Format Axis*>*Number* (Figure 12.9).

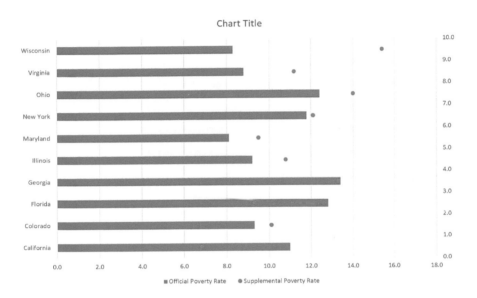

FIGURE 12.9

7. For labels, we could keep the legend where it is, move it to the top, or integrate it directly into the chart by labeling the bars and dots. We could accomplish the latter approach by:

   a. Select the bars and click on the top bar (for California) so it's the only bar selected. Right-click and add the data label. Right-click the label, and in the *Format Data Label* menu, select the check box for *Series Name* rather than *Value*. Change the *Label Position* to *Inside Base*, which will place the label along the vertical baseline. (Excel will likely add data labels to every bar, so you may need to manually delete those one at a time.)

Setting

Making

Moving

b. We can do a similar thing for the dots. Select the series and click on the top dot, right-click, and add data labels. Again, once we change the label format to the *Category Name*, Excel will add labels to every dot, so we'll need to select and manually delete each one (Figure 12.10).

We could also add an entirely different scatterplot series for just the labels. In that series, there would be two values for *x* (1 and 13.4) and two equal values for *y* (9.5 and 9.5).

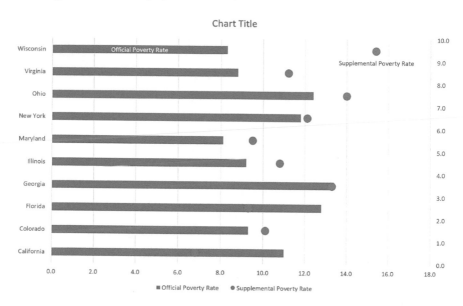

FIGURE 12.10

Finally, it might be better to sort the data by the values for this graph. Remember when we sort the data, we want to make sure the y-values for the scatterplot line up with the bars—just do a quick check to make sure they are lined up correctly! Personally, I like to sort on the bars in this graph (by the *Official Poverty Rate* series) because they are more visually prominent. This switch makes fitting the *Supplemental Poverty Rate* label by the dot for Georgia a little difficult, so I placed the label next to the dot for Florida instead (I don't think that's going to confuse anyone) (Figure 12.11).

Setting

Making

Moving

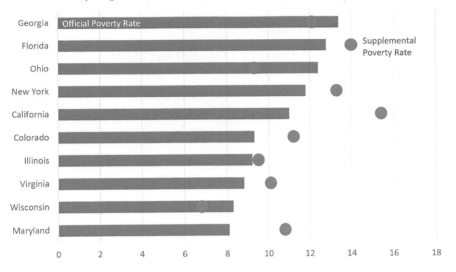

FIGURE 12.11

Quick Instructions

Vertical Layout

1. Select cells A1:C11 and insert a *Clustered Column* chart

2. Change the *Supplemental Poverty Rate* series to a *Line with Markers:*

   a. **On PCs**: select *Supplemental Poverty Rate series Chart Design > Change Chart Type > Combo > Supplemental Poverty Rate > Line with Markers*

   b. **On Macs**: select *Supplemental Poverty Rate series > Chart Design > Change Chart Type > Line with Markers*

3. Select line for *Supplemental Poverty Rate* series:

   a. Right-click > *Format Data Series > Line > No Line*

   b. Right-click > *Format Data Series > Marker > format as needed*

Horizontal Layout

1. Arrange data and formulas

2. Select cells A1:C11 and insert a *Clustered Bar* chart

3. Format vertical axis:

   a. Right-click > *Format Axis* > *Axis Options* > *Categories in reverse order*

   b. Right-click > *Format Axis* > *Axis Options* > *Horizontal axis crosses* > *At maximum category*

4. Change the *Supplemental Poverty Rate* series to a scatterplot:

   a. **On PCs**: select *Supplemental Poverty Rate series* > *Chart Design* > *Change Chart Type* > *Combo* > *Supplemental Poverty Rate* > *Scatter*

   b. **On Macs**: select *Supplemental Poverty Rate series* > *Chart Design* > *Change Chart Type* > *Scatter*

5. Insert the correct cell references for the *Supplemental Poverty Rate* series: right-click > *Select Data* > *Supplemental Poverty Rate* > *Edit* > *X Values: C2:C11* and *Y Values: D2:D11*

6. Delete secondary vertical axis

Chapter 13

Broken Stacked
Bar Chart

Broken Stacked Bar Chart	
Level: **Intermediate**	
Data Type: **Categorical**	
Combine Charts: **No**	
Formulas Used: **MAX**	

Although stacked bar or column charts can show differences in frequency for multiple data series, they can make it difficult to compare series that do not lie on the same y-axis. In the standard stacked bar chart shown in Figure 13.1, it's hard to figure out the relative values of the gray series because the bars are not aligned on the same axis. This tutorial shows how to break up a stacked bar chart and have each series sit on its own y-axis.

At its core, a broken stacked bar chart is a series of aligned bar charts. Creating multiple charts and aligning them in Excel can be a challenge, so it's better to do it all in a single graph. We are going to use the survey results from a 2021 Gallup Poll on respondents' agreement with the following statement: *I have role models in computer science.* The data includes four levels of agreement or disagreement (strongly agree, somewhat agree, somewhat disagree, and strongly disagree) across four areas (large cities, suburbs, small towns, and rural areas).

DOI: 10.1201/9781003321552-15

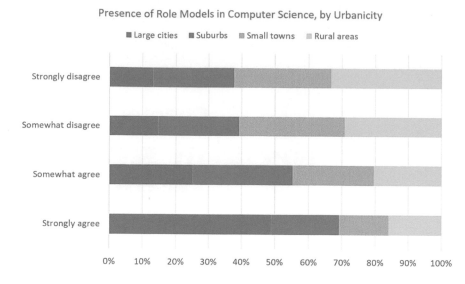

Presence of Role Models in Computer Science, by Urbanicity

■ Large cities   ■ Suburbs   ■ Small towns   ■ Rural areas

FIGURE 13.1

1. Although the original data are set up as a 4×4 grid with row and column labels (cells A1:E5), I've created a new data table in rows 8–12 that intersperses a "Filler" data series between each column. Each filler series is equal to 50 minus the neighboring cell. To create these filler series, I've used a formula with an absolute reference to cell A7. The first value in the *Filler1* series (cell C9), for example, is =$A7-B9. I used the number 50 because it's larger than the maximum value in the data (46), which I found using a MAX formula (=MAX(B2:E5)) (Table 13.1).

2. Using the data in cells A8:I12, create a *Stacked Bar* chart, which is the second option in the *2-D Bar* area of the *Insert Chart* menu. We do not want to include the *Total* series in column J—that's just a reminder that we've transformed our data from percentages that sum to 100% to a new set of values that includes the filler series (Figure 13.2).

3. Notice how the chart groups the series by columns rather than by rows. To switch the organization of the chart, select the chart and select *Chart Design > Switch Row/Column*. The chart is now grouped by rows instead of columns (Figure 13.3).

4. As we saw in the second Gantt chart tutorial, the order of the bars in the graph doesn't match the order of the data in the spreadsheet. To format the y-axis so they match, we can right-click on the axis (or use the CTRL+1 keyboard shortcut) and make two changes in the same menu: *Format Axis > Axis Options > At maximum category* and *Format Axis > Axis Options > Categories in reverse order* (Figure 13.4).

TABLE 13.1

	A	B	C	D	E	F	G	H	I	J
1		Strongly Agree	Somewhat Agree	Somewhat Disagree	Strongly Disagree					
2	Large cities	46	26	13	15					
3	Suburbs	19	31	22	28					
4	Small towns	14	25	28	33					
5	Rural areas	15	21	26	38					
6										
7	50									
8		Strongly Agree	Filler 1	Somewhat Agree	Filler 2	Somewhat Disagree	Filler 3	Strongly Disagree	Filler 4	Total
9	Large cities	46	4	26	24	13	37	15	35	200
10	Suburbs	19	31	31	19	22	28	28	22	200
11	Small towns	14	36	25	25	28	22	33	17	200
12	Rural areas	15	35	21	29	26	24	38	12	200
13										
14	Scatter	X	Y							
15	Strongly agree	0	4.0							
16	Somewhat agree	50	4.0							
17	Somewhat disagree	100	4.0							
18	Strongly disagree	150	4.0							

Setting

Making

Moving

5. We can hide the *Filler* series by changing the fill color to *No Fill* in the *Format* menu. Excel will remember that we selected *No Fill*, so we can easily click back and forth between the bars and the paint can icon instead of having to reselect each time (Figure 13.5).

6. We need to change the spacing of the vertical gridlines to match the vertical alignment of the data bars. Select the x-axis and right-click or CTRL+1 to format. Change the axis to span from 0 (in the *Minimum*

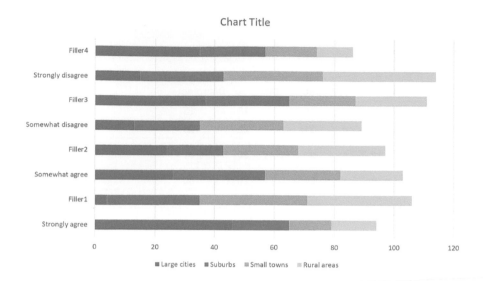

FIGURE 13.2

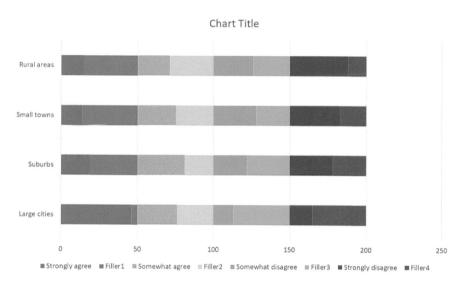

FIGURE 13.3

section) to 200 (in the *Maximum* section), and change the *Major Unit* to 50 to match the value used to construct the spacing (Figure 13.6).

If we don't want the final gridline on the chart, we can cheat a bit and change the minimum value to 0 and the maximum value of the x-axis to 199.9. (Excel might change the minimum value to something other than 0 to generate an even length, so you may need to change it back.) On PCs, the button to the right of the input boxes will change from "Auto" to "Reset," which is a good indication that the limits have been manually set. On Macs, a light gray arrow will change to dark gray.

Setting

Making

Moving

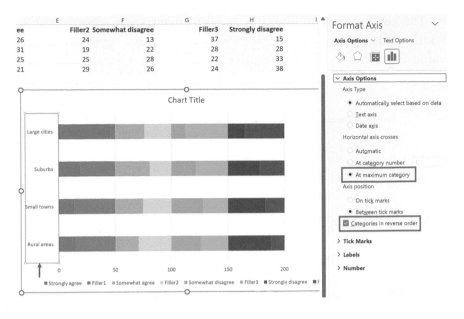

FIGURE 13.4

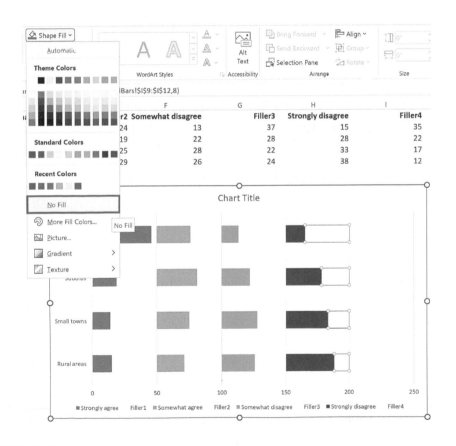

FIGURE 13.5

Setting

Making

Moving

The key for a graph like this one is to make each segment the same width. Otherwise, it might appear that the bars represent a greater value than they really do because they take up a greater share of the space between the gridlines.

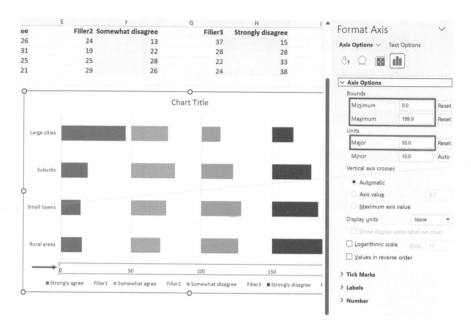

FIGURE 13.6

7. We can also delete the four *Filler* series labels in the legend by selecting each entry and deleting it. We can delete the x-axis because the markers don't make much sense at this point. And finally, if we want to make the bars wider, we can click and adjust using *Format Data Series > Gap Width* (Figure 13.7).

Adding Custom Labels above the Bars

You might have noticed that having a legend at the top of the chart does not necessarily allow us to integrate the graphics and text. In this section of this tutorial, we are going to add data labels to the top of each bar instead of using a legend. There are a few ways to do this (aren't there always?), but my preference is to add a scatterplot. We're going to use this "combo chart" technique a lot in this book, so you'll see this approach many more times.

1. We need to set up separate data that we can plot as a scatterplot, which means we need an x-dimension and a y-dimension. Here, the x-values will sit on our vertical gridlines (0, 50, 100, 150), and the y-values are set

Presence of Role Models in Computer Science, by Urbanicity

■ Strongly agree   ■ Somewhat agree   ■ Somewhat disagree   ■ Strongly disagree

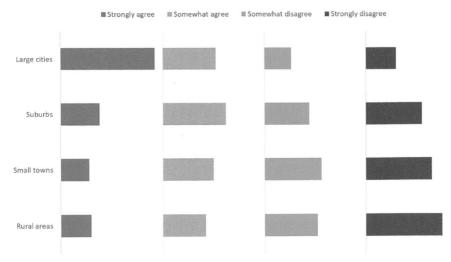

FIGURE 13.7

arbitrarily just above the bars. I set the y-values to 4.0 to start because there are four groups along the y-axis (Table 13.2).

TABLE 13.2

	A	B	C
14	Scatter	X	Y
15	Strongly agree	0	4.0
16	Somewhat agree	50	4.0
17	Somvewhat disagree	100	4.0
18	Strongly disagree	150	4.0

2. Now, we'll add these data to the existing broken bar chart and convert them to a scatterplot, which will end up on the secondary y-axis. On the original chart, right-click > *Select Data* > *Add*. Use cell A14 ("Scatter") as the *Series Name* and cells C15:C18 for the *Series values:* box. Press OK twice (Figure 13.8).

3. Notice that our new series does not appear anywhere on the chart! It's there but it's difficult to find because we fixed the horizontal axis dimension to go from 0 to 200, and our new "Scatter" series is stacked on top of the last series beyond the maximum horizontal axis value. We can select the new series by selecting the chart, going to the *Format* tab, and using the *Current Selection* drop-down menu (on the far left of the tab) to select the series. With the series selected, we can use the *Chart Design* > *Change Chart Type* > *Combo* option

Setting

Making

Moving

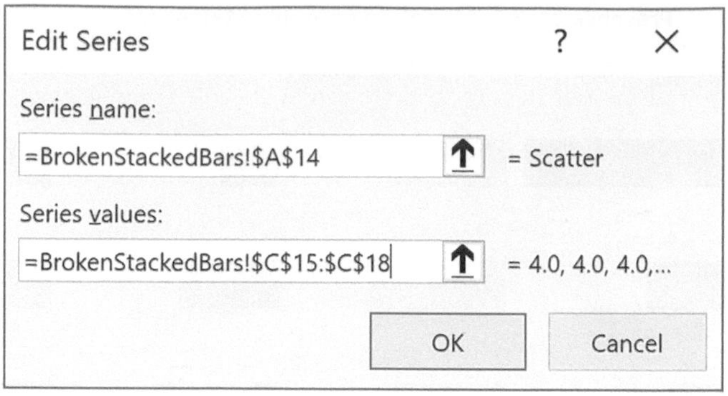

Setting

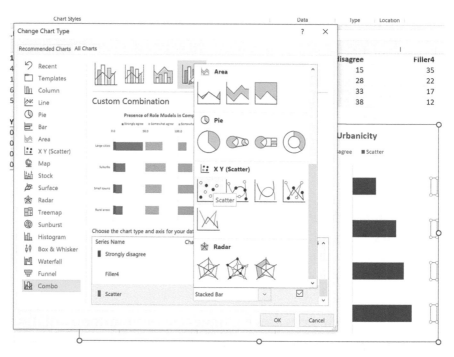

FIGURE 13.8

to convert this new series to a *Scatter* chart (Figure 13.9). (If you're on a Mac, use the same process to select the series but use the *Chart Design > Change Chart Type* menus to select the *Scatter* option directly.) Excel will add a secondary vertical axis on the right side of the graph, which we can modify like any other axis.

Making

Moving

FIGURE 13.9

4. Now that the new series has been converted to a scatterplot, we need to assign x-values to it. Select the chart, right-click > *Select Data > Scatter > Edit*,

and insert the references for the x-values in cells B15:B18. Press OK (Figure 13.10). The points will now spread out along the chart, situated on the left edge of each bar segment for each vertical gridline.

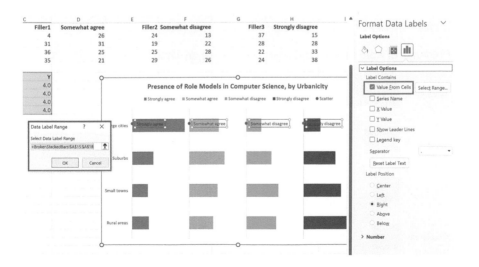

Edit Series	? ✕
Series name:	
=BrokenStackedBars!$A$14 ⬆	= Scatter
Series X values:	
=BrokenStackedBars!$B$15:$B$18 ⬆	= 0, 50, 100, 15…
Series Y values:	
=BrokenStackedBars!$C$15:$C$18 ⬆	= 4.0, 4.0, 4.0,…
	OK Cancel

FIGURE 13.10

5. With the markers on the chart, we can select them and right-click to add data labels. First, right-click on the *Scatter* series and select *Add Data Labels*. Next, right-click on the labels, select *Format Data Labels > Value from Cells* to reference cells A15:A18 as the labels, and press OK. Be sure to uncheck the *Y Value* box because we don't want them to appear in the label (Figure 13.11).

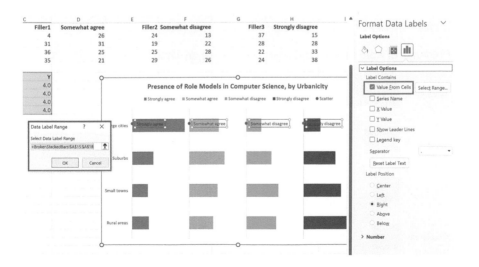

FIGURE 13.11

Setting

Making

Moving

6. We need to do a little manipulation here to get the labels situated just right. Let's lock the secondary y-axis—right-click on that axis > *Format Axis* and change the *Minimum* value to 0 and the *Maximum* value to 4. The value doesn't really matter, but we must have a range we can use to place the labels where we want. With a y-value of 4.0, the labels will sit at the very top, but we can move them down if we want by changing the values for the scatterplot series (in cells C15:C18) to a lower value like 3.8 or 3.9 (Figure 13.12).

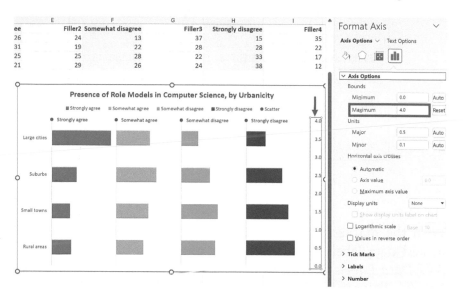

FIGURE 13.12

7. With the labels in place, we can style them by changing the font size, font color, and alignment. We can also hide the dots using *Format Data Series* > *Marker* > *Marker Options* > *None* (Figure 13.13).

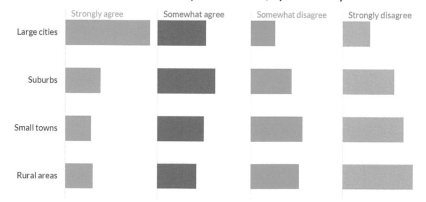

FIGURE 13.13

Setting

Making

Moving

Quick Instructions

1. Select cells A8:I12 and insert a *Stacked Bar* chart

2. Switch order of the chart: *Chart Design > Switch Row/Column*

3. Format vertical axis:

   a. Right-click > *Format Axis > Axis Options > Categories in reverse order*

   b. Right-click > *Format   Axis > Axis   Options > Horizontal   axis crosses > At maximum category*

4. Change color of each *Filler* series: right-click on each > *Format Data Series > Fill > No Fill*

5. Edit range of horizontal axis: right-click > *Format Axis > Bounds > 0* for *Minimum* and 200 for *Maximum*

6. Edit horizontal axis units: right-click > *Format Axis > Units > 50* for *Major*

7. Delete the four *Filler* series labels in legend: click on legend > click on each *Filler* label > delete

8. Delete the horizontal axis

Setting

Making

Moving

Chapter 14

Diverging Bar Chart

Diverging Bar Chart
Level: **Intermediate**
Data Type: **Categorical**
Combine Charts: **No**
Formulas Used: **SUM**

The diverging bar chart is a great way to show the difference between negative and positive values, such as a survey that asks respondents to rank their opinion from Strongly Agree to Strongly Disagree. Because the responses align around a central (neutral) value, it can be clearer to show these categories diverging from a single midpoint. To demonstrate, we'll use the same Gallup Poll data from the previous chapter.

1. As in the Broken Stacked Bars tutorial, we're going to make some small changes to the table structure to get started. We're going to add two new empty data series between the two "disagree" and two "agree" categories, and we're going to change the values in the two "disagree" series to negative numbers. To make these changes, we can use a formula to multiply the values by -1 (e.g., B2*-1), or we can type -1 into a cell, copy it, select the data, and use the *Multiply* option in the *Paste Special* menu. (I show a different way to make this chart at the end

DOI: 10.1201/9781003321552-16

of the chapter without modifying the data in this way, but I like this approach better.)

We are going to use these two empty data series because, as you will see, Excel doesn't align the bar segments and the labels correctly when we combine negative and positive numbers (Table 14.1).

TABLE 14.1

	A	B	C	D	E	F
1		Strongly Agree	Somewhat Agree	Somewhat Disagree	Strongly Disagree	
2	Large cities	46	26	13	15	
3	Suburbs	19	31	22	28	
4	Small towns	14	25	28	33	
5	Rural areas	15	21	26	38	
6						
7		Somewhat Disagree	Strongly Disagree	Somewhat Disagree	Strongly Disagree	Somewhat Agree	Strongly Agree
8	Large cities	−13	−15			26	46
9	Suburbs	−22	−28			31	19
10	Small towns	−28	−33			25	14
11	Rural areas	−26	−38			21	15

2. Now, select cells A7:G11 to create a *Stacked Bar* chart (Figure 14.1).

3. As in previous chapters, Excel does not plot the data in the direction we want, so we can select *Chart Design > Switch Row/Column* to reshape the chart to our preferred layout (Figure 14.2).

4. Once again, Excel has ordered the bars opposite to how they appear in the spreadsheet, so we need to fix the alignment by selecting the y-axis, right-clicking to format, and arranging: *Format Axis > Axis Options > At maximum category* and *Format Axis > Axis Options > Categories in reverse order* (Figure 14.3).

5. Take a look at the legend in the resulting graph. Notice how the *Strongly disagree* bars are in the (correct) far left position of the chart but the label is to the right of the *Somewhat disagree* category? It's backward, so we need to make some slight changes.

Setting

Making

Moving

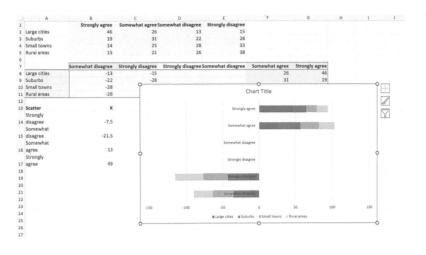

FIGURE 14.1

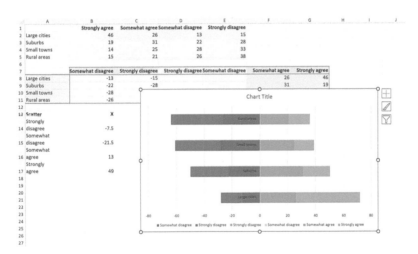

FIGURE 14.2

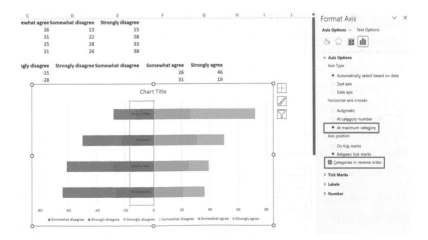

FIGURE 14.3

Setting

Making

Moving

To align the bars and the legend entries, we are going to edit the legend directly. We can delete the first two "disagree" series in the legend—the ones that are tied to actual data. Don't worry, we can delete those two entries in the legend but the data will remain in the chart. Click the legend then click again on the *Somewhat disagree* label and delete; repeat for the *Strongly disagree* label (Figure 14.4).

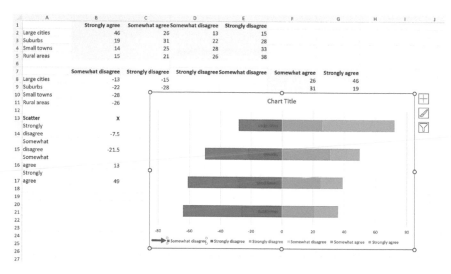

FIGURE 14.4

6. With the remaining two "disagree" series—the ones with empty cells in the table (columns D and E)—we can again click in the legend and use the *Home > Shape Fill* menu to select colors that match the bars in the chart (Figure 14.5).

7. Now we can do a bit of styling:

    a. Move the Legend to the top of the chart (right-click > *Format Legend > Legend Position > Top*).

    b. The category labels (e.g., *Large cities, Suburbs,* etc.) are probably best positioned on the left side of the chart, so right-click on the y-axis and select *Format Axis > Labels > Label Position > Low.*

    c. We want the zero-axis line to stand out, so with the y-axis labels still selected, change the color of the line to another color by modifying the settings in *Format Axis > Line* (Figure 14.6).

    d. If we want to add data labels to each segment, right-click on each bar and select the *Add Data Labels* option from the menu and format as needed.

Setting

Making

Moving

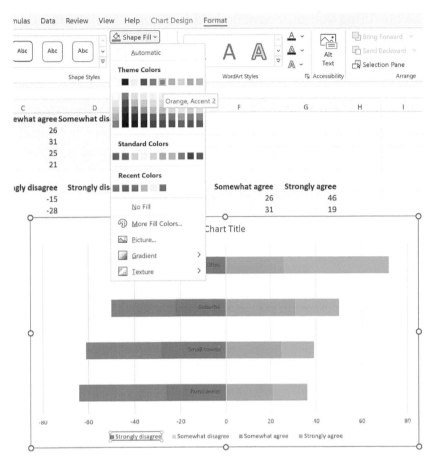

FIGURE 14.5

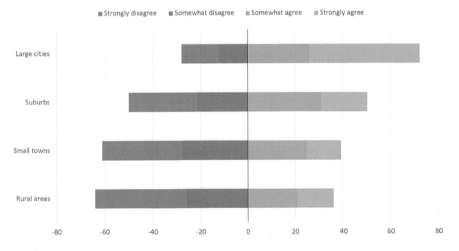

FIGURE 14.6

8. The one thing you may have noticed is that the horizontal axis labels don't make much sense—there's not −13% of people who strongly disagreed with the statement! We used the negative numbers to make the chart, but now we need to make those negative axis labels *look* like they are positive numbers using the *Number Formatting* menu.

   Select the x-axis labels, right-click (or use CTRL+1), select *Format Axis > Number > Custom*, and replace whatever is in the *Format Code* box (*Type* on Macs) with the following number format: #, ###;#, ###;0. Click *Add* (Figure 14.7).

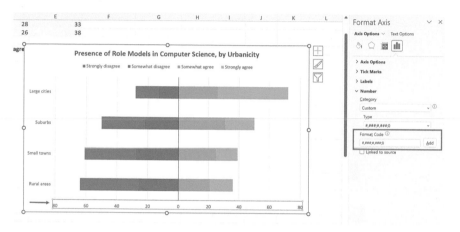

FIGURE 14.7

As noted in Chapter 4, this number format styles positive numbers, negative numbers, and zeros in each position. The "#, ###" code before the first two semicolons tells Excel to include a comma for numbers that are at least 1,000; include no decimals; and show negative numbers as positive numbers. The zero after the second semicolon tells Excel to show the zero number.

9. We can also use all positive numbers to create this chart. With this version, we create a different filler series equal to the sum of the two "disagree" series: =80-SUM(C8:D8). We use 80 because the original chart extended from −80 to +80, so we want to repeat that range here. With this new *Filler* series, we insert a *Stacked Bar Chart*, reverse the vertical axis again, and set the fill color on the *Filler* series to *No Fill*. Here, the axis labels go from 0 to 160, which doesn't make any sense, so we have to delete the axis labels.

   If we want to add the dark line to the middle of the chart where the two "agree" categories are separated from the two "disagree" categories (labeled 80 on the x-axis), we can format the x-axis to have the y-axis cross at 80. To make this change, right-click on the x-axis and type 80 into the box in the *Vertical axis crosses > Axis value* section of the menu. To place the labels back to the far-left part of the chart, right-click on the y-axis, set the position of the labels to *Low*, and change the color/thickness of the line (Figure 14.8).

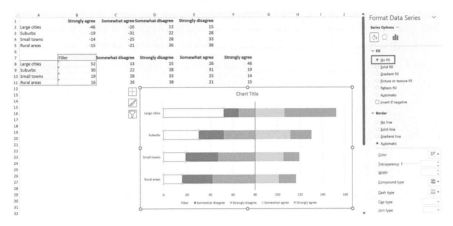

FIGURE 14.8

10. If we want to remove the legend and replace it with direct labels, we can follow the same process as described in the previous chapter for the Broken Stacked Bar chart: add a new series, change it to a scatterplot, label the dots, and adjust the new secondary vertical axis to place the labels in the right place. In the spreadsheet, the x-values are equal to the midpoint of each segment and the y-values are set to 4.0. Each of the labels (e.g., "Strongly agree") is placed on two lines by inserting a carriage return between the words, which we can do by clicking in the cell, placing the cursor between the words, and using the ALT+ENTER keyboard combination (Option+RETURN on Macs) (Figure 14.9).

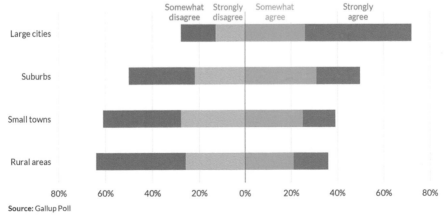

FIGURE 14.9

Setting

Making

Moving

One last point about diverging bar charts. When you have a "neutral" or "no answer" category, such responses are neither agree nor disagree by definition and should not be grouped with either category. In other words, don't place the neutral category in the middle of the chart along the vertical baseline. Instead, consider placing it off to the side along its own vertical axis. You can do so by creating a separate "filler" series that will add a blank space between the segments on the far right (the Strongly disagree category) and segments for the "neutral" category.

Quick Instructions

1. Select cells A7:G11 and insert a *Stacked Bar* chart

2. Switch order of the chart: *Chart Design > Switch Row/Column*

3. Format vertical axis:

    a. Right-click > *Format Axis > Axis Options > Categories in reverse order*

    b. Right-click > *Format Axis > Axis Options > Horizontal axis crosses > At maximum category*

    c. Right-click > *Format Axis > Labels > Low*

    d. Right-click > *Format Axis > Line > Solid line*

4. Delete the legend entries for the *Strongly disagree* and *Somewhat disagree* categories, and change the colors of the other *Strongly disagree* and *Somewhat disagree* categories.

5. Format x-axis labels: right-click > *Format Axis > Number > Custom >* insert #, ###;#, ###;0 into *Format Code* box

Chapter 15

Block Shading
(Same Frequency)

Block Shading (Same Frequency)
Level: **Beginner**
Data Type: **Categorical**
Combine Charts: **Yes**
Formulas Used: **None**

Block Shading charts are typically used to highlight a span of time within a line or column chart. These charts might be used to add a forecast period, mark recession dates, or highlight when a specific policy was in place. When the frequencies of the data match up—for example, when both series are measured annually—the chart is relatively easy to make. In this case, we're going to make a line chart of the monthly US unemployment rate from January 2007 to January 2022 and add shaded bands to show the official recession periods, also measured in months.

1. We start by inserting a line chart with two series in cells B1:D182. The unemployment rate data are in column C, and months in which there was a recession are marked with a 16 in column D. If we include the "Year" label at the top of column B, Excel will plot that series as data, so I've left it out of the practice file (Figure 15.1).

DOI: 10.1201/9781003321552-17

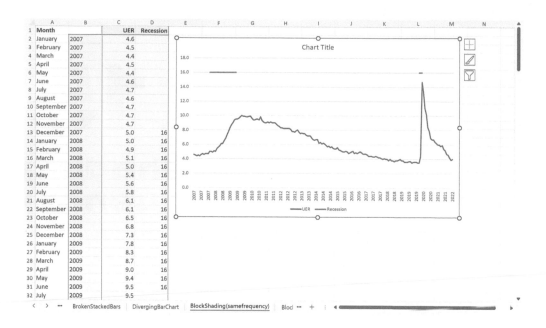

FIGURE 15.1

2. Select the *Recession* series then *Chart Design > Change Chart Type > Combo* and change the *Recession* series to a *Clustered Column* chart in the drop-down menu (Figure 15.2).

    On Macs, select the *Recession* series, then select the *Clustered Column* chart directly in the *Change Chart Type* menu. There is no *Combo* chart option on Macs, so we have to make the chart type change directly (see Chapter 4 for a more detailed description).

3. We originally set the values for the *Recession* series to 16 because they are slightly greater than the maximum value in the unemployment rate series. Notice that with these two series, Excel set the maximum value of the y-axis to 18 because Excel won't let us plot data to the top of the y-axis. We want the bars to extend the entire height of the chart, so we can format the y-axis by right-clicking or using the CTRL+1 keyboard shortcut to change the *Maximum* y-value to 16 (Figures 15.3 and 15.4).

4. Let's close up the space between the bars. Select the *Recession* (orange bars) series and right-click to format. In the *Series Options* tab, change the *Gap Width* to 0% (Figure 15.5).

5. We can style the graph as we like by deleting the legend, changing the color of the bars (I like gray for these purposes), and altering the number or appearance of the gridlines. We can also change the frequency of

Setting

Making

Moving

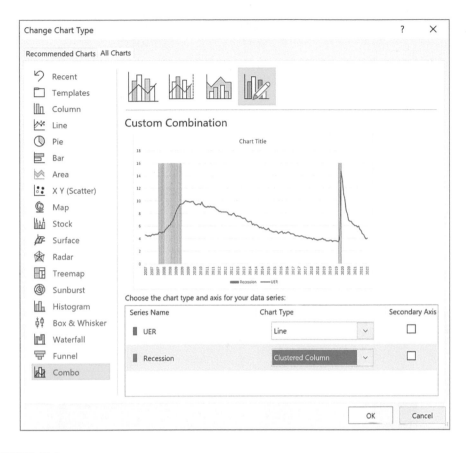

FIGURE 15.2

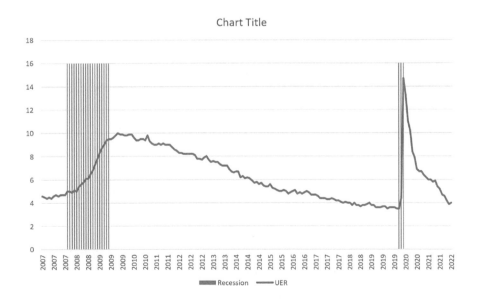

FIGURE 15.3

Setting

Making

Moving

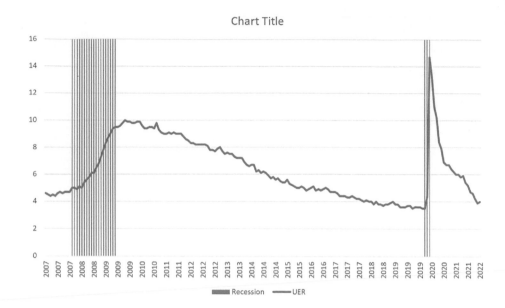

FIGURE 15.4

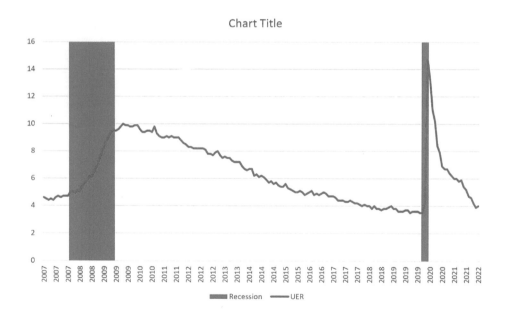

FIGURE 15.5

the x-axis labels within the chart options menu by changing the interval of the labels (*Format Axis > Labels > Interval between labels > Specify interval unit*) to 12 (as in 12 months) (Figure 15.6).

If we want the y-axis labels to have a percentage sign for the top value but not on the others, we can use *Number Formatting* to get the labels just right.

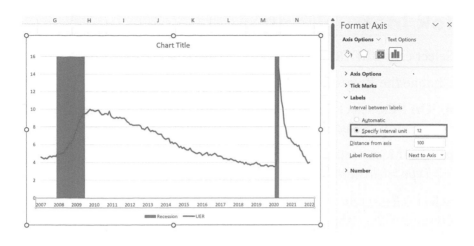

FIGURE 15.6

Select the y-axis labels and under the *Custom* option of the *Number Formatting* menu, type the following:

$$[=16]\#,\#\#\#"\%";\#,\#\#\#\_\%;0\_\%$$

This formula dictates that if the number is equal to 16, add a percentage sign at the end ("%"), but if the number is positive or zero, add a space *after* the number the width of a percentage sign ("_%") so the labels (kind of) line up.

We can also add a label at the bottom (like the "Shading denotes..." one above) by adding a text box. Or, better yet, we can select a single point on any of the series, add a data label, and move it where we want it. I like this approach better because Excel then treats the chart as a single object rather than a chart and a text box (Figure 15.7).

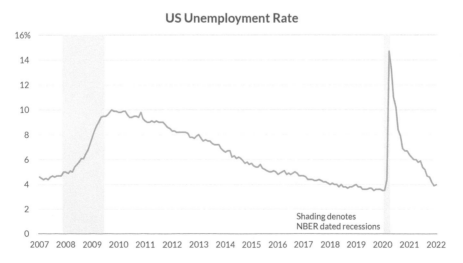

FIGURE 15.7

Setting

Making

Moving

Quick Instructions

1. Select cells B1:D182 and insert a *Line* chart

2. Change the *Recession* series to a *Clustered Column* chart:

   a. **On PCs**: select *Recession series > Chart Design > Change Chart Type > Combo > Recession > Clustered Column*

   b. **On Macs**: select *Recession series > Chart Design > Change Chart Type > Clustered Column*

3. Select *Recession* series > right-click > *Format Data Series > Series Options > Gap Width* to 0%

4. **Change vertical axis dimensions**: right-click > *Format Axis > Axis Options >* 0 for *Minimum* and 16 for *Maximum*

Setting

Making

Moving

Chapter 16

Block Shading (Different Frequencies)

Block Shading (Different Frequencies)
Level: **Intermediate**
Data Type: **Categorical**
Combine Charts: **Yes**
Formulas Used: **None**

Whereas the frequency of the data in the block shading chart we just discussed lined up, this version does not, which makes it more complicated. In this case, we'll plot *annual* estimates of the unemployment rate with *monthly* values for the recessions, so building the chart requires using the secondary axes.

1. Create a line chart using the data in cells A1:B16, which is the annual unemployment rate from 2007 to 2021 (Figure 16.1).

2. To add the monthly recession data, right-click on the chart and choose *Select Data > Add*. Insert the reference to cell E1 for the *Series Name* and that series (cells E2:E169) for the *Series values*. Press OK. This step will slide the **blue** series to the far left of the chart area because Excel now views the chart as a line chart with 168 spaces (corresponding to the number of observations in the *Recession* series) (Figure 16.2).

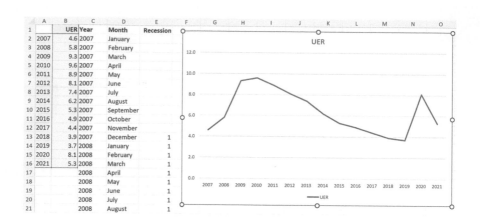

	A	B	C	D	E
1		UER	Year	Month	Recession
2	2007	4.6	2007	January	
3	2008	5.8	2007	February	
4	2009	9.3	2007	March	
5	2010	9.6	2007	April	
6	2011	8.9	2007	May	
7	2012	8.1	2007	June	
8	2013	7.4	2007	July	
9	2014	6.2	2007	August	
10	2015	5.3	2007	September	
11	2016	4.9	2007	October	
12	2017	4.4	2007	November	
13	2018	3.9	2007	December	1
14	2019	3.7	2008	January	1
15	2020	8.1	2008	February	1
16	2021	5.3	2008	March	1
17			2008	April	1
18			2008	May	1
19			2008	June	1
20			2008	July	1
21			2008	August	1

FIGURE 16.1

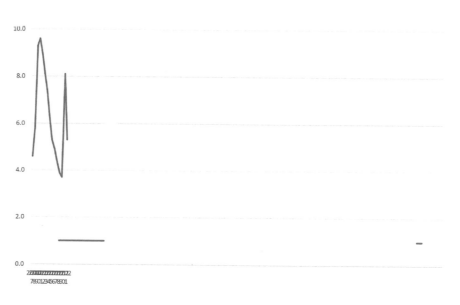

FIGURE 16.2

3. Now, select the orange (*Recession*) series in the chart, right-click, and select the button for *Secondary Axis* in the *Format Data Series > Series Options* tab (Figure 16.3).

Just like the original vertical axis, Excel arbitrarily sets the minimum and maximum values, and we can style and edit the secondary axes just like we would the primary axes.

Setting

Making

Moving

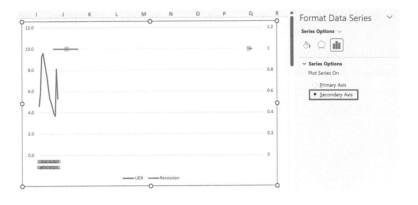

FIGURE 16.3

4. The chart still looks a little weird, but don't worry, we're getting there. As we did in the previous chapter, we want to change the *Recession* series from a line chart to a *Clustered Column* chart. On PCs, select the line, then *Chart Design > Change Chart Type > Combo* to change the chart type for the *Recession* series to a *Clustered Column* chart in the drop-down menu (Figure 16.4). On Macs, select the *Recession* series and change the chart type to a *Clustered Column* directly in the *Change Chart Type* menu.

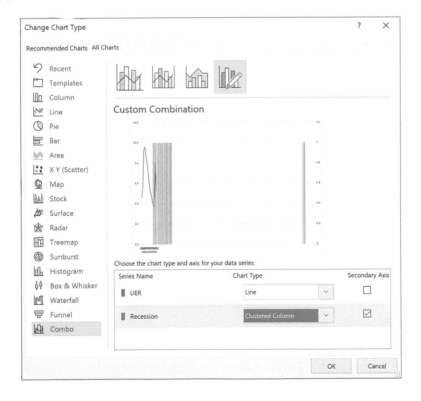

FIGURE 16.4

5. With a column chart now created—and tagged to the secondary axis—we need to "turn on" the secondary x-axis. To do so, select the chart and click *Chart Design > Add Chart Element > Axes > Secondary Horizontal* from the top ribbon. The orange column chart flips to the secondary axis, and the **blue** line stretches out as it did initially (Figure 16.5).

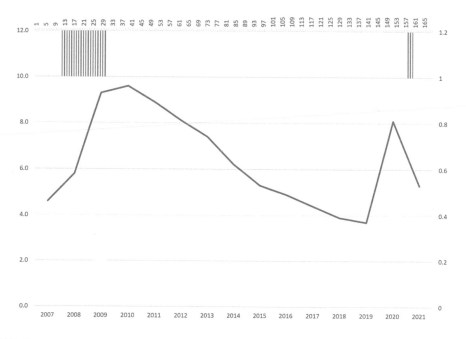

FIGURE 16.5

6. We're closer now, but we still want the bars to stretch along the entire y-axis. Select the secondary vertical axis > *Format Axis > Axis Options* and change the *Minimum* value to 1 and the *Maximum* value to 2. Think of this step as extending the bars from infinity *above* the chart down to 1 at our new secondary x-axis. (Note that this step works because the values in the *Recession* series are set to 1. We can use a different number, but these minimum/maximum values would also change.) (Figure 16.6).

7. Remove the space between the columns by formatting the column chart: right-click > *Format Data Series > Series Options > Gap Width* to 0%. In that same menu, we can also change the colors of the bars using the *Fill* options (Figure 16.7).

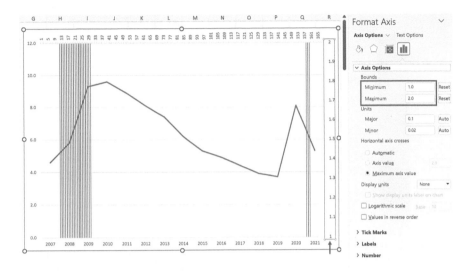

FIGURE 16.6

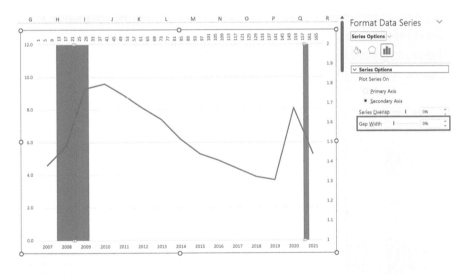

FIGURE 16.7

8. Clean up the graph by hiding the secondary horizontal and vertical axes. For each axis, right-click and make three changes:

a. *Format Axis > Line color > No line*

b. *Format Axis > Axis Options > Tick Marks > None*

c. *Format Axis > Axis Options > Labels > None*

The chart will sometimes break if we simply select and delete the axes, so it's better to turn off everything (Figure 16.8).

Setting

Making

Moving

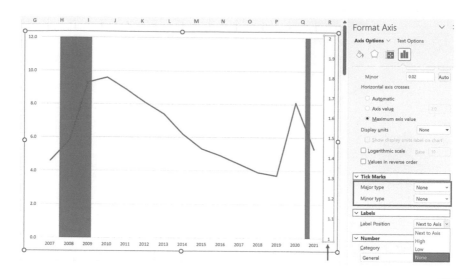

FIGURE 16.8

9. Finally, to get everything lined up just right, we need to put the line chart *on the tick marks* and leave the bars *between the tick marks*. Select the primary x-axis (for the line chart), right-click, and select the button for *On tick marks* in the *Axis position* area of the menu (Figure 16.9).

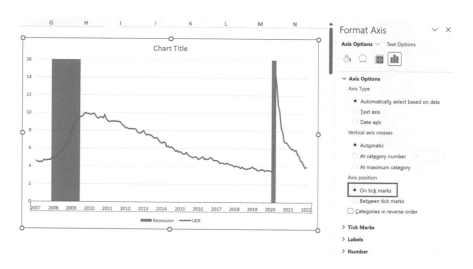

FIGURE 16.9

10. As always, we can style the text, titles, and other elements. In charts like this one with just a few data points, I sometimes add data markers to the line to give it more visual heft. If I think my reader wants to know the exact values, I might add the data labels inside those markers.

To add those stylings, right-click on the line and select the *Add Data Labels* option. Now select the labels, right-click, and *Format Data Labels > Label Position > Center*. Go back to the chart and select the line again, right-click, and in *Format Data Series > Marker Style > Built-in*, increase the size of the markers to be larger than the labels. We can also change some of the other formatting options—in this example, I added a white fill and changed the border of the dots to match the color and thickness of the line using the options in the *Format Data Series > Marker > Fill* and *Format Data Series > Marker > Border* menus (Figure 16.10).

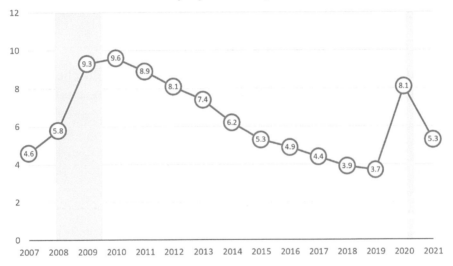

FIGURE 16.10

Quick Instructions

1. Select cells A1:B16 and insert a *Line* chart

2. Add *Recession* data: right click > *Select Data > Add > Series Name: Recession (cell E1)* and *Y Values: E2:E169*

3. Select *Recession* series > right-click > *Format Data Series > Series Options > Plot Series On > Secondary Axis*

4. Change the *Recession* series to *Clustered Column* chart:

   a. **On PCs**: select *Recession series > Chart Design > Change Chart Type > Combo > Recession > Clustered Column*

   b. **On Macs**: select *Recession series > Chart Design > Change Chart Type > Clustered Column*

Setting

Making

Moving

5. Turn on secondary horizontal axis: select chart > *Chart Design > Add Chart Element > Axes > Secondary Horizontal*

6. Change the dimensions of the secondary vertical axis (on the right): right-click > *Format Axis > Axis Options >* 1 for *Minimum* and 2 for *Maximum*

7. Select *Recession* series > right-click > *Format Data Series > Series Options > Gap Width* to 0%

8. Format secondary horizontal and secondary vertical axis:

   a. *Format Axis > Line color > No line*

   b. *Format Axis > Tick Marks > None*

   c. *Format Axis > Labels > Label Position > None*

9. **Adjust Primary Horizontal Axis Tick Marks**: right-click > *Format Axis > Axis Options > Axis position > On tick marks*

Chapter 17

Mark an Event with a Line

Mark an Event with a Line
Level: **Intermediate**
Data Type: **Time**
Combine Charts: **Yes**
Formulas Used: **IF, OR, VALUE, RIGHT**

Sometimes, we need to mark an event, a policy change, or add some other annotation on our chart. This tutorial shows you how to do this by adding a vertical line that is part of the graph, can be moved to other programs (e.g., PowerPoint), and is linked to the data for easier updating and replication. Here, we'll plot the total pounds of beef Americans have consumed annually since 1930 and add a line to denote when the first McDonald's restaurant opened in April 1955 in San Bernardino, California.

There are two primary ways to make this graph, and I'm not sure which one I prefer. Both ways have pros and cons, so you can decide which method works best for you.

DOI: 10.1201/9781003321552-19

The Dual Line Chart Method

In this first version, we'll combine two line charts and use the fact that Excel doesn't plot values shown as #N/A in the chart to our advantage.

1. We'll plot a standard line chart with two series: The first is the full data series (column C) and the second plots only the value in 1955 (column D) when the first McDonald's opened. That series will use a simple IF formula: =IF(B2=1955,100,NA()), which says that if it's the year 1955, enter a value of 100 in the cell, and if it's any other year, place a #N/A in the cell (NA() is rendered as #N/A in the cell). Excel will ignore the #N/A symbol when we create the graph (Table 17.1).

TABLE 17.1

	A	B	C	D	E
1			Beef	First McDonald's Restaurant Opens	1955 Value
2	1930	1930	33.7	#N/A	#N/A
3		1931	33.4	#N/A	#N/A
4		1932	32.1	#N/A	#N/A
5		1933	35.5	#N/A	#N/A
6		1934	43.9	#N/A	#N/A
7		1935	36.6	#N/A	#N/A
8		1936	41.6	#N/A	#N/A
9		1937	38.0	#N/A	#N/A
10		1938	37.4	#N/A	#N/A
11		1939	37.6	#N/A	#N/A
12	1940	1940	37.8	#N/A	#N/A
13		1941	42.6	#N/A	#N/A
14		1942	45.9	#N/A	#N/A
15		1943	43.0	#N/A	#N/A
16		1944	46.6	#N/A	#N/A
17		1945	48.0	#N/A	#N/A
18		1946	44.2	#N/A	#N/A
19		1947	49.2	#N/A	#N/A
20		1948	44.2	#N/A	#N/A
21		1949	44.7	#N/A	#N/A
22	1950	1950	44.6	#N/A	#N/A
23		1951	41.2	#N/A	#N/A
24		1952	43.9	#N/A	#N/A
25		1953	54.5	#N/A	#N/A
26		1954	56.0	#N/A	#N/A
27		1955	57.2	100	57.2
28		1956	59.5	#N/A	#N/A

Setting

Making

Moving

If we insert a *Line with Markers* chart using cells B1:D91 (leave column E alone for now—we'll come back to it), we can see our lone point in 1955 near the top of the chart. If you don't see the orange dot, it's probably because you inserted a standard *Line* chart. For this example, we want to start with the *Line with Markers* chart (Figure 17.1).

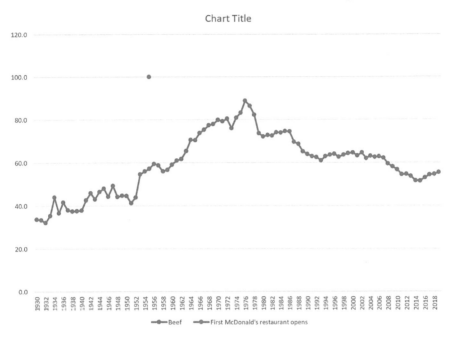

FIGURE 17.1

2. We now select the single orange point and add an Error Bar (*Chart Design > Add Chart Element > Error Bars > More Error Bars Options*). Then, in the error bar formatting menu, we'll make three changes:

   a. Set the *Direction* to *Minus*

   b. Set the *End Style* to *No Cap*

   c. Set the *Percentage* to 100%

   Together these three options create a straight line that goes from our marker down to the x-axis. If you don't see the *More Error Bars Options* button—this option can randomly disappear on some computers—select any of the other options, like *Percentage*, and modify the error bar in the format menu just the same (Figures 17.2 and 17.3).

3. We can now annotate the point by right-clicking and adding a data label. Because we named the series "First McDonald's restaurant opens," we can use it as the label on the chart. Right-click on the label, select *Format*

Setting

Making

Moving

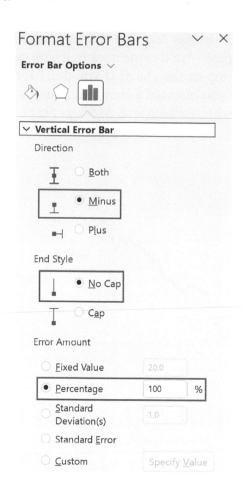

FIGURE 17.2

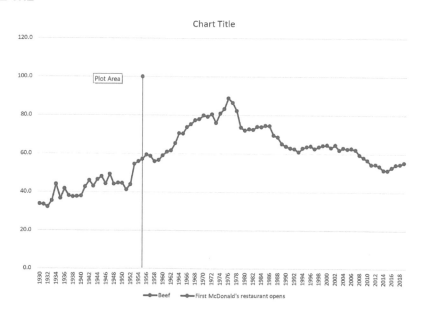

FIGURE 17.3

Data Label, select the checkbox next to the *Series Name* option, and unselect the checkbox next to the *Value* option. We can move the label to the left of the point in the *Label Position* area at the bottom of the menu. If we want to left-align the text within the label itself, we can click on it and use the standard alignment menu in the *Home* tab (Figure 17.4).

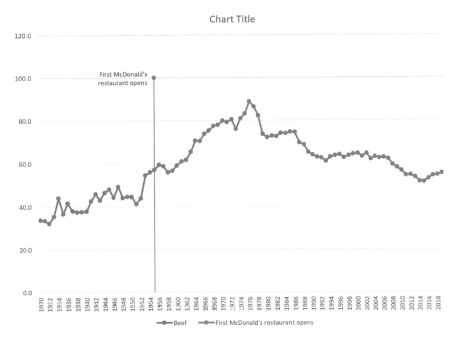

FIGURE 17.4

4. There are just a few smaller things to finish up this graph:

   1. Set the y-axis to go from 0 to 100—remember, Excel won't let us plot the data to the top of the y-axis, so we need to manually set it to 100 (select axis > right-click > *Format Axis* > *Minimum/Maximum*).

   2. Select the **blue** series and change the chart type to a regular line chart, either by using the *Combo* chart option in the *Change Chart Type* menu or by hiding the markers in the *Format Data Series Marker* > *Marker Options* > *None* menu. (If the right-click menu says *Format Data Point*, you have selected a single point. In that case, click out of the chart and click on the line again.)

   3. Hide our orange annotation point: *Format Data Point* > *Marker* > *Marker Options* > *None*.

   4. We can also manually move the label or add a white fill so the gridline doesn't cut through the label (Figure 17.5). Excel may add a "leader line"—a line that connects the label to the dot—if we move the label, but we can turn it off in the *Format Data Labels* menu.

Setting

Making

Moving

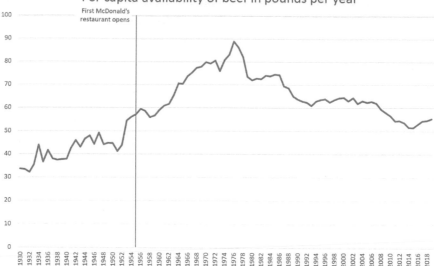

FIGURE 17.5

5. Finally, we can adjust the x-axis labels. The easy way is to select the x-axis and set the *Format Axis > Labels > Interval between labels > Specify interval unit* to the preferred interval (I've used 10 years). But by using 10-year increments, we lose the last (2019) label.

As an alternative, we can create an entirely different data series for the horizontal labels. In column A (Table 17.1), I've created those alternative labels using a formula:

```
=IF(OR(VALUE(RIGHT(B2,1))=0,B2=2019),B2,"")
```

That's a complex formula, but let's break it down. It's an entire IF statement, so inside are three arguments:

1. *The evaluation:* OR(VALUE(RIGHT(B2,1))=0,B2=2019). There are two statements within this OR statement, which I've highlighted in different colors. The RIGHT(B2,1) formula in blue looks at the first character in the cell starting at the right—in other words, the last number of the year. Wrapping that statement inside a VALUE() formula means Excel will enter the value as a number in the cell. That number is evaluated to see whether it is equal to zero. The second part of the OR formula in green is to see if the year is 2019.

2. *When True:* The second argument is the TRUE part of the IF statement. If either piece is true—the last digit of the year is zero *or* the year is 2019—the formula will put the year value in the cell.

3. *When False*: The last argument is the FALSE part of the IF statement. If both are false, the formula will put a space ("").

As you can see, we end up with a series that has years that end in zero *and* 2019 in it, with empty spaces in between.

To use this new series for the x-axis labels, we need to do two things:

1. First, set the x-axis label increments back to every year: select the x-axis > right-click > *Format Axis* > *Labels* > *Interval between labels* > *Automatic*.

2. Now we can reference the new series for the x-axis labels: select chart > *Select Data* > *Horizontal Category Axis Labels*: > *Edit* > cells A2:A91. This new set-up gives us the first year of each decade and 2019 at the end (Figure 17.6).

A Century of Beef

Per capita availability of beef in pounds per year

FIGURE 17.6

6. We can extend or change the look of the vertical line using this method in a few ways. First, we can shorten the line so it stops at the data line. Instead of using the *Percentage* option in the error bar menu, select the *Custom* option and input the difference between 100 and the data value (in this case, per capita beef consumption was 57.2 billion pounds in 1955, so the difference from 100 is 42.8) (Figure 17.7).

Setting

Making

Moving

Second, if we want to add a marker to the point where the error bar meets the data line, we can add yet *another* line to the chart (column E). In this case, the values of the line are #N/A except in 1955, where we want to mark the point. We can style the marker of that single point—say a big dot with a white fill—to make it clearer to the reader. (Excel does offer an option to style the end of the error bar with an arrow or a dot—see the Dot Plot chapter—but the dot sits behind the original line, so that approach doesn't quite work here.) (Figures 17.7 and Table 17.2).

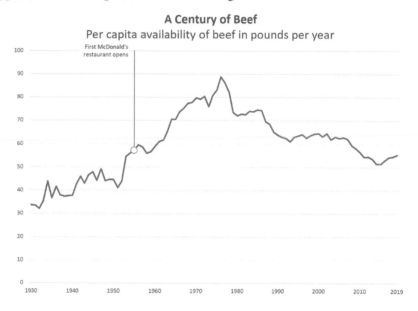

FIGURE 17.7

TABLE 17.2

	A	B	C	D	E	F
1			**Beef**	**First McDonald's Restaurant Opens**	**1955 Value**	**Difference**
20		1948	44.2	#N/A	#N/A	
21		1949	44.7	#N/A	#N/A	
22	1950	1950	44.6	#N/A	#N/A	
23		1951	41.2	#N/A	#N/A	
24		1952	43.9	#N/A	#N/A	
25		1953	54.5	#N/A	#N/A	
26		1954	56.0	#N/A	#N/A	
27		1955	57.2	100	57.2	42.8
28		1956	59.5	#N/A	#N/A	

Setting

Making

Moving

The Combo Chart Method

The second way to make this graph combines a line chart and a scatterplot.

1. Start by making the *Line* graph of just the *Beef* series in cells B1:C91 (Table 17.1 and Figure 17.8).

FIGURE 17.8

2. We'll add the vertical line by adding a scatterplot chart and dropping a vertical error bar from that point. Right-click on the chart and choose *Select Data > Add* to add the new series (Figure 17.9).

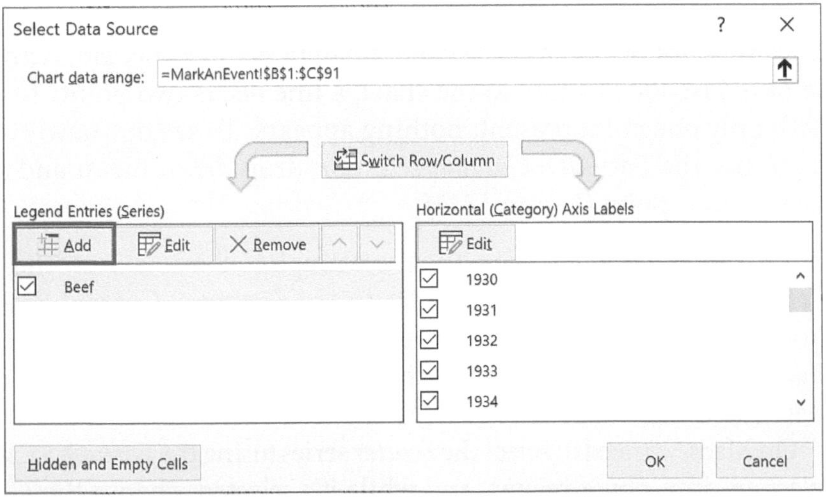

FIGURE 17.9

Setting

Making

Moving

3. From there, input the *Series name* ("First McDonald's restaurant opens" in cell H2) and a y-value of 100 into the *Series values* (cell I4) box. Click OK (Figure 17.10).

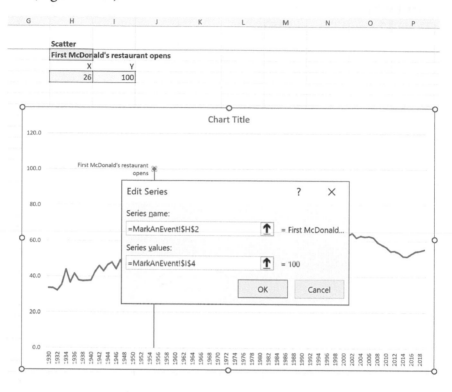

FIGURE 17.10

4. Two things happen. First, the y-axis moves from a maximum of 100 to a maximum of 120—again, Excel will not allow us to put a data series at the maximum of the chart. Second, no data marker appears. Although we have just added a line to the chart, a line needs two points to exist. With only one point present, nothing appears. To see our newly added point, use the *Format > Current selection* drop-down menu and select the new data point (Figure 17.11).

5. To change the new series to a scatterplot chart, select the *First McDonald's restaurant opens* series in the *Format > Current Selection* drop-down menu. With it still selected, use the *Chart Design > Change Chart Type > Combo* option to change the *Scatter* series to a *Scatter* chart (Figure 17.12).

On Macs, we need to select the *Scatter* series (using the *Format > Current Selection* drop-down menu), and while it's selected, choose the *Change Chart Type > Chart Design > Scatter* option.

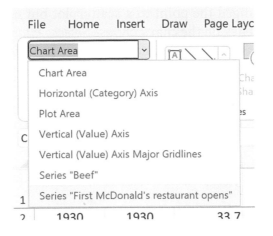

FIGURE 17.11

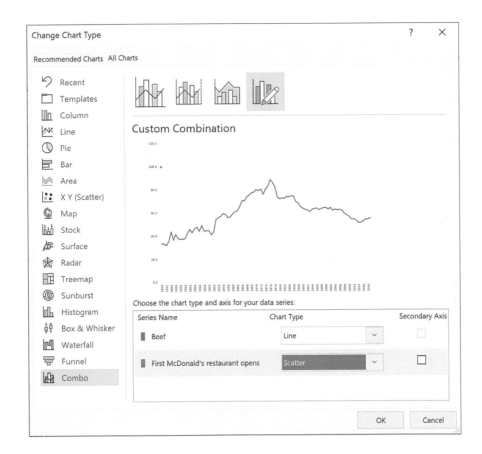

FIGURE 17.12

6. We've now changed the point to a scatterplot but need to assign it an x-value. Right-click on the chart, choose *Select Data > First McDonald's restaurant opens > Edit*, and input the x-value (cell H4) into the *Series X Values:* box (Figure 17.13).

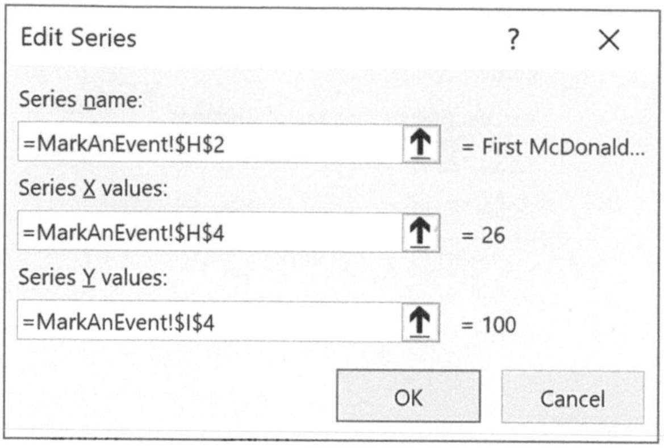

FIGURE 17.13

The scatterplot point now appears on the chart at the y-value of 100 and an x-value of 26—note that this is the 26th position, not the year 1955. If cell H4 was set to 1955 instead of 26, Excel would set the point at the 1,955th position on the x-axis, as illustrated in Figure 17.14.

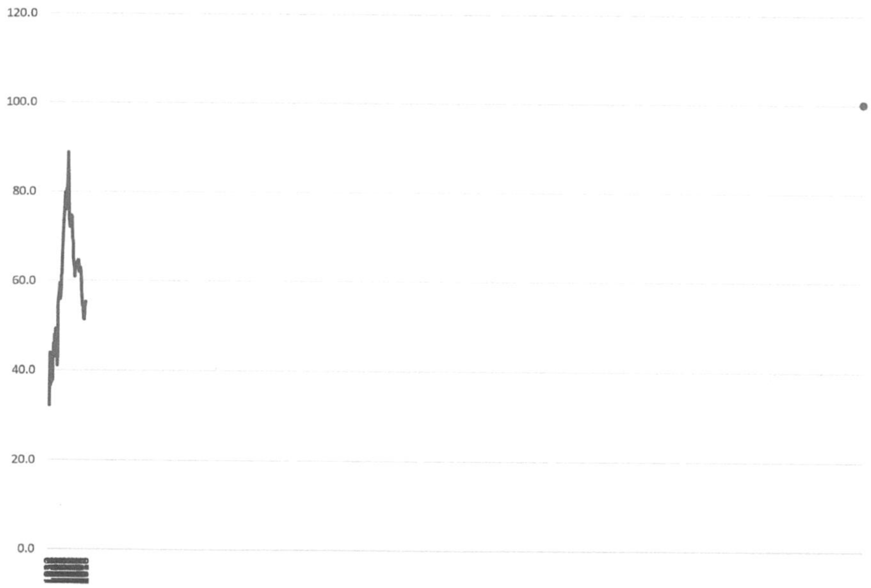

FIGURE 17.14

Setting

Making

Moving

7. Time to add the vertical error bar, which mimics how we did it using the line chart. Select the scatterplot point and navigate to the error bar formatting menu by selecting *Chart Design > Add Chart Element > Error Bars > More Error Bars Options*. Unlike the line chart where Excel added a vertical error bar only, Excel adds both horizontal and vertical error bars for a scatterplot.

Excel automatically brings us to the *Vertical Error Bars* formatting menu. If we click out of the chart, we can grab the vertical error bars directly or by using the *Format > Current Selection* drop-down menu. Once the vertical error bars are selected, make three changes:

a. Change the *Direction* to *Minus*

b. Change the *End Style* to *No Cap*

c. Select the *Percentage* option in the *Error Amount* menu and type 100% into the box. The vertical error bar will drop to the x-axis (Figure 17.15).

FIGURE 17.15

8. We still have a horizontal error bar, which we don't need, so select it and delete. (Remember, we can also use the *Format > Current Selection* drop-down menu to select the error bar.)

9. Let's add some annotation. Select the orange marker, right-click, and *Add Data Label*. As before, we can select and format the label by using the *Format Data Label > Series Name* (we already named it the labels we want to use!). Uncheck the box for *Y Value*, and position the label using *Label Position > Left* (Figure 17.16).

Setting

Making

Moving

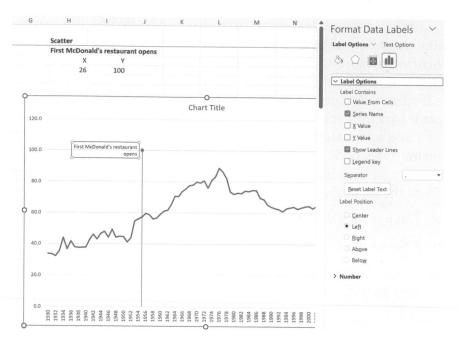

FIGURE 17.16

10. Finally, adjust the maximum of the y-axis to 100 by formatting the axis (right-click or CTRL+1) and changing the *Maximum* value to 100. To hide the scatterplot marker, right-click and use *Format Data Series > Marker > Marker Options > None* (Figure 17.17).

A Century of Beef
Per capita availability of beef in pounds per year

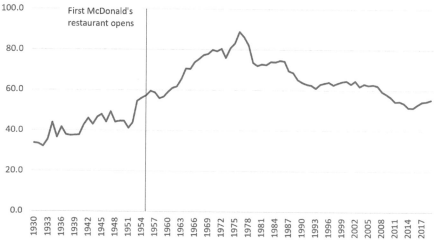

FIGURE 17.17

As with the line chart method, we can make the line shorter by changing the value from 100 to the difference between 100 and our data value (again, 48.2) and using the *Custom* error bar option rather than setting the *Percentage* to 100% (Figure 17.18). We can also mark the point on the line by adding an "arrow" to the end of the error bar (in the formatting area of the menu) because there's an option to use a circle rather than an arrowhead. This dot, however, cannot be styled the way we did for the additional series in the line chart version (Figure 17.7).

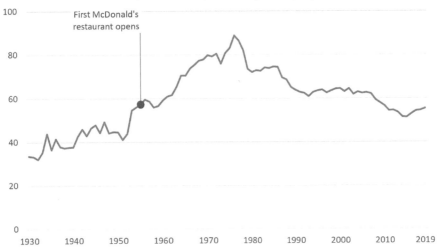

FIGURE 17.18

In either case, extending the technique to add more annotation lines simply requires adding more data to the series (be it line or scatterplot) and referencing (and placing) the correct labels.

The PowerPoint Method

There is a third way to make this graph, but I reserve it for special cases. We can create a basic chart in Excel, paste it into PowerPoint (or a similar tool), and add the annotations there. Because PowerPoint is a blank canvas, it's easier to add and align objects and text boxes. We can also size our slides to be any dimension we want.

Keep in mind, of course, that when inserting a line or marker manually, it can be more difficult to identify the *specific data value* where the line or label should be placed. I use this manual approach when I need to add more detailed or custom labels, annotations (e.g., curved arrows), or when I'm confident

Setting

Making

Moving

the graph won't need to be updated or replicated. Once the graph is built in PowerPoint, we can export it as an image using the *Export* option in the *File* menu and selecting the file type (e.g., JPEG, PDF, PNG, TIFF, etc.).

Quick Instructions

Method #1

1. Arrange data and formulas

2. Select cells B1:D91 and insert a *Line with Markers* chart

3. Add an *Error Bar* to the orange dot (the *First McDonald's restaurant opens* series in column D): select dot > *Chart Design* > *Add Chart Element* > *Error Bars* > *More Error Bars Options*

4. **Format Error Bar**: select > right-click > *Format Error Bars* >

   a. Set *Direction to Minus*

   b. Set *End Style to No Cap*

   c. Set *Error Amount* > *Percentage* > *100%*

5. **Select Scatterplot Marker**: right-click, and *Add Data Label*

6. **Hide Markers for Both Series**: right-click on each > *Format Data Series* > *Marker* > *Marker Options* > *None*

7. **Change Vertical Axis Dimensions**: right-click > *Format Axis* > *Axis Options* > 0 for *Minimum* and 100 for *Maximum*

8. To add or adjust year labels, see full tutorial

Method #2

1. Arrange data and formulas

2. Select cells B1:C91 and insert a *Line* chart

3. **Add a New Series**: right-click > *Select Data* > *Add* > *Series Name: First McDonald's restaurant opens (cell H2)* and *Series Values: I4*

4. Change the new series to a scatterplot:

   a. **On PCs**: select *McDonald's series (use the Format > Current Selection menu) Chart Design* > *Change Chart Type* > *Combo* > *McDonald's drop-down menu* > *Scatter*

   b. **On Macs**: select *McDonald's series (use the Format > Current Selection menu)* > *Chart Design* > *Change Chart Type* > *Scatter*

Setting

Making

Moving

5. **Assign the x-Value**: right-click > *Select Data* > *First McDonald's restaurant opens* > *Edit* > *Series X Values: H4*

6. **Add Error Bars to Scatterplot Point**: select dot > *Chart Design* > *Add Chart Element* > *Error Bars* > *More Error Bars Options*

7. **Format Vertical Error Bar**: select > right-click > *Format Error Bars* >

   a. Set *Direction to Minus*

   b. Set *End Style to No Cap*

   c. Set *Error Amount* > *Percentage* > *100%*

8. Delete horizontal error bars

9. **Select Scatterplot Marker**: right-click, and *Add Data Label*

10. **Hide Scatterplot Point**: right-click > *Format Data Series* > *Marker* > *Marker Options* > *None*

11. **Change Vertical Axis Dimensions**: right-click > *Format Axis* > *Axis Options* > 0 for *Minimum* and 100 for *Maximum*

12. To add or adjust year labels, see full tutorial

Setting

Making

Moving

Chapter **18**

Dot Plot

Dot Plot
Level: **Intermediate**
Data Type: **Categorical**
Combine Charts: **No**
Formulas Used: **IF, AVERAGE**

The dot plot is a nice alternative to a paired or stacked bar chart when you want to compare values across categories or over time. At its core, a dot plot in Excel is just a scatterplot with some additional considerations about how and where to place the data labels. We'll again use *Error Bars* to create the final chart, but instead of stretching them vertically, we will use them to draw horizontal lines.

We'll use the World Bank's maternal mortality ratio, defined as the "number of women who die from pregnancy-related causes while pregnant or within 42 days of pregnancy termination per 100,000 live births." Globally, the maternal mortality ratio fell from 342 deaths per 100,000 live births in 2000 to 211 deaths per 100,000 live births in 2017, but more recent estimates (Gates Foundation, 2021) suggest that the ratio increased during the COVID-19 pandemic.

DOI: 10.1201/9781003321552-20

1. To start, create a *Scatter* chart from cells A1:C8. The *Height* variable in column B represents the height/row of our dots in the dot plot (recall Chapter 12). When we insert those three columns in the chart, Excel inserts two series, so we need to adjust them (Figure 18.1).

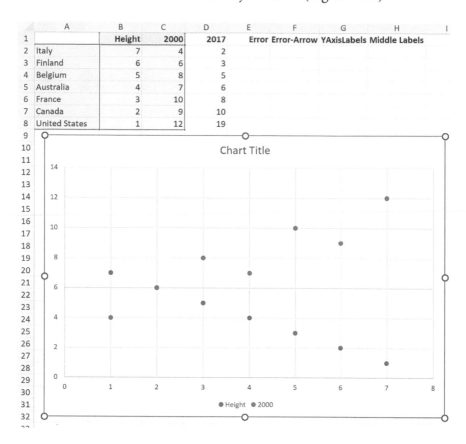

FIGURE 18.1

2. Right-click on the chart and select the *Select Data* option. We're going to make a number of changes here. We want two scatterplot series in this chart—one with the *2000* series (column C) as the x-values and the *Height* values (column B) as the y-values, and the second with *2017* (column D) as the x-values and the *Height* values (column B) as the y-values.

    First, let's edit the *2000* series to include the data we want. Select that series and click the *Edit* button. We need to change both series here: change the cell references to cells C2:C8 (the *2000* series) in the *Series X Values:* box and change the cell reference to cells B2:B8 (the *Height* series) for the *Series Y Values:* box. Click OK (Figure 18.2).

Next, edit the second series. Here, the *Series name:* should be cell D1 (*2017*), the *Series X Values:* is the data in cells D2:D8, and the *Series Y Values:* is the *Height* series in cells B2:B8 again. Click OK twice.

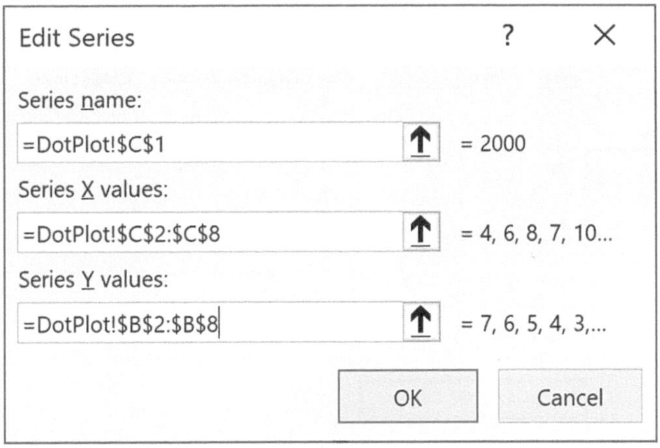

Edit Series   ?   ×

Series name:

=DotPlot!$C$1   ↑   = 2000

Series X values:

=DotPlot!$C$2:$C$8   ↑   = 4, 6, 8, 7, 10...

Series Y values:

=DotPlot!$B$2:$B$8   ↑   = 7, 6, 5, 4, 3,...

                                OK   Cancel

FIGURE 18.2

3. With the dot pairs now in the graph, we can use *Error Bars* to connect the dots with horizontal lines. First, we need to calculate the value for the error bars. Because we are creating a horizontal linking line, the value of the error bars is equal to the value in the *2017* column minus the value in the *2000* column. For Italy, that would be $2-4=-2$. In cell E2, insert the formula =D2−C2 and copy that formula down the length of the column to row 8. To add the error bars onto the chart, select the *2017* series (the blue series in the earlier image) and navigate to the *Chart Design > Add Chart Element > Error Bars > More Error Bars Options* menu (Figure 18.3).

4. With scatterplots, Excel adds both vertical and horizontal error bars. We don't need the vertical error bars for this chart, so we can select them and click delete. (Remember, we can also use the *Format > Current Selection* drop-down menu to grab them.) (Figure 18.4).

5. Now, select and right-click on the horizontal error bars to format. We're going to make three changes in the *Format Error Bars* menu:

   a. Set *Direction to Minus.*

   b. Set *End Style to No Cap.*

   c. Select the button for *Custom* for the *Error Amount* and click on the *Specify Value* button. In the resulting menu, insert the reference for the "Error" series we created (cells E2:E8) in the *Negative Error Value box.* Click OK.

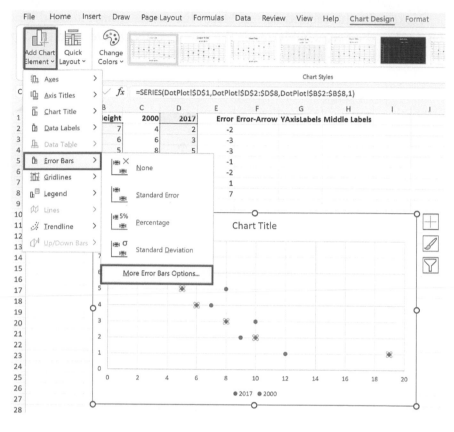

FIGURE 18.3

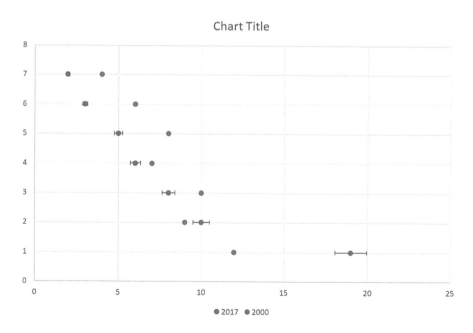

FIGURE 18.4

If you find that the error bars are not pointing in the right direction, you may have selected the wrong series or the wrong Plus/Minus option in the *Direction* part of the menu (Figure 18.5).

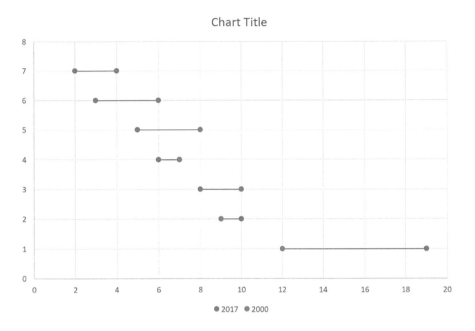

FIGURE 18.5

6. We now have the core graph and can do some basic formatting like deleting the horizontal and vertical axis gridlines, deleting the vertical axis labels, increasing the marker size, and changing the colors. But we also need to add labels, so before we polish this chart, let's look at three ways we can add labels.

   a. **Next to the Left-most Dot.** This approach is probably the most basic, the easiest, and the one I see most often. Select the dots on the left, right-click, and add data labels. Then, select the data labels and right-click to format. We'll make a few changes (Figure 18.6):

      i. Check the *X Value* box.

      ii. Uncheck the *Y Value* box.

      iii. Select the *Value From Cells* option and add the A2:A8 reference to the menu to add the country names to the labels.

      iv. Change the *Separator* to *space* (if you want—comma is fine too)

      v. Change the *Label Position* to *Left.*

Setting

Making

Moving

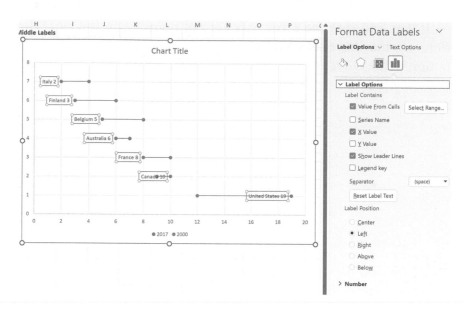

FIGURE 18.6

We're basically set here, though the labels for the bottom two series (Canada and the US) are not lined up correctly. Excel is following our directions correctly, but the values for 2017 are to the *right* of the values for 2020. We can fix this misalignment by selecting each point and changing the *Label Position* to *Right*. Or we can create a separate scatterplot series to use for the labels only. With this option, we can specify one series for labels to the left and another to the right.

To place series year labels above the first pair of dots, we need to either add data labels to a different series and manually move them or add another scatterplot series for just those two points, add labels, align them above the points, and hide the points. I left the year labels just a bit misaligned in Figure 18.7 so you can see the potential hazards of manually adding labels this way. Unless you plan on using this graph as a template over and over, doing a bit of manual work is not the end of the world.

b. **Aligned along the Vertical Axis.** If we would rather have the labels aligned along the y-axis, I prefer to add another scatterplot series where the x-values are equal to zero and the y-values are equal to the *Height* variable. I then add the country labels to the *left* of those points. Fill in the *YAxisLabels* series with zeros and add another scatterplot series (right-click > *Select Data* > *Add* > insert cell references G2:G8 for the x-values and cells B2:B8 for the y-values, and click OK) (Figure 18.8). With those dots added, right-click to add the labels and right-click on the labels to format, followed by three edits:

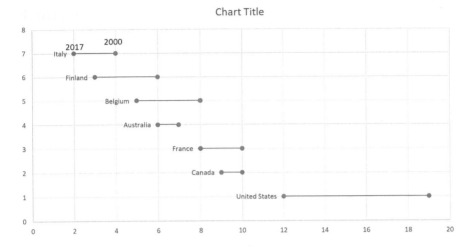

FIGURE 18.7

   i. Check the box next to *Value From Cells* and insert the reference to cells A2:A8.

  ii. Uncheck the box next to *X Value* box

 iii. Set the position to the *Left*. Remember, if the labels do not look left-aligned, you may need to shrink the width of the *Plot Area* by selecting the left edge and sliding it to the right.

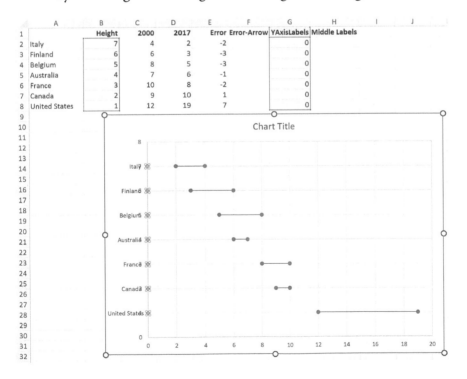

FIGURE 18.8

Setting

Making

Moving

c. **Sitting on Top of the Line.** Placing labels on top of the error bars can be a nice touch. Again, one additional scatterplot series will do the trick. In this case, the y-values stay the same (*Height*), but the x-values are calculated as the average of the two data values. In the *Middle Labels* series, insert a formula to calculate the average of the two data series (for Italy: =AVERAGE(C2:D2)) and add it as the x-series in another scatterplot. Right-click to add the labels, format to place them *Above* the dots, reference cells A2:A8 in the *Values From Cells* option, hide the marker, and we're all set (Figure 18.9).

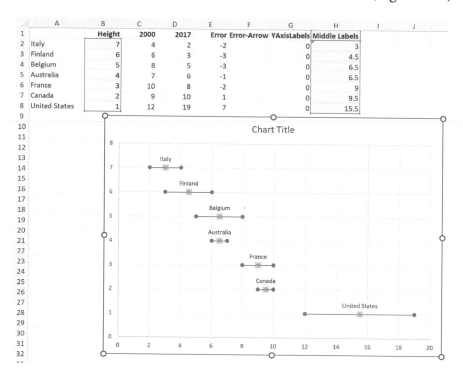

FIGURE 18.9

We can also add data labels directly to the points. Remember for Canada and the US, we'll need to select those labels individually and move the label to the other side of the dot (Figure 18.10).

One last thing: Personally, I don't like it when I can see the gridlines cut through my data labels, so I usually add a white fill to the labels. You can see this clearly in the labels for Belgium and Australia in Figure 18.10.

7. A final technique you might want to employ with a dot plot—especially when showing changes over time—is using arrows for the lines. We can create the graph the same way as above, with the only difference being the length and formatting of the error bars.

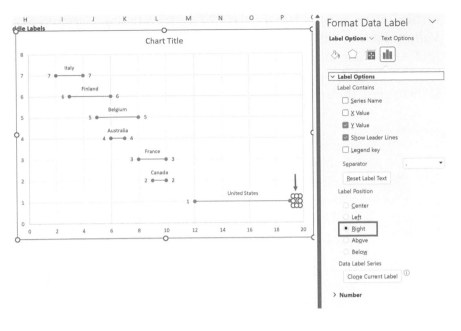

FIGURE 18.10

To make it so the arrowheads are not hidden behind the dots, we need to shorten the error bars slightly. Because there are two countries for which the change between 2000 and 2017 goes in the opposite direction as the other countries, the formula for our new error bar series is more complicated. In column F ("Error-Arrow"), we can insert this formula:

$$=IF(E2<0,D2-C2+\$F\$9,D2-C2-\$F\$9)$$

It's a basic IF statement that evaluates the first *Error* series (which is calculated as the value in *2017* minus the value in *2000*). If that difference is negative, indicating that the mortality rate declined over this period, the calculation in the second part of the formula takes the difference *plus* a fixed value in cell $F$9, which I've set to 0.25 and inserted into that cell. If the difference is positive, indicating that the mortality rate increased over the period, we *subtract* that fixed value.

As a result, every country except Canada and the US has new error bars that are slightly larger (less negative) than the original. For Canada and the US, they are slightly smaller (less positive).

8. With the value of our error bars adjusted, we can now add horizontal error bars to the *2000* series by selecting and using the standard steps: *Chart Design > Add Chart Element > Error Bars > More Error Bar Options*. In the horizontal error bar formatting menu (don't forget to delete the

vertical error bars), reference the F2:F8 series in the *Custom > Specify Value > Positive Error Value* box and change the *End Arrow type* and *End Arrow Size* to the arrow type and size we prefer. Here, the arrowheads are plainly visible but note that if we change the 0.25 value in cell $F$9 to zero, the arrowheads are hidden behind the dots (Figure 18.11).

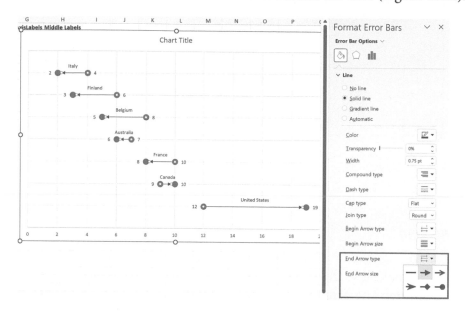

FIGURE 18.11

We can now add some colors to the labels, add some labels to the dots, or even add a text box (yikes) to provide an important comment or annotation (Figure 18.12).

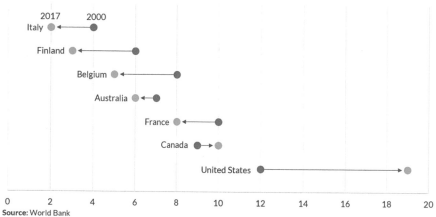

FIGURE 18.12

Quick Instructions

1. Select cells A1:C8 and insert a *Scatter* chart

2. Edit both series:

   a. Right-click > *Select Data > 2000 > Edit > Series Name: 2017 (cell D1)*; *X values: D2:D8*; and *Y values: B2:B8*

   b. Right-click > *Select Data > Height > Edit > Series Name: 2000 (cell C1)*; *X values: C2:C8*; and *Y values: B2:B8*

3. Add error bars to the 2017 series: select series > *Chart Design > Add Chart Element > Error Bars > More Error Bars Options*

4. Format horizontal error bars: select > right-click > *Format Error Bars >*

   a. Set *Direction to Minus*

   b. Set *End Style to No Cap*

   c. Set *Error Amount > Custom > Specify Values > Negative Error Value >* cells E2:E8

5. Delete vertical error bars

6. Add labels or modify lines to arrows, see full tutorial for more details and options

Setting

Making

Moving

Chapter 19

Slope Chart

Slope Chart
Level: **Intermediate**
Data Type: **Time**
Combine Charts: **No**
Formulas Used: **&**

The slope chart is another good alternative to a paired bar chart if we want a user to compare levels and changes within and across groups. The slope chart, which is created in Excel as a modified line chart, makes that task easier. To demonstrate, we will use the same data we used for the dot plot: estimates of maternal mortality in 2000 and 2017 for seven countries.

We can make and add labels to a slope chart in two ways. Both have different forms of manual work. I find the first method to be more tedious, but it doesn't require managing multiple data series.

The chart itself is relatively easy to create—but adding the labels at the start and end of each line takes longer. With either of these methods, the labels will be neatly aligned and tagged to the data, which is better than text boxes that are manually created and aligned (and which will never look quite right).

DOI: 10.1201/9781003321552-21

Method 1: Adding Data Labels

1. Create a *Line with Markers* chart using the data in cells A2:C9. (We can ignore columns D:H for now as we'll use those in Method 2.) (Figure 19.1).

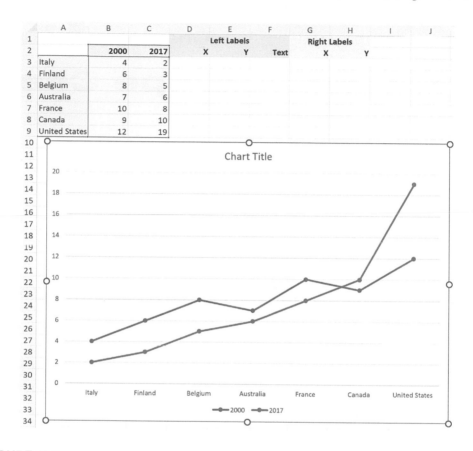

FIGURE 19.1

2. Excel will create a line chart along the columns, but we want to flip it. Click on the chart and select the *Chart Design > Switch Row/Column* button (Figure 19.2).

3. We're already getting pretty close, but we need to add our labels. Select one of the lines, right-click, and select *Add Data Labels* in the menu. This step will add a data label to either end of the line. At both ends, the data label will be aligned to the right of the point and show the value. For the point on the right, this placement is perfect, but on the left, we want the data marker to be to the left of the point and to include the country name (Figure 19.3).

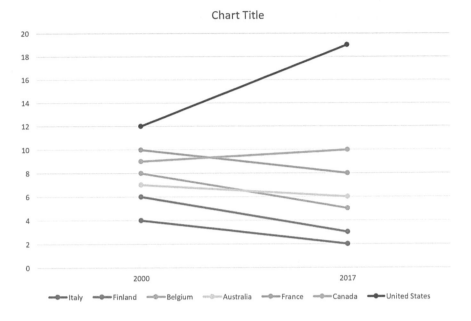

FIGURE 19.2

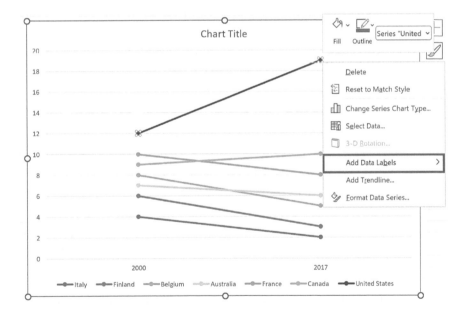

FIGURE 19.3

4. To change the formatting, select the data labels and click on the left label again so only that label is selected. (The box will change from one with four circles on the corners to one with eight larger circles.) With that label selected, right-click and select the *Format Data Label* option

Setting

Making

Moving

in the menu. Check the box next to *Series Name* (in addition to the *Value* box that is already selected), and select the *Left* option under the *Label Position* section of the menu. We can also change the separator from a comma to a space if we want (Figure 19.4).

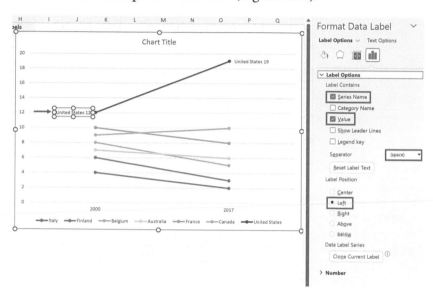

FIGURE 19.4

5. Now we've reached the tedious part: repeat this step for each of the remaining lines, going one by one. Add the data labels, select them, re-click on the left label, and change the formatting (Figure 19.5).

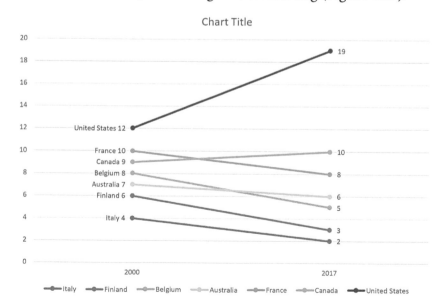

FIGURE 19.5

6. Let's get the graph to use the full horizontal space. Select the x-axis and format. In the *Axis Options* menu, select the *On tick marks* option in the *Axis position* area of the menu (Figure 19.6).

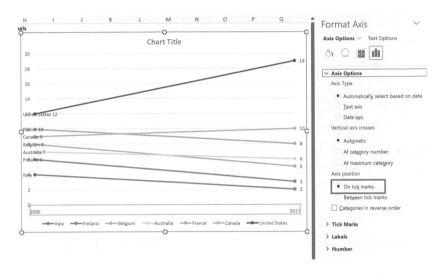

FIGURE 19.6

7. Doing so stretches the *Plot Area* to the full width of the *Chart Area*, but now our labels are sitting on top of the points. We can fix this alignment by grabbing the left edge of the *Plot Area* and pulling it to the right. The labels will right-align, and we are good to go (Figure 19.7).

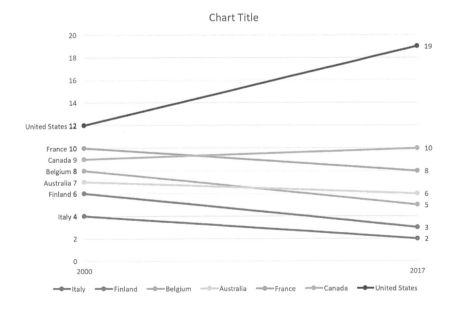

FIGURE 19.7

Setting

Making

Moving

8. The last part is a simple bit of styling: delete the y-axis labels, legend, and gridlines (select and delete) and format the title as you like. We can also manually color the labels to match the color of the lines (Figure 19.8).

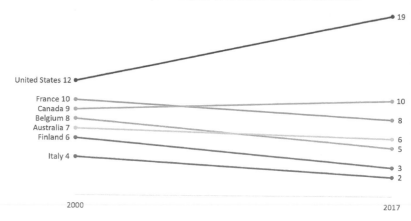

Maternal Deaths per 100,000 Live Births in 2000 and 2017

FIGURE 19.8

Method 2: Using a Combo Chart

For the second method, we will combine a line chart and a scatterplot. Although it requires many different steps, it's a technique—creating a combination chart—that we have used already and will use even more in later chapters.

1. Start as we did before and create a *Line with Markers* chart with cells A2:C9, then switch the row/column data. We can delete the gridlines, y-axis labels, and legend (Figure 19.9).

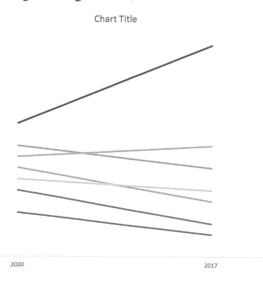

Chart Title

FIGURE 19.9

Setting
Making
Moving

2. To add the data labels, we will use the new data inserted into columns D:H.

   a. **Column D**. We want one set of labels aligned with the 2000 tick mark, which Excel views as the first position (recall Chapter 17), so type a series of 1s.

   b. **Column E**. We want the data values for 2000, so this column is the same as column B.

   c. **Column F**. Remember, we want the labels on the left to be the country name and the data value separated by a space. We can use a little concatenate function here: =A3&" "&B3 to merge the three elements together.

   d. **Column G**. We want the other set of labels aligned with the 2017 tick mark in the second position, so this is a series of 2s.

   e. **Column H**. Here, we need the data values for 2017, so this column is the same as column C (Table 19.1).

TABLE 19.1

	A	B	C	D	E	F	G	H
						Left Labels	Right Labels	
1								
2		2000	2017	X	Y	Text	X	Y
3	Italy	4	2	1	4	Italy 4	2	2
4	Finland	6	3	1	6	Finland 6	2	3
5	Belgium	8	5	1	8	Belgium 8	2	5
6	Australia	7	6	1	7	Australia 7	2	6
7	France	10	8	1	10	France 10	2	8
8	Canada	9	10	1	9	Canada 9	2	10
9	United States	12	19	1	12	United States 12	2	19

3. To add the first scatterplot series, which we'll use to add labels on the left side, right-click on the graph and choose the *Select Data* option. We'll add a new series and reference cell D1 (*Left Labels*) for the name of the series and cells E3:E9 for the *Series values*. After you press OK, the data will render as a line chart, similar to how this tutorial started—again, Excel assumes we want to plot the data down the column as a time series (Figure 19.10).

1. Instead of adding these data as a line, we are going to change the series to a scatterplot. Select the *Chart Design > Change Chart Type > Combo* option to change the chart type for the *Left Labels* series to a *Scatter*

Setting

Making

Moving

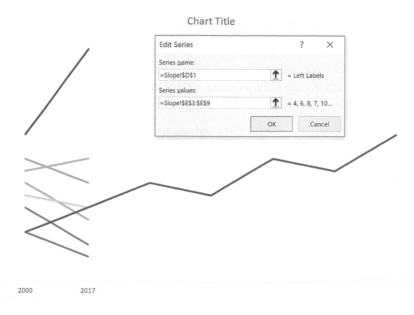

FIGURE 19.10

chart. Now, if Excel has magically changed some of the other series to bar charts, we will need to change those back to line charts using the drop-down menus. Remember, Excel is just following built-in defaults, but we have the ultimate say as to what happens.

(Again, if you're using a Mac, you will need to use a slightly different approach. First, select the series and with that series selected, go to the *Change Chart Type* menu in the *Chart Design* tab. There, select the *Scatter* chart option.) (Figure 19.11).

2. Because a scatterplot requires both x- and y-values, we need to return to the chart data menu and add in the x-values. Select the chart, right-click, and choose the *Select Data* option. Scroll down to the *Left Labels* series, select *Edit*, and a new box appears where we can insert the x-values. Click inside the box and insert the reference to the x-values in cells D3:D9 (labeled with a capital *X* in the spreadsheet) and click OK (Figure 19.12).

3. We now have dots at the beginning of each line, which is where we can add our data labels. But first, let's add markers to the right end of the lines. Go back to the *Select Data* menu and add a new series. Now, Excel prompts us for both x- and y-values. Because we've added a scatterplot to the graph, Excel (correctly this time!) thinks we want to add another scatterplot series. In the boxes, reference cell G1 for the series title, cells G3:G9 for the x-values, and cells H3:H9 for the y-values. Click OK when done (Figure 19.13).

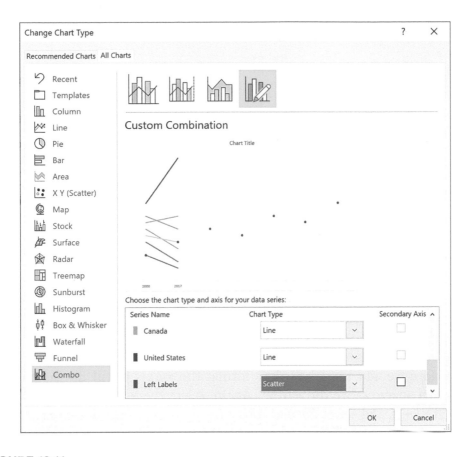

FIGURE 19.11

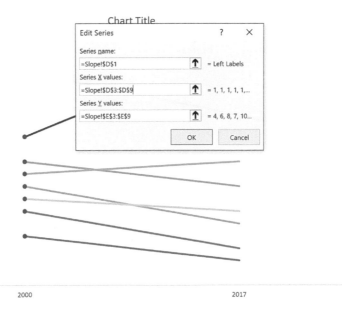

FIGURE 19.12

Setting

Making

Moving

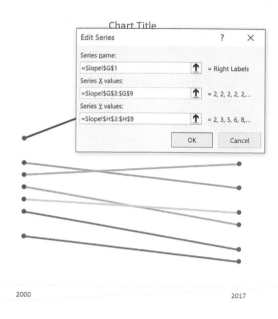

FIGURE 19.13

4. Before we add the labels, let's format the x-axis to fill up the entire chart space, as we did earlier. Again, select the x-axis, right-click (or CTRL+1), and select *Format Axis > Axis position > On tick marks*. This step lines up the data markers with the tick marks and uses the whole chart space (Figure 19.14).

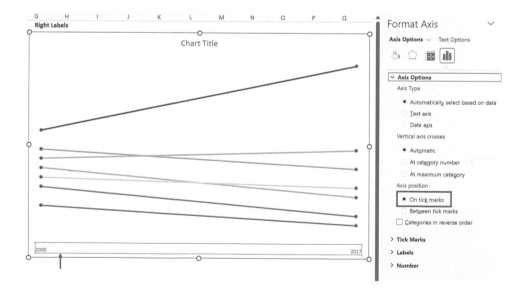

FIGURE 19.14

5. For the data labels on the left side of the graph, we select those dots, right-click, and select *Add Data Labels*. To format, select the labels>right-click>*Format Data Labels*> *Value From Cells*>enter cells F3:F9 in the box. Then, unselect the *Y Value* checkbox. In the same *Data Labels* menu, place the labels to the *Left* of the point in the *Label Position* menu (Figure 19.15).

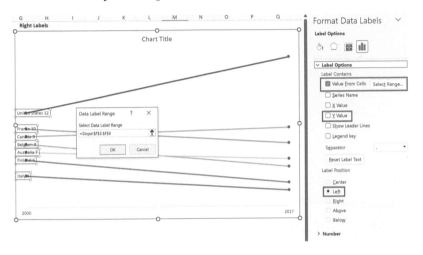

FIGURE 19.15

6. As before, the *Plot Area* is too close to the edge of the *Chart Area*, so the labels are sitting on top of the dots. Grab the left edge of the *Plot Area* and slide it to the right, giving the chart more room and letting the labels sit to the left of the points (Figure 19.16).

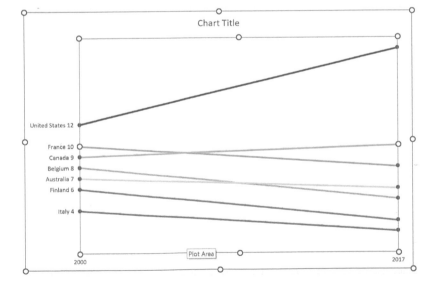

FIGURE 19.16

Setting

Making

Moving

7. To add the other data labels, select the dots on the right side and *Add Data Labels.* In this case, because the default Excel behavior is to add the y-value to the right of the point, we don't have any additional formatting to do (Figure 19.17).

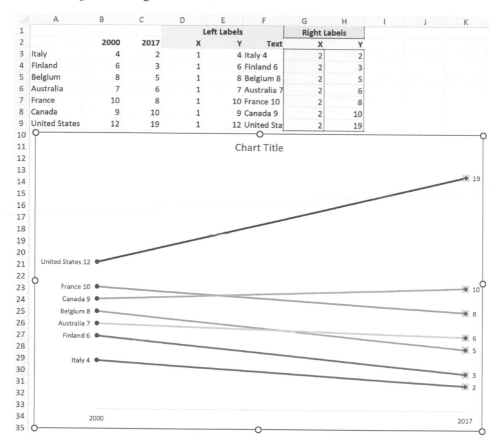

FIGURE 19.17

8. Lastly, we need to do a bit of styling.

a. If we want, we can remove the dots at the end of the lines, but because the labels are connected to the dots, we can't just hit delete. Instead, we can hide the dots using the *Marker > Marker Options > None* menu. If we want to keep dots at the end of the lines, we can do so because there are dots *behind* the scatterplot points from the *Line Chart with Markers* that we inserted at the start.

b. Finally, we can modify the colors of the lines and/or labels to match. The version in Figure 19.18 uses different colors for each country, and the version in Figure 19.19 has one color for increases and another color for decreases.

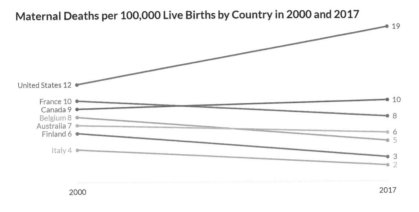

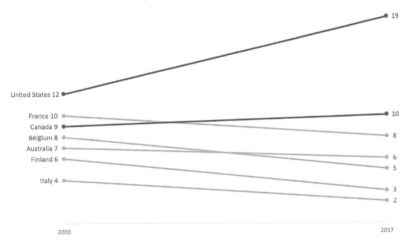

FIGURE 19.18

FIGURE 19.19

Quick Instructions

Method #1

1. Select cells A2:C9 and insert a *Line with Markers* chart

2. Switch order of the chart: *Chart Design > Switch Row/Column*

3. Select one line, right-click, and *Add Data Labels*

4. Select left data label only, right-click, select *Format Data Label*, and make three changes:

   a. *Label contains > Series Name and Value*

   b. Change *Separator to Space*

   c. Change *Label Position to Left*

Setting

Making

Moving

5. Repeat data labeling and formatting steps (3 and 4) for each series

6. Delete legend, vertical axis, and horizontal gridlines

7. Format horizontal axis: right-click > *Format Axis* > *Axis Options* > *Axis position* > *On tick marks*

8. Adjust *Plot Area* by selecting the left edge and moving it to the right to fit labels

Method #2

1. Arrange data and formulas

2. Select cells A2:C9 and insert a *Line with Markers* chart

3. Switch order of the chart: *Chart Design* > *Switch Row/Column*

4. Add scatterplot for left labels: right-click > *Select Data* > *Add* > *Series Name: Left Labels (cell D1)* and *Series values: E3:E9*

5. Change the *Left Labels* series to a scatterplot:

   a. **On PCs**: select *Left Labels series* > *Chart Design* > *Change Chart Type* > *Combo* > *Left Labels* > *Scatter*

   b. **On Macs**: select *Left Labels series* > *Chart Design* > *Change Chart Type* > *Scatter*

6. Add x-values to *Left Labels* series: right-click > *Select Data* > *Left Labels* > *Edit* > *X values: D3:D9*

7. Add *Right Labels* series: right-click > *Select Data* > *Add* > *Series Name: Right Labels (cell G1)*; *X values: G3:G9*; and *Y values: H3:H9*

8. Add and format labels for the *Left Labels* series:

   a. Right-click > *Add Data Labels*

   b. Select data labels > right-click > *Format Data Labels and make two changes*:

      i. *Label contains* > *Value from Cells* > F3:F9 (and uncheck the box next to *Y Value*)

      ii. Change Label *Position to Left*

9. Add labels to the *Right Labels* series: right-click > *Add Data Labels*

10. Format horizontal axis: right-click > *Format Axis* > *Axis Options* > *Axis position* > *On tick marks*

11. Adjust *Plot Area* by selecting the left edge and moving it to the right to fit labels

12. Delete legend, vertical axis, and horizontal gridlines

Chapter **20**

Overlaid Gridlines

Overlaid Gridlines

Level: **Intermediate**

Data Type: **Categorical**

Combine Charts: **Yes**

Formulas Used: **None**

The overlaid gridline chart places gridlines on top of a bar chart, which can allow viewers to absorb the data as segments rather than single bars. Overlaid gridline charts can also offer a useful way to plot an average or total for all groups in a way that stands out from the other data. This tutorial will start with the more complex, though perhaps less interesting strategy of creating these gridlines. The chapter concludes with the simpler and more interesting version of showing the average value.

In this version, we'll combine a bar chart and a scatterplot, then add horizontal error bars to the scatterplot points to mimic the gridlines. We'll use the 2017 maternal mortality data to make our chart.

1. Create a bar chart with the *2017* data in column B (cells A2:B9). Delete the existing horizontal gridlines and chart title (Figure 20.1).

DOI: 10.1201/9781003321552-22

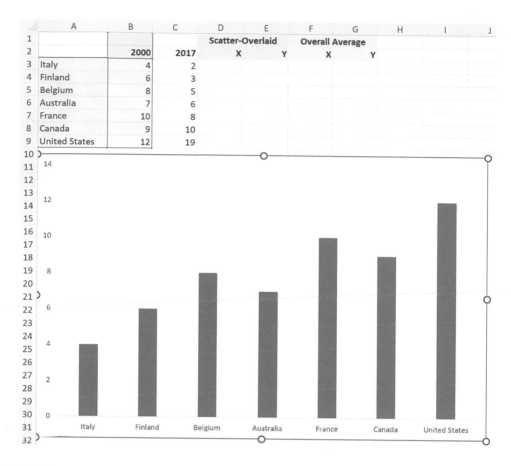

FIGURE 20.1

2. To make our gridlines, we are going to add a scatterplot where the x-values are equal to the midpoint along the x-axis and the y-values are equal to the gridlines. In this case, we'll add 10 horizontal gridlines corresponding to the original y-axis increments. In column C, enter the number four in 10 cells, from cell C3 to C12. Why the number four? Remember Excel views the values on the x-axis as *positions*, so four is in the middle of these seven bars. In column D, we'll add the 10 y-values corresponding to the horizontal gridlines, starting at 2 and going to 20.

To insert this new series as a scatterplot, right-click on the chart and choose *Select Data > Add*. Click cell C1 for the *Series name* and enter cells D3:D12 in the *Series values:* box so they become the y-values of our scatterplot. Click OK, and a paired column chart with a bunch of extra bars should appear (Figure 20.2).

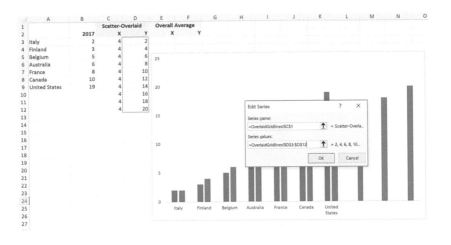

FIGURE 20.2

3. Select the *Scatter-Overlaid* series in the chart and, as we've done before, change this new series to a scatterplot: *Chart Design > Change Chart Type > Combo* (Figure 20.3). (If you're on a Mac, select the orange bars and navigate to *Chart Design > Change Chart Type > Scatter* and click.).

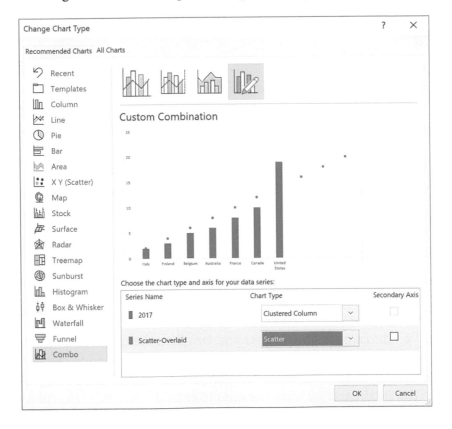

FIGURE 20.3

Setting

Making

Moving

4. We have only assigned y-values to the scatterplot series, so we now need to assign x-values. Right-click on the chart and choose *Select Data > Scatter-Overlaid > Edit*. In the *Series X values:* box, click on cells C3:C12, and click OK (Figure 20.4).

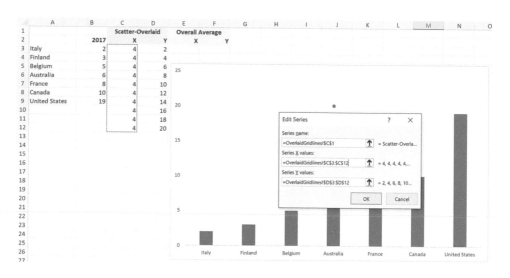

FIGURE 20.4

5. We now have the scatterplot overlaid on the bar chart, so we need to add the horizontal error bars. Select the dots and navigate to *Chart Design > Add Chart Element > Error Bars > More Error Bars Options*. By default, Excel adds vertical and horizontal error bars. After we right-click on the error bars and select *Format*, take note of which menu we're in—the horizontal or vertical error bars menu.

6. We want to style the horizontal error bars. Select those error bars (again, by right-clicking or using CTRL+1) to go to the *Horizontal Error Bar* formatting pane. We'll make three changes here:

a. Change the *End Style* to *No Cap*.

b. In the bottom area, go to *Error Amount > Fixed Value*. Here, we can choose how far our error bars extend. If we type in "3," the error bars don't quite extend *through* the first or the last bar. And if we type in "4," the error bars go too far and lengthen the entire graph. But if we take the difference and use "3.5," the lines will extend to just the right length. Why 3.5? Because the error bars refer to the position along the x-axis, and we want the lines to extend from the scatterplot point to just beyond the first and last bars, meaning we need to extend the lines slightly more than three positions to clear the edges of the bars.

(Alternatively, we could use the *Custom* option and specify the data in the worksheet, but for this example, we can just type in the numbers.) (Figures 20.5–20.7).

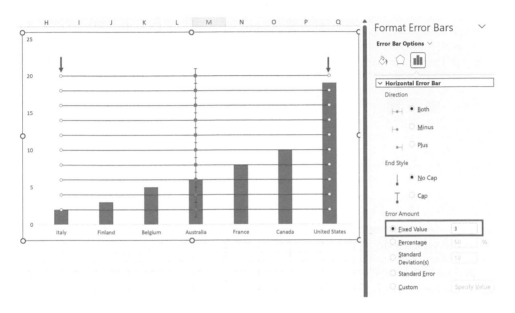

FIGURE 20.5

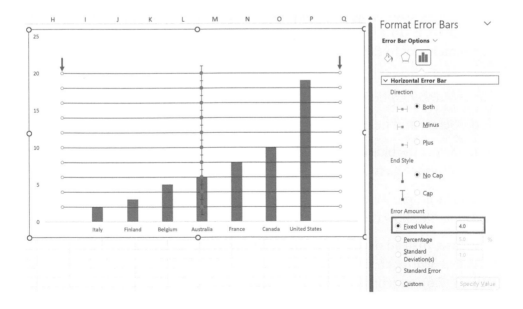

FIGURE 20.6

Setting

Making

Moving

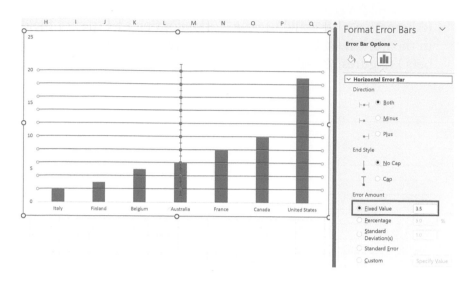

FIGURE 20.7

7. Now we can do a little styling:

a. In the *Line Color* tab of the error bar menu, change the line color to white, and in the *Line Style* tab, change the line width to 1.5 point.

b. Adjust the increments on the y-axis to match our new "gridlines" and change the y-axis limits to match. Right-click on the y-axis to format and change the *Maximum* bound to 20 and the *Major Units* to 2. In this case, and for demonstration purposes, we've placed a white gridline at increments of two maternal deaths per 100,000 live births. (In a final version, I'd probably put the gridlines at increments of five, only because two seems like too many gridlines.)

c. Hide the markers: select the dots > *Format Data Series* > *Marker* > *Marker Options* > *None* (Figure 20.8).

d. Select and delete the vertical error bars.

e. Select the blue bars and adjust the *Series Overlap* (e.g., to 0%) and *Gap Width* (e.g., to 100%) sliders to make the bars wider.

In this next graph, we use the same technique—combine a column chart and a scatterplot—to show the average value across these seven countries (Figure 20.9).

In this case, instead of selecting the values in cells C3:D12 to add the gridlines, we create a *Scatter* chart with a single x-value (4 in cell E3) and a single y-value in cell F3 (7.6), which is equal to the average across all the values in cells B3:B9, using the formula =AVERAGE(B3:B9).

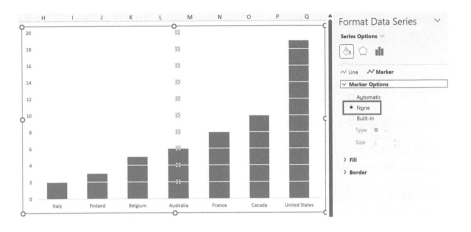

FIGURE 20.8

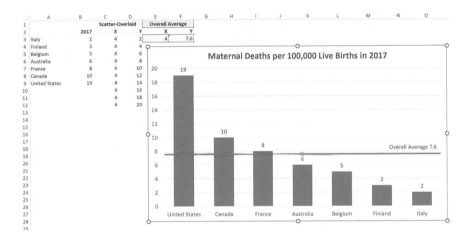

FIGURE 20.9

We can make this change easily by right-clicking on the chart, *Select Data > Scatter-Overlaid > Edit*, and changing the reference in the *Series X values:* box to cell E3 and the reference in the *Series Y values:* box to cell F3. Click OK twice and change the color of the error bar to something solid.

After adding the line, I also added a data label (by right-clicking on the point) and moved it to the right side of the graph so it doesn't interfere with the label above the bar for Australia.

Other points worth highlighting here. First, I used a scatterplot rather than a line chart because the line in the line chart extends only to the middle of the first and last bars. We could use a secondary-axis approach with a line chart, but I find it much easier to use the scatterplot approach. Second, we could place the scatterplot points in other positions and use only positive or negative error bars. I prefer putting them in the middle because I find it easier to control the length of the lines.

Quick Instructions

1. Select cells A2:B9 and insert a *Clustered Column* chart

2. Right-click > *Select Data* > *Add* > *Series Name: Scatter-Overlaid (cell C1)* and *Series values: D3:D12*

3. Change the *Scatter-Overlaid* series to a scatterplot:

   a. **On PCs**: select *Scatter-Overlaid series* > *Chart Design* > *Change Chart Type* > *Combo* > *Scatter-Overlaid* > *Scatter*

   b. **On Macs**: select *Scatter-Overlaid series* > *Chart Design* > *Change Chart Type* > *Scatter*

4. Add x-values to *Scatter-Overlaid* series: right-click > *Select Data* > *Scatter-Overlaid* > *Edit* > *X values: cells C3:C12*

5. Add error bars to the *Scatter-Overlaid* series: select > *Chart Design* > *Add Chart Element* > *Error Bars* > *More Error Bars Options*

6. Format horizontal error bars: select > right-click > *Format Error Bars* >

   a. Set *Direction to Both*

   b. Set *End Style to No Cap*

   c. Set *Error Amount* > *Fixed Value* > *3.5*

   d. Set color: *Line* > *Solid Line* > *Color* > *change to white*

7. Delete vertical error bars

8. Delete existing gridlines

9. Hide *Scatter-Overlaid* markers: right-click > *Format Data Series* > *Marker* > *Marker Options* > *None*

10. Edit vertical axis limits: right-click > *Format Axis* > *Axis Options* > 0 for *Minimum* and 20 for *Maximum*

11. If keeping the vertical axis, adjust the labels to match new gridlines: right-click > *Format Axis* > *Bounds* > *Units* > *Major* > 2

Chapter 21

Lollipop Chart

Lollipop Chart
Level: **Intermediate**
Data Type: **Categorical**
Combine Charts: **No**
Formulas Used: **None**

A lollipop chart is basically a bar chart, but the end of the bar is replaced with a dot (the candy) and the bar itself is replaced with a line (the stick). A lollipop graph reduces the amount of ink used and helps the reader focus on where the data are encoded. We'll use the maternal mortality data again to create our lollipop graph, focusing on the values in 2017.

1. Insert a bar chart with the data in cells A1:B8. Notice that Excel places the data with the value in the bottom row (for the US) at the top of the chart rather than at the bottom (Figure 21.1).

2. As we've had to do several times, flip the order of the bars by formatting the y-axis. Select the axis and right-click or use the CTRL+1 shortcut to make two changes: *Format Axis > Axis Options > At maximum category* and *Format Axis > Axis Options > Categories in reverse order* (Figure 21.2).

DOI: 10.1201/9781003321552-23

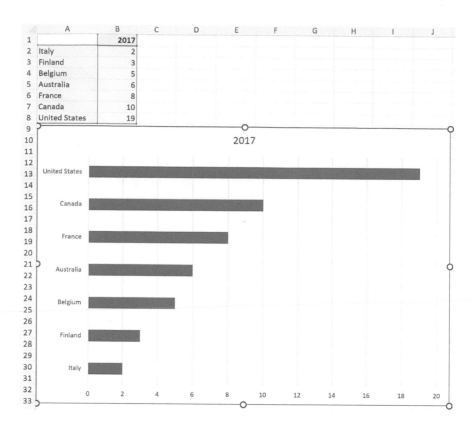

FIGURE 21.1

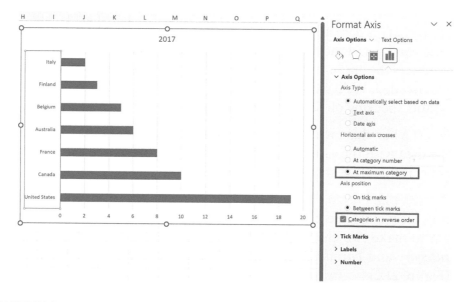

FIGURE 21.2

3. To change this bar chart to the lollipop chart, we'll use error bars. Click on the bars and select *Chart Design > Add Chart Element > Error Bars > More Error Bars Options* (Figure 21.3).

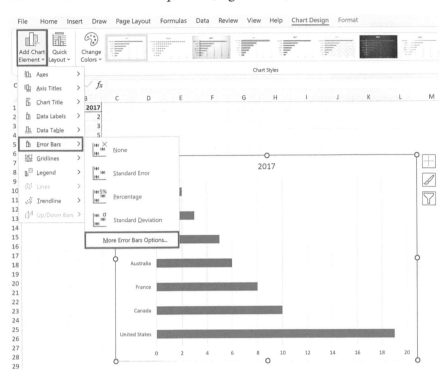

FIGURE 21.3

4. Excel automatically adds horizontal error bars in both directions from the end of the bar, so we need to make a few changes in the *Horizontal Error Bar* menu:

   a. Change the *Direction* to *Minus*

   b. Change the *End Style* to *No Cap*

   c. Select the *Error Amount > Percentage >* type 100% in the box. This step will create a horizontal error bar that extends to the y-axis, regardless of the length of the bar (Figure 21.4).

5. To add the dots at the ends of the error bars, select the paint can icon in the *Error Bar* menu and change the *Begin Arrow type* to the oval and increase its size (if you like) in the *Begin Arrow size* menu (Figure 21.5).

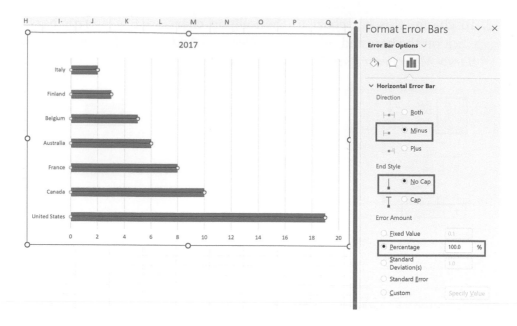

FIGURE 21.4

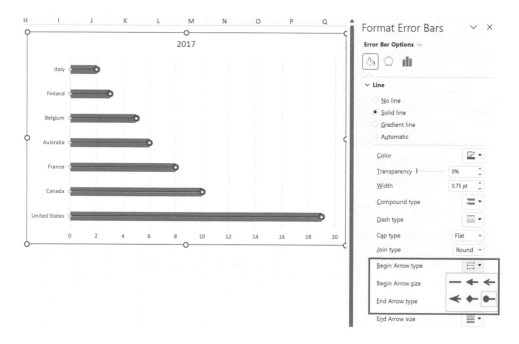

FIGURE 21.5

6. Finally, we can hide the bars by selecting them and changing the color to *No Fill* (Figure 21.6).

Setting

Making

Moving

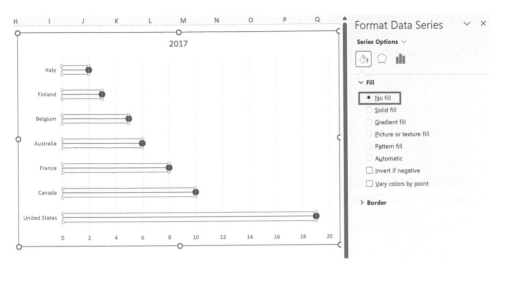

FIGURE 21.6

7. We can change the color of the error bars in the *Line Color* area of the *Error Bar* formatting menu, though the dots and lines will be the same color. If we want more control over the size of the dots or if we want to make the colors of the lines and dots different, we can make this chart with a simple scatterplot and error bars (see Figure 21.7 and the dot plot tutorial in Chapter 18).

Maternal Deaths per 100,000 Live Births by Country in 2000 and 2017

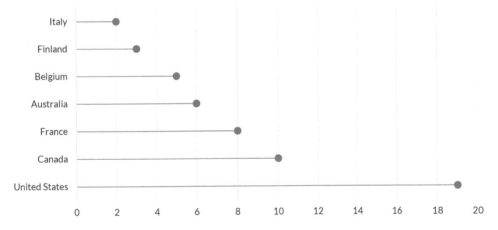

FIGURE 21.7

Setting

Making

Moving

Quick Instructions

1. Select cells A1:B8 and insert a *Clustered Bar* chart

2. Format vertical axis:

   a. *Format Axis > Axis Options > Categories in reverse order*

   b. *Format Axis > Axis Options > Horizontal axis crosses > At maximum category*

3. Select bars and add error bars: *Chart Design > Add Chart Element > Error Bars > More Error Bars Options*

4. Format error bars: select > right-click > *Format Error Bars >*

   a. Set *Direction to Minus*

   b. Set *End Style to No Cap*

   c. Set *Error Amount > Percentage > 100%*

5. More error bar formatting (paint can icon):

   a. Change *Begin Arrow Type* to circle

   b. Change *Begin Arrow Size* to the largest size

6. Change color of the bars: right-click > *Format Data Series > Fill > No Fill*

Chapter **22**

Bullet Chart

Bullet Chart

Level: **Advanced**

Data Type: **Categorical**

Combine Charts: **No**

Formulas Used: **MAX, AVERAGE, MATCH, TEXT, CHAR, &**

The standard bullet chart enables us to make many comparisons simultaneously as it facilitates more and easier comparisons across multiple values. The typical bullet chart contains at least five data series: an observed (actual) value, a target value, and three (or more) ranges (e.g., poor, good, and excellent). I find bullet charts are often used in the financial services field because they can enable investors to compare actual returns, targeted returns, and a range of expected returns, for example.

We'll use a dataset consisting of receiving yards for the top five receivers in the history of the National Football League (NFL): Jerry Rice, Larry Fitzgerald, Terrell Owens, Isaac Bruce, and Randy Moss. For each player, we have the total number of receiving yards in each year of their careers. In this tutorial, we will create a vertical bullet chart using a stacked bar chart and secondary axes.

1. Before we get to the graph itself, let's talk a bit about getting the data ready. From the raw data, which are in cells A1:F37, we are going to do some calculations and place our modified data for the graph in the shaded cells in A38:F46 (Table 22.1).

TABLE 22.1

	A	B	C	D	E	F
38		Jerry Rice	Larry Fitzgerald	Terrell Owens	Isaac Bruce	Randy Moss
39	0–500	500	500	500	500	500
40	500–1,000	500	500	500	500	500
41	1,000–1,500	500	500	500	500	500
42	1,500–2,000	500	500	500	500	500
43	Best	1,848	1,431	1,451	1,781	1,632
44	Average	1,145	1,029	1,062	951	1,143
45	Best Year	1995	2008	2000	1995	2003
46	Label	1,848 (1995)	1,431 (2008)	1,451 (2000)	1,781 (1995)	1,632 (2003)

Setting

Making

Moving

- The first four rows of the data (cells A39:F42) are our ranges: simple increments of 500 yards. We can type in the number 500 into those 20 cells. These ranges can be anything we like—even quartiles or quintiles in the data—but for purposes of this graph, increments of 500 yards seem straightforward.

- The fifth row of the data (*Best*) is each player's best individual year. We can grab this number from the raw data with a simple MAX formula. For Jerry Rice, we enter the formula =MAX(B2:B37) in cell B43, yielding a result of 1,848.

- The sixth row (*Average*) is each player's average number of yards. Again for Jerry Rice, we can enter the formula =AVERAGE(B2:B37) in cell B7, yielding a result of 1,145.

- The seventh row (*Best Year*) will feed into the eighth row (*Label*) for our custom labels. To fill the seventh row, we need to use a formula we didn't cover in Chapter 5: the MATCH formula. This formula looks for a value in a set of cells and generates the position of that value in the list. For Jerry Rice, we can enter the following formula in cell B45:

=MATCH(B43,B2:B37,0)+1984

The formula looks for the value in B43, which is Rice's best year of 1,848 yards, in cells B2:B37. The zero in the last part of the formula tells Excel to look for the *exact* value specified in cell B43. Rice had his best year in 1995, but the MATCH function just pulls the *position* of that value in the series, which is 11. To get the actual year Jerry Rice recorded his best value, we need to add 1984 (the year before our data started) to 11 (the position) to get 1995 for the *Best Year* value.

- Finally, in the last row of the graphing data, we can create a label that has the highest number of yards in a single year *and* the year in which that occurred. But doing so is not trivial—the formula we use in cell B9 is:

```
=TEXT(B43,"#,##0")&CHAR(10)&"("&B8&")"
```

Phew, that's a lot going on! Although this formula is a basic concatenation, it has three parts, which are joined by ampersand (&) symbols. Let's break it down:

- **TEXT(B43,"#, ##0")**. For the receiving yards, we want to keep the basic number formatting of #,##0. But when we join numbers in this way, Excel doesn't keep the commas. We have to use the TEXT function to turn the number in cell B43 into text, so we can format it how we want.

- **CHAR(10)**. This little trick adds a character break in the formula so our first value (number of yards) appears on a different line than the next number (year). Don't worry if the year doesn't wrap on two lines in the cell itself because it will render with a break in the chart labels. If we want to test whether the return worked correctly, select the cell and press the *Wrap Text* button in the *Alignment* section of the *Home* tab.

- **"("&B8&")"**. Three things are joined here—an open parenthesis, cell B45 (the year of most yards), and a closed parenthesis.

So yeah, it looks complicated, but in the end, it's just two numbers pulled together with a space between them (Figure 22.1 and Table 22.2).

Once we've entered these four formulas in column B for Jerry Rice, we can simply to copy and paste across the five columns so the values fill for each of the receivers.

Setting

Making

Moving

| SUM | ⌄ | ⋮ | ✕ ✓ f_x | =TEXT(B43,"#,##0")&CHAR(10)&"("&B45&")" |

FIGURE 22.1

TABLE 22.2

	A	B	C	D	E	F
38		Jerry Rice	Larry Fitzgerald	Terrell Owens	Isaac Bruce	Randy Moss
39	0–500	500	500	500	500	500
40	500–1,000	500	500	500	500	500
41	1,000–1,500	500	500	500	500	500
42	1,500–2,000	500	500	500	500	500
43	Best	1,848	1,431	1,451	1,781	1,632
44	Average	1,145	1,029	1,062	951	1,143
45	Best Year	1995	2008	2000	1995	2003
46	Label	1,848 (1995)	1,431 (2008)	1,451 (2000)	1,781 (1995)	1,632 (2003)

2. Okay, onto the graph itself. First, we need to create a stacked bar chart using the data in cells A38:F44 (Figure 22.2).

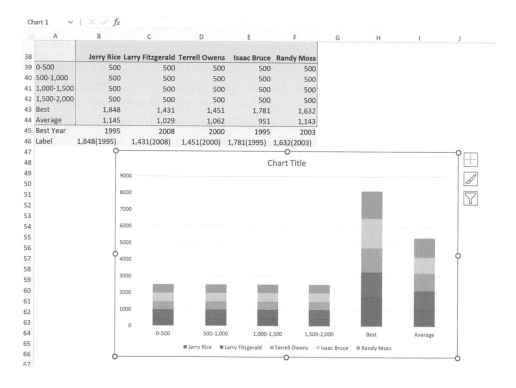

FIGURE 22.2

3. We want these series to be stacked for each receiver, so we need to use the *Chart Design* > *Switch Row/Column* button (Figure 22.3).

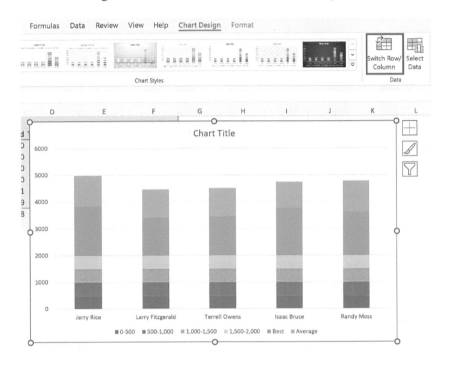

FIGURE 22.3

4. We'll move the *Best* and *Average* series to the secondary axis by selecting each, right-clicking (or CTRL+1), and selecting the *Format Data Series* option at the bottom of the menu (Figure 22.4).

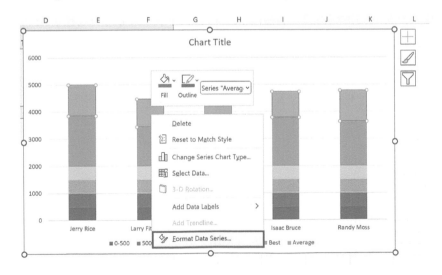

FIGURE 22.4

Setting

Making

Moving

5. With one of the series selected, click on the *Secondary Axis* option in the *Format* menu (Figure 22.5).

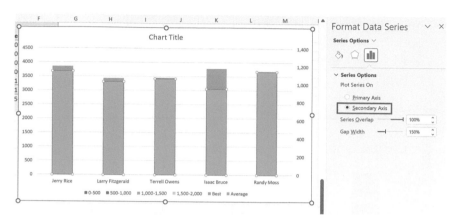

FIGURE 22.5

6. After we move the first series to the secondary axis, we might not be able to see the other series to select it. Remember, we can always use the *Format* > *Current Selection* drop-down menu and click *Format Selection* (Figure 22.6).

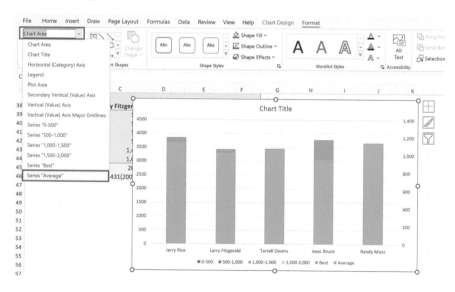

FIGURE 22.6

7. Once we've moved both series to the secondary axis, select those bars and *Format Data Series* > *Gap Width* > 400%. (We'll only need to do this step for one of the series.) Basically, we've put two series on the secondary axis, which puts them on top of the other bars, so we thinned out the bars on the secondary axis to see the bars behind them (Figure 22.7).

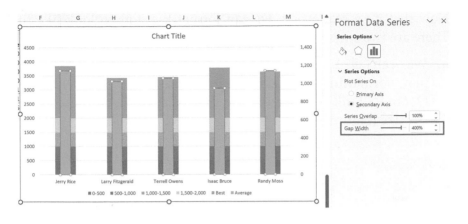

FIGURE 22.7

8. We'll now change the *Best* series (the green bars) to a *Scatter* chart to create the marker. Select the bars for the *Best* series, then *Chart Design > Change Chart Type > Combo* (Figure 22.8).

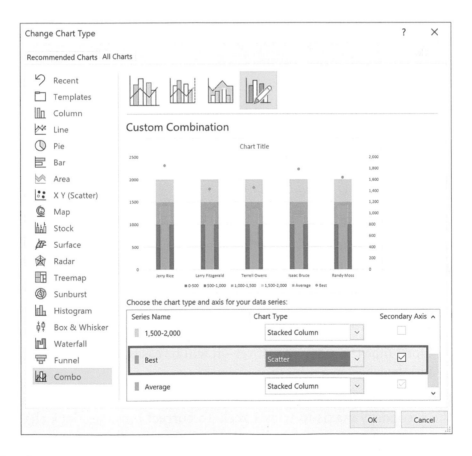

FIGURE 22.8

Setting

Making

Moving

9. Now that it's a scatterplot, we can format the dots to look like lines. There are two ways to do so:

a. We can change the *Marker Type* by selecting the scatterplot, formatting by right-clicking, and under *Marker > Marker Options > Built-In*, selecting the dash shape. We can also increase the size (Figure 22.9).

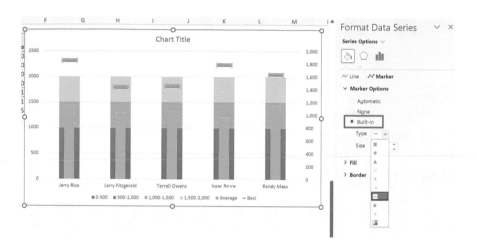

FIGURE 22.9

b. Alternatively, we can add a horizontal error bar to the scatterplot point by selecting the point and using *Add Chart Element > Error Bars > More Error Bars Options*. Delete the vertical error bar and format the horizontal error bars:

i. Keep the *Direction at Both*.

ii. Change the *End Style to No Cap*.

iii. Change the *Fixed value to 0.2*.

c. We can also change the appearance of the horizontal error bar:

i. In the *Line Style* menu, change the width.

ii. In the *Line Color* menu, change the color (Figure 22.10).

Don't hide the markers just yet—it will be easier to have them there to add the labels in a minute.

10. Currently, the two vertical axes are not the same because we are using the secondary y-axis to trick Excel. To correct our axes, let's change the range of both vertical axes to 0–2,000 in the *Format Axis* menu (Figure 22.11).

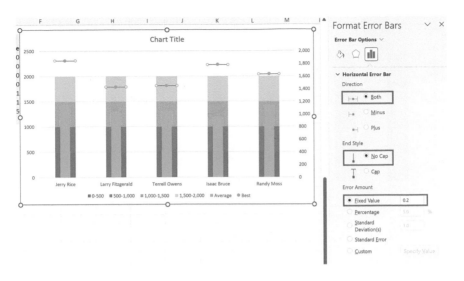

FIGURE 22.10

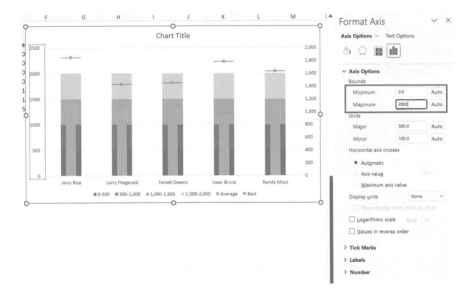

FIGURE 22.11

11. There are lots of ways to think about adding labels here. For this chart, let's just add labels to the *Average* series (the thinner bar) and the *Best Year* series (the marker/error bar). For the *Average* series, right-click, select *Add Data Labels*, then select the labels to format: right-click > *Format Data Labels* > *Label Position* > *Inside End* (Figure 22.12).

For the *Best Year* series, we're going to use the *Labels* we created in row 46 with the concatenation function. Select the dots/error bars,

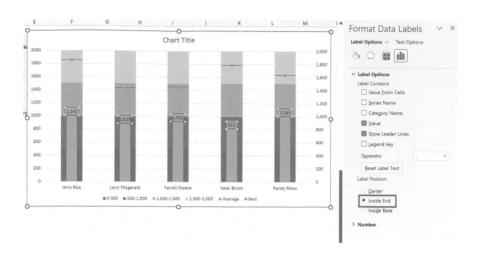

Setting

Making

Moving

FIGURE 22.12

right-click, and select *Add Data Labels*. Right-click to format the labels, change the label reference to *Value From Cells*, and select the values in cells B8:F8. As expected, the labels wrap on two lines because of the CHAR(10) piece of our formula. Be sure to uncheck the box for *Y Value* in the *Label Options* area of the menu. Finally, change the *Label Position* to *Above* (Figure 22.13).

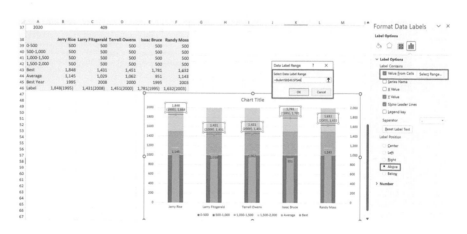

FIGURE 22.13

12. Now we can clean this up:

    a. Let's hide our markers: select the dots > right-click > *Format Data Series* > *Marker* > *Marker Options* > *None*.

    b. Make the error bars (in the *Format Error Bars* menu) a different color and make them a little thicker (I used 2 points).

   c. Delete the legend.

   d. Change the y-axis increments to every 500 yards. We can keep or delete the secondary y-axis here. In this case, I don't think it looks so bad, so I'm going to keep it.

   e. Change the colors of all the series—I'll use shades of gray for the ranges in the background.

   f. Update the title—I'll also add a subtitle that explains what each part of the chart shows. We can also manually move some of the labels around if they are too close to the top of the chart. I moved the labels for Jerry Rice and Isaac Bruce below the marker.

With our final chart, we can see that Jerry Rice had the best individual season and the highest average yards of our five receivers. Our graph also clearly shows that despite having the second-best individual season, Isaac Bruce fell into a lower range for average receiving yards than the other receivers (Figure 22.14).

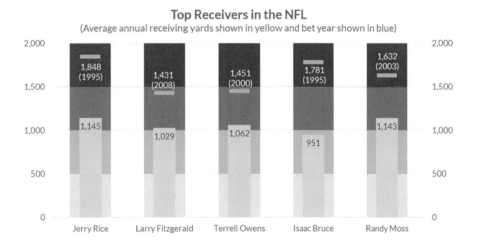

FIGURE 22.14

Quick Instructions

1. Arrange data and formulas

2. Select cells A38:F44 and insert a *Stacked Column* chart

3. Switch order of the chart: *Chart Design > Switch Row/Column*

4. Move *Best* and *Average* series to the secondary axis: right-click on each > *Format Data Series > Secondary Axis*

Setting

Making

Moving

5. Change width of *Average* series: right-click > *Format Data Series* > *Series Options* > *Gap Width* to 400%

6. Change the *Best* series to a scatterplot:

   a. **On PCs**: select Best series > *Chart Design* > *Change Chart Type* > *Combo* > *Best* > *Scatter*

   b. **On Macs**: select Best series > *Chart Design* > *Change Chart Type* > *Scatter*

7. Format scatterplot point (*Best* series) to a line:

   a. **Method 1.** Change marker format: right-click > *Format Data Series* > *Marker* > *Marker Options* > *Built-In* > select dash shape and adjust size

   b. **Method 2.** Add error bar: select dots > *Chart Design* > *Add Chart Element* > *Error Bars* > *More Error Bars Options*. Format the horizontal error bars:

      i. Set *Direction to Both*

      ii. Set *End Style to No Cap*

      iii. Set *Fixed value to 0.2*

   c. Hide Best marker: right-click > *Format Data Series* > *Marker* > *Marker Style* > None

   d. Delete vertical error bars (may need to use the Format > *Current Selection menu*)

8. Edit ranges of the primary and secondary vertical axis:

   a. Right-click > *Format Axis* > *Bounds* > *0 for Minimum and 2,000 for Maximum*

   b. Right-click > *Format Axis* > *Bounds* > *Units* > *Major* > *500*

Setting

Making

Moving

Chapter 23

Tile Grid Map

Tile Grid Map
Level: **Advanced**
Data Type: **Geospatial**
Combine Charts: **No**
Formulas Used: **VLOOKUP, MIN, MAX**

When plotting geographic data on a standard map, the size of the geographic unit, say, a state or country, may not necessarily correspond to the importance of the data value. Take the US. Alaska and Montana are very large states, accounting for 20% of total land area, but are not very populous, accounting for <1% of the country's total population. Tile grid maps try to address that distortion by using shapes of uniform size—usually a square—and arranging the tiles to approximate their real-world position. We can construct tile graph maps fairly easily in Excel once we've spent some upfront time with cell formatting and formula building.

Conceptually, the biggest issue with this version of the tile grid map is that it *approximates* the location of the geographic units. These maps don't always work. For example, I created the tile grid map of the world in Figure 23.1, but it really doesn't make much sense. On the one hand, it addresses the geographic distortion of very large countries, allowing us to see all of the countries of the world. On the other hand, it forced me to make a lot of arbitrary decisions about where to place certain countries, and in many cases, placing the tiles in reasonable proximity to each other was virtually impossible.

FIGURE 23.1

In this section, we are going to build two different tile grid maps—a standard grid map with a single value and another grid map made up of slope charts with multiple values. For the first map, we'll plot the share of people who did not vote in the 2020 US Presidential election. In the second map, we'll plot the share of people who voted for Democrats and the share who voted for Republicans in 1976 and 2020.

There are final, formatted versions of both maps in the Excel file available at https://www.routledge.com/Data-Visualization-in-Excel-A-Guide-for-Beginners-Intermediates-and-Wonks/Schwabish/p/book/9781032343266, so you can skip the tedious formatting work. Unlike many of the other tabs in the file, I have included the formulas and formatting in the worksheet. Following the tutorial here will enable you to create your own tile grid map of a region, country, city, or any geography you think might work.

Before we create the tile grid map, let's create a standard geographic map using the built-in Excel graph as a comparison. The state names and share of people who did not vote in 2020 are included in cells A1:B52 of the spreadsheet.

1. Select the data and go to the *Maps* option in the *Insert* tab, to the right of the standard graph area (Figure 23.2).

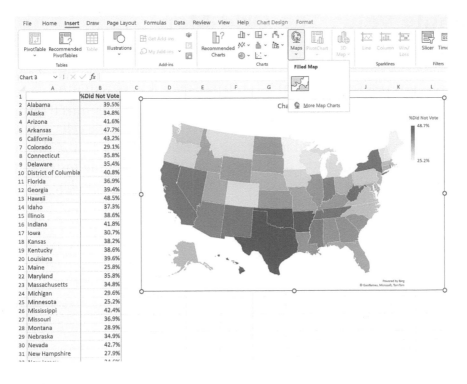

FIGURE 23.2

2. Excel will insert a map of the US with our data values, and by right-clicking on the chart and entering the *Format Data Series* menu, we can change the map projection, how the labels appear, colors, and more (Figure 23.3).

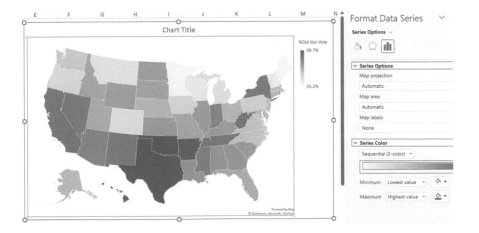

FIGURE 23.3

Setting

Making

Moving

Single Value Tile Grid Map

Setting

Making

Moving

1. To start building the tile grid map, we need to first set up the worksheet with the same data as above. We'll place the data in columns P and Q (we can use a VLOOKUP formula in column Q to pull different data series from other worksheets) and set up the map in columns B through L, which is a manual process that involves laying out the cells, pointing to the correct data, and formatting the labels (Figure 23.4). (The practice file already has the data filled in, so if you're not interested in this part, you can skip to the next section starting in step number 4.)

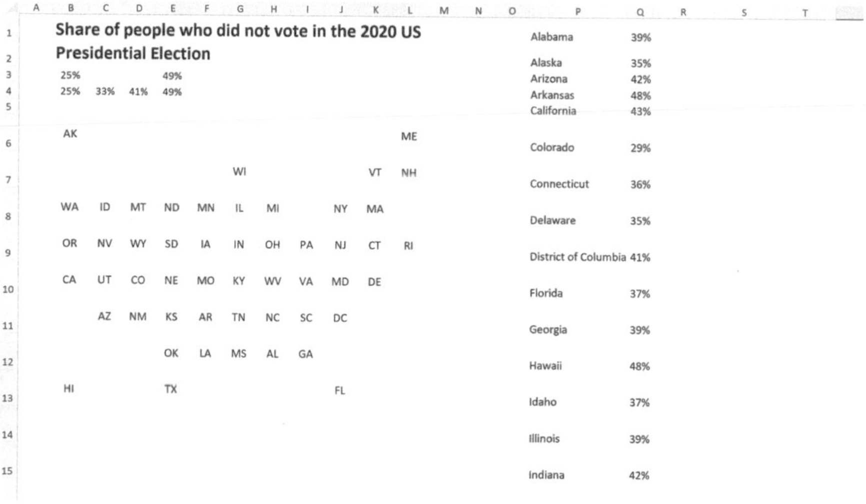

FIGURE 23.4

2. To format the map, we'll change the size of the rows and columns to create squares. In this example, I've set the column height and row width to 36 pixels (we can also see these dimensions in inches in the *Page Layout* option in the *View* tab).

3. We need to do two things in each cell of the map: reference the data value for each state and change the cell format. Take Alaska, for example, in cell B6. The formula in that cell is simply "=Q2," which refers to the actual data value. Instead of showing the data value, we want to show the state abbreviation ("AK"). We can right-click > *Format Cells* > *Number* > *Custom* > type "\AK" in the *Type* box and click OK (the backslash tells Excel to display the text in the cell and not the number; see the *Number Formatting* section in Chapter 4). This step will

overwrite the value and show the state abbreviation rather than the data value. Again, I've already completed this step in the practice file, but you can apply the technique to a tile grid map for a different geography (Figure 23.5).

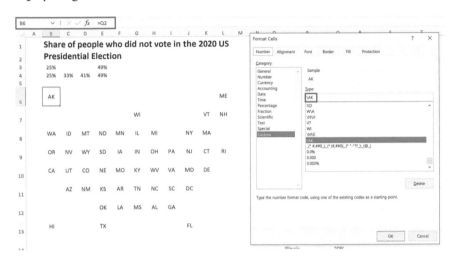

FIGURE 23.5

Changing from the data values to the state abbreviations is the tedious part of setting up this tile grid map. We need to click each state, reference the correct data value, and change the format to manually insert the state abbreviation. If you want to create your own tile grid map, you can similarly adjust the rows and columns to create squares, reference the correct data values, and change the formatting in each cell.

4. To create the actual map, we'll use *Conditional Formatting*. First, we'll create the legend at the top, so we need to assign numbers to the cells B3:E3.

For the legend, we need to create a linear scale that goes from the smallest value to the largest value. In cell B4, we can use a MIN (minimum) formula to find the smallest value in our data. Insert this formula into cell B4: =MIN(Q1:Q51). In cell E4, we use a MAX (maximum) formula to find the largest value: =MAX(Q1:Q51) (Figure 23.6).

To fill in the other two cells (C4 and D4), we need to remember a bit of sixth-grade math. We want to calculate the slope of a line, which is equal to the change in y divided by the change in x. In cell C4, we use the formula =B4+($E$4-$B$4)/3. This formula takes the value in B4 and adds the difference between the maximum and minimum

Setting

Making

Moving

value (change in *y*) divided by three (change in *x*). Because this formula includes absolute references with the dollar signs, we can copy and paste it to cell D4 to find that value. We now have four values in this row of cells: 25%, 33%, 41%, and 49%, which if we plotted them in a line chart, would look like a straight line (Figure 23.6).

Setting

Making

Moving

SUM		✓ ⋮ ✕ ✓ *fx*	=MIN(Q1:Q51)														

Share of people who did not vote in the 2020 US Presidential Election

	Alabama	39%
25% 49%	Alaska	35%
=MIN(Q1:Q51) 41% 49%	Arizona	42%
MIN(number1, [number2], …)	Arkansas	48%
	California	43%

AK   ME

                                        WI   VT   NH

WA   ID   MT   ND   MN   IL   MI   NY   MA

OR   NV   WY   SD   IA   IN   OH   PA   NJ   CT   RI

CA   UT   CO   NE   MO   KY   WV   VA   MD   DE

     AZ   NM   KS   AR   TN   NC   SC   DC

               OK   LA   MS   AL   GA

HI   TX   FL

	Colorado	29%
	Connecticut	36%
	Delaware	35%
	District of Columbia	41%
	Florida	37%
	Georgia	39%
	Hawaii	48%
	Idaho	37%

FIGURE 23.6

5. Now we'll use *Conditional Formatting* to assign the colors based on the data values. Highlight all of the cells (B4:L13)—including the map and the legend—and select *Home > Conditional Formatting > Color Scales > More Rules* (remember the heatmap in Chapter 8). Choose the colors—a light color for the *Lowest Value* and a dark color for the *Highest Value*—and click OK (Figure 23.7).

6. For the state abbreviations, we can manually change the text color of the state labels to white when the fill colors are dark or, better yet, use *Conditional Formatting*. We'll set up our formatting, so the abbreviation for any state in which the value is greater than 40 percent will be white. Select the same group of cells (B4:L13) and select *Home > Conditional Formatting > Highlight Cells Rules > Greater Than*. In the menu, type 0.40 in the box.

   Next, select *Custom Format > Font > Color,* and in the drop-down menu, change the text color to white. Click OK twice (Figure 23.8).

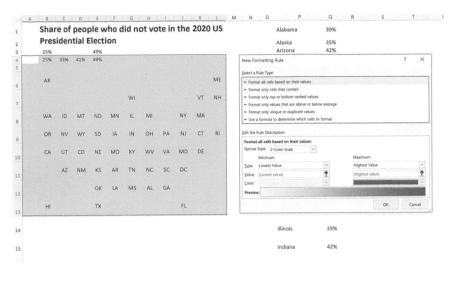

FIGURE 23.7

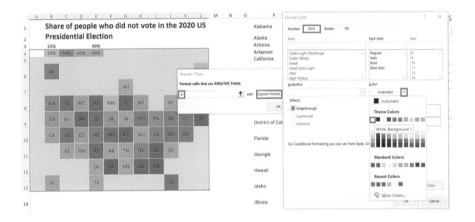

FIGURE 23.8

7. Finally, if we don't want to show the numbers in the legend, we can use our number format trick from Chapter 8: right-click > *Format Cells* > *Number* > *Custom* and type three semicolons (;;;) into the *Type* box. Above the legend, we can re-add the numbers we do want by typing them in the empty cells or using a reference equation (Figure 23.9).

8. As a final note, we can also create this kind of map with distinct categories rather than continuous ones (this version is already completed in the practice file). If we want to break the data into three groups of

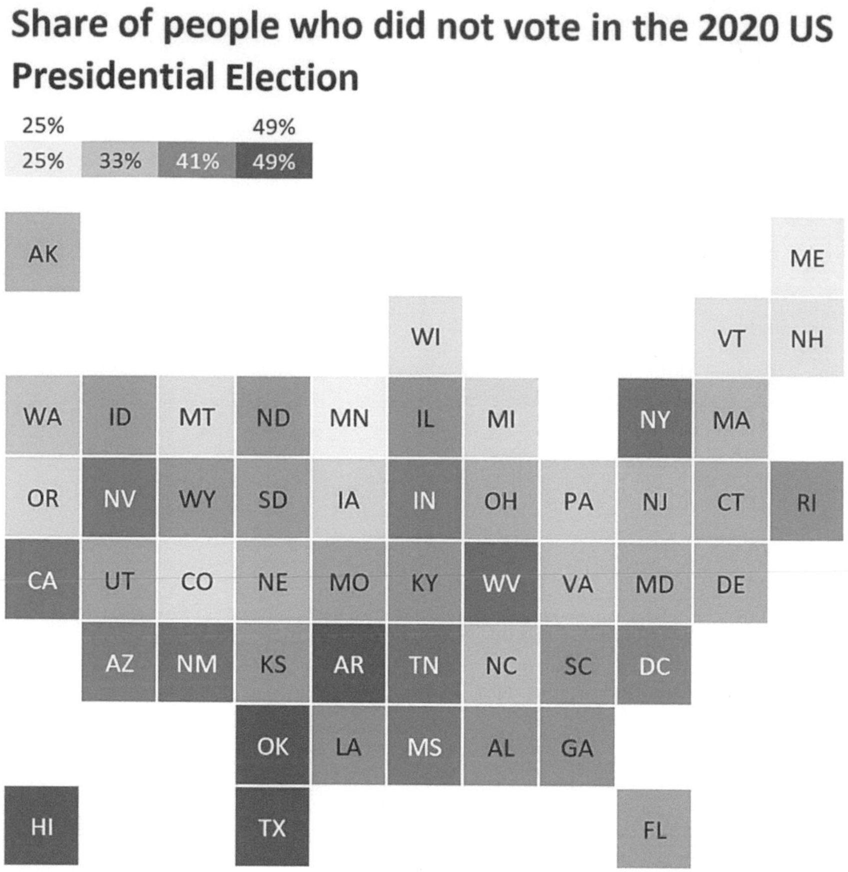

Share of people who did not vote in the 2020 US Presidential Election

FIGURE 23.9

Setting

Making

Moving

voting thresholds—25% to 35%; 35% to 45%; and 45% and over—we could reset the data we use in the map and change the conditional formatting rules.

In Figure 23.10, I moved the voting percentage data over to column R, and in column Q—which is what the state tiles reference—I inserted counter values of 1, 2, and 3 to correspond to the three groups. (Of course, we can do this manually, but I used the *approximate match* option in the VLOOKUP formula to look up the shares in columns U1:V3 to pull the correct number; see Chapter 5 for more details.).

9. We can use *Conditional Formatting > Highlight Cells Rules > Exact Values* again to set the fill and font colors. The legend format changes a bit here, but it's nothing we can't handle by resizing the rows/columns and typing in the labels. If we want to see all the *Conditional Formatting* rules in the selected cells, we can go to *Home > Conditional Formatting > Manage Rules* (Figure 23.11).

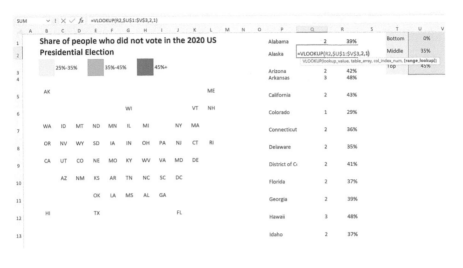

FIGURE 23.10

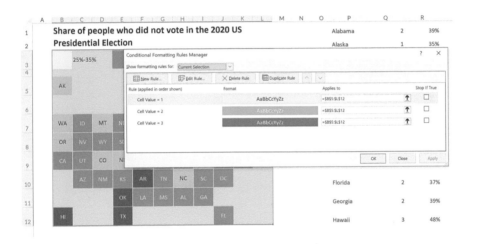

FIGURE 23.11

Multiple Value Tile Grid Map

If we have multiple values we want to display on a map, we can expand the tile grid map to include small slope charts in each state. In this case, we are going to show the share of people who voted for the Democratic candidate and the share who voted for the Republican candidate in the 1976 and 2020 presidential elections. (This map is a redesign of a map originally created by Philip Bump at the *Washington Post*.) Instead of plotting the map in the spreadsheet cells, we are going to create a line chart-scatterplot combination. For this map, most of the work consists of preparing the data, but if you're not interested in learning how to prepare the data, you can use the practice file, which has the data already set up, and skip to the next section starting with step number 5.

1. The raw data are shown in columns A through F, with the state names, abbreviations, and vote shares for each party in 1976 and 2020. (We'll come back to columns G, H, and I in a moment.)

2. Similar to how we made the waffle chart in Chapter 10, we will set up a "key" so we can match the data to the state abbreviations. In columns K:R, type each state's two-letter abbreviation. Each state will have four data points, two for each party in each year. If you imagine rotating the cells to the right and flipping it, you can envision the US laid out how it was in the first tile grid map (and how it will ultimately look). In this layout, we'll have three states along the bottom "row" of the map (Florida, Texas, and Hawaii in column H) and two states in the top "row" (Maine and Alaska in column K).

   This manual set-up requires a lot of organization and typing. The blank cells between each group of states (e.g., row 6) will be used to add vertical space between the states (Figure 23.12).

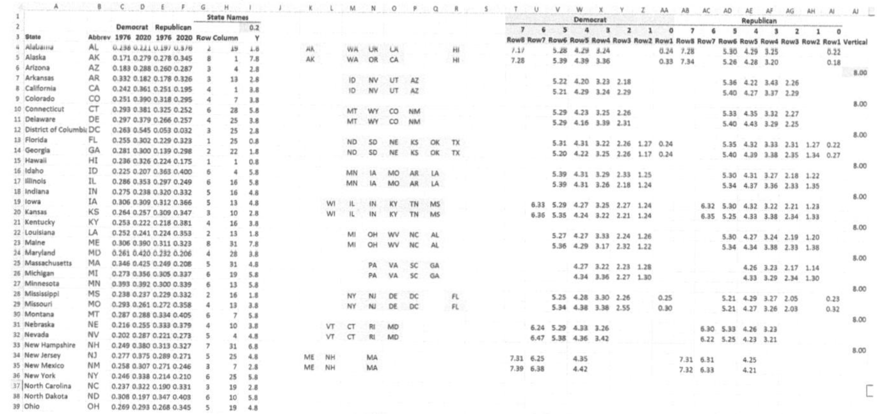

FIGURE 23.12

3. The next part of the spreadsheet (columns T:AI) assigns the data for each state in the map layout. Columns T:AA will hold the data for Democrats and columns AB:AI hold the data for Republicans. Here's the VLOOKUP in cell T4, the top cell for Alaska, that brings the raw data over for graphing:

=VLOOKUP(K4,$B$4:$F$54,2,0)+T$2

   There are four arguments in the formula plus an extra number in cell T2:

   a. **K4.** The state abbreviation we want to search for in the raw data.

b. **$B$4:$F$54.** The reference to the raw data in column B:F. Remember that the VLOOKUP formula needs to have what we are searching for in the first column of the data table, so column B has the state abbreviations.

c. **2.** A reference to the second column in the raw data callout, which is the Democrat vote share in 1976. This reference changes in the second row of each state (e.g., "row 5") and for the data for Republicans (columns AB:AI).

d. **0.** A reference to an *exact match* (see Chapter 5), where Excel looks for the exact thing in the first argument of the formula (Figure 23.13).

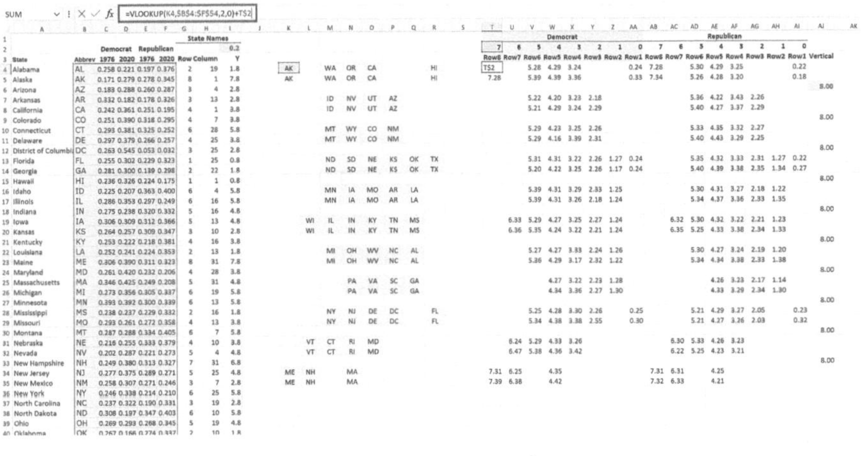

FIGURE 23.13

Setting

Making

Moving

What about the reference to cell T$2? The tile grid map is arranged in rows and columns. I place the states at the bottom of the map—Florida, Texas, and Hawaii—in "row 1." States at the top—Maine and Alaska—are in "row 8." Cell T$2 references the row number. In the Alaska example, we take the actual vote share numbers and add a value of 7 (cell T2) to place it in the top row. By contrast, the formula in cell AA4 for Hawaii is =VLOOKUP(R4,$B$4:$F$54,2,0)+AA$2. The VLOOKUP works in the same way, but the value of cell AA$2 is 0 because that state is on the bottom row.

Because the column reference for the vote shares differs in the raw data (columns B:F), we need to copy and paste the formula for each party separately for the 1976 and 2020 values and for the Democrat and Republican vote shares. In other words, cell T4 can be pasted into the cells from V4 to AA4, but the formula needs to be tweaked for cells T5:AA5 and for the Republican vote shares in columns AB:AI.

The formulas are already included in the practice file, so you can play around with it without breaking them!

4. There are two more data series we need for the chart.

   a. **Column AJ ("Vertical").** We are going to add a separate line chart at the top of the map and use vertical error bars to add breaks between the states. The *Vertical* series is equal to the maximum value in the chart and placed between the states (e.g., "row 8").

   b. **Columns G:I ("State Names").** We are going to add state abbreviations in the top-left part of each tile in the map using a scatterplot. Column G ("Row") is the (manually-entered) row reference for each state. Column H ("Column") is the (manually-entered) column reference for each state. The label for Alaska will be positioned in the first "column" of the chart, and the label for "Alabama" will be positioned in the 19th "column" of the chart. For each state, just count the number of dots (and spaces!) starting with the first dot on the left of the map. Finally, column I is going to be the y-position of the scatterplot. We want this position to be equal to the row position minus a fixed value (0.2) shown in cell I2. I chose the value 0.2 because it looked like the right amount of space to add above the label. If we wanted the label in the middle of the cell, we could change this value to 0.5 and everything would update automatically.

5. With the core data set up, let's make the chart! Insert a *Line Chart with Markers* with cells T4:AJ35. Already, we are pretty close to having this chart in shape. (Well, after a ton of work getting the data prepared!) (Figure 23.14).

6. Now, we're going to separate the states by using the *Vertical* series to add white vertical lines. Using the same process as in Chapter 17, select the series and choose *Chart Design > Add Chart Element > Error Bars*. In the *Vertical Error Bar* menu, we will make three changes:

   a. Change *Direction* to *Minus*

   b. Change *End Style* to *No Cap*

   c. Select the *Error Amount > Percentage* and type "100%" in the box.

   We can also change the color of the error bars to white and increase the *Width* to whatever size works (I've used 12 point) (Figure 23.15).

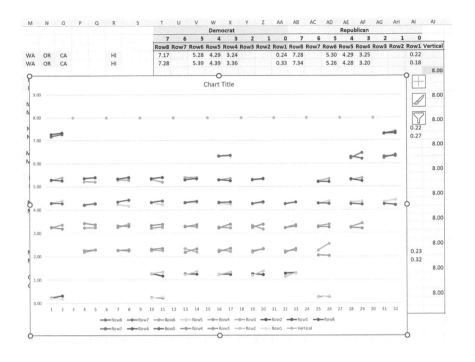

FIGURE 23.14

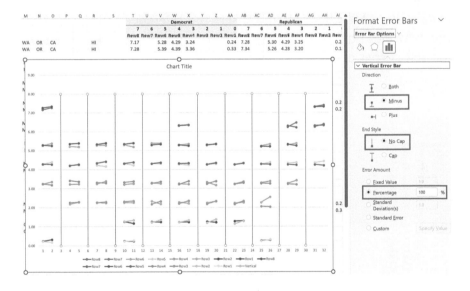

FIGURE 23.15

7. We'll use a scatterplot in cells H4:I54 to add the state abbreviation labels. Right-click on the chart and click *Select Data > Add* to add the *State Names* series by inserting cell G1 in the *Name* box and cells I4:I54 in the *Y Values:* box. Click OK twice (Figure 23.16).

Setting

Making

Moving

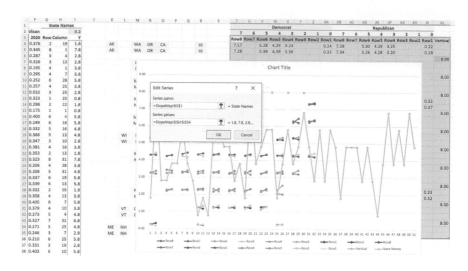

FIGURE 23.16

8. We get a crazy looking graph because we haven't changed the new series to a scatterplot and assigned the x-values. Use the standard method: right-click > *Chart Design* > *Change Chart Type* > *Combo* and change the *State Names* series to a *Scatter* chart. In the graph, *Select Data* > *State Names* > *Edit* and insert the reference to cells H4:H54 in the *X Values* box. After we click OK twice, dots should appear in the top-left corner of each state's square (Figure 23.17).

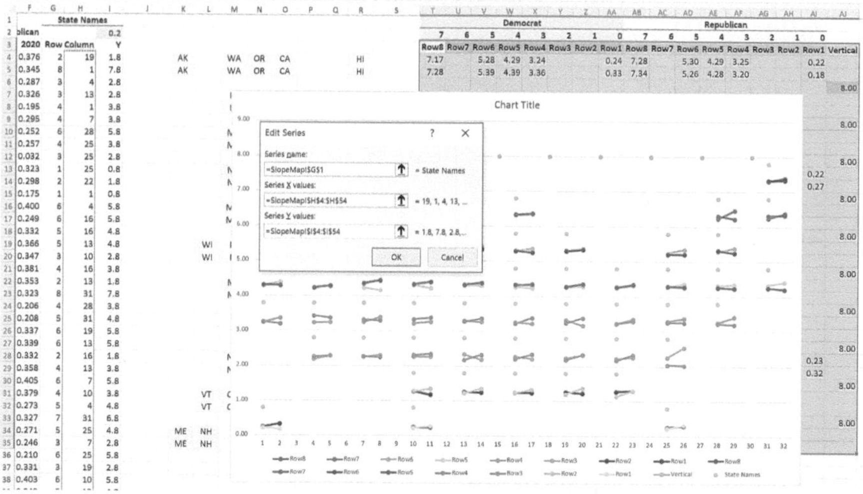

FIGURE 23.17

9. We can now add the state abbreviations as labels. Right-click on the scatterplot points and select *Add Data Labels*. Right-click on the labels to format and select *Values From Cells*. Insert the reference to cells B4:B54 in the box and click OK. Uncheck the *Y Value* box and set the position in *Label Position > Center* (Figure 23.18).

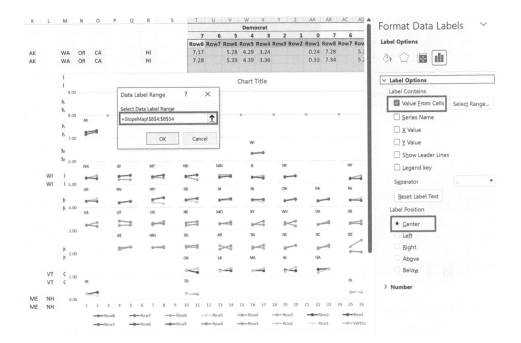

FIGURE 23.18

10. Now we can clean it up:

    a. Delete the legend and x-axis labels.

    b. Hide the markers for the *State Names* and *Vertical* series by right-clicking on each and selecting *Format Data Series > Marker > Marker Options > None*.

    c. Change the range on the y-axis to go from 0 to 8 (*Format Axis > Minimum/Maximum*) and delete the axis.

    d. Finally, the tedious part: select each series and recolor (*Format Data Series*). Unfortunately, we have to recolor each line and change the colors for the *Line*, *Marker fill*, and *Marker outline*, but once we are done, this tile grid map can be updated with new data with less effort (Figure 23.19).

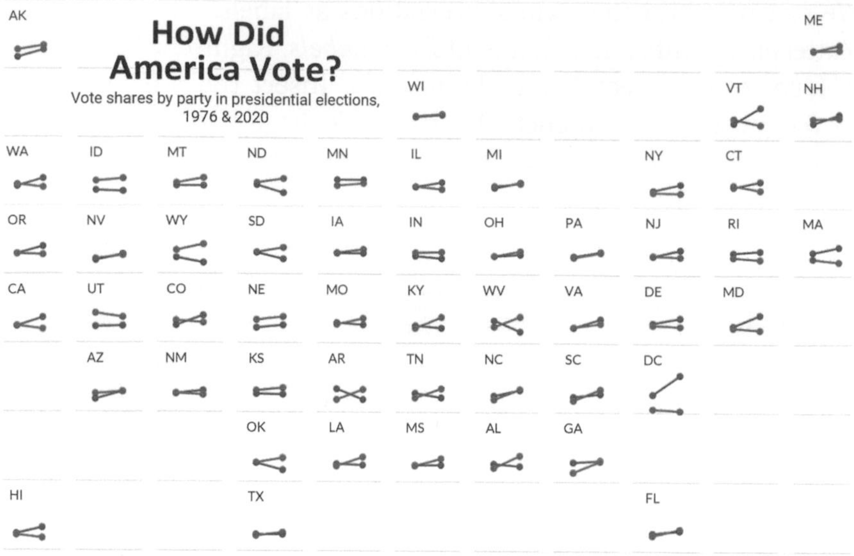

FIGURE 23.19

Quick Instructions

Map #1: Default Map

1. Select cells A1:B52 and insert *Maps* in the *Insert* tab

2. Right-click > *Format Data Series* to modify colors, projection, labels, and more

Map #2: Single Values with Continuous Legend

1. Arrange data, formulas, and tiles

2. Select cells B4:L13

3. Set tile colors: *Home* > *Conditional Formatting* > *Color Scales* > *More Rules*

   a. Set *Minimum* and *Maximum* colors

4. Set text colors: *Home* > *Conditional Formatting* > *Highlight Cells Rules* > *Greater Than* > 0.40 > *Custom Format* > *Font* > *Color* > white

Map #3: Single Values with Discrete Legend

1. Arrange data, formulas, and tiles

2. Select cells B5:L12

3. Set tile colors for first category: *Home > Conditional Formatting > Highlight Cells Rules > Equal To > 1 > Custom Format > Fill > Background color*

    a. Repeat for other categories

4. Set text colors: *Home > Conditional Formatting > Highlight Cells Rules > Greater Than > 0.40 > Custom Format > Font > Color >* white

Map #4: Multiple Values

1. Arrange data and formulas

2. Select cells T4:AJ32 and insert a *Line with Markers* chart

3. Add error bars to the *Vertical* series (dots along the top): *Chart Design > Add Chart Element > Error Bars > More Error Bars Options*

4. Format error bars: select > right-click > *Format Error Bars >*

    a. Set *Direction* to *Minus*

    b. Set *End Style* to *No Cap*

    c. Set *Error Amount > Percentage >* 100%

    d. Set color: *Line > Solid Line >* white

    e. Increase line width: *Line > Width*

5. Add *State Names* series for state abbreviation labels: right-click > *Select Data > Add > Series Name: State Names (cell G1)* and *Series values: H4:H54*

6. Change the *State Names* series to a scatterplot:

    a. **On PCs**: select *State Names* series > *Chart Design > Change Chart Type > Combo > State Names > Scatter*

    b. **On Macs**: select *State Names* series > *Chart Design > Change Chart Type > Scatter*

Setting

Making

Moving

7. Insert x-values: right-click > *Select Data* > *State Names* > *X Values: H4:H54*

8. Add and format data labels:

   a. Right-click on the *State Names* series > *Add Data Labels*

   b. Right-click on labels > *Format Data Labels* > *Value From Cells* > *B4:B54* (and uncheck the box next to *Y Value*)

   c. Right-click on labels > *Format Data Labels* > *Label Position* > *Center*

9. Hide scatterplot markers for labels (*Vertical* and *State Names* series): right-click on each > *Format Data Series* > *Marker* > *Marker Options* > *None*

10. Edit range of vertical axis: right-click > *Format Axis* > *Bounds* > 0 for *Minimum* and 8 for *Maximum*

11. Delete legend, horizontal axis, and vertical axis

Setting

Making

Moving

Chapter 24

Histogram

Histogram
Level: **Advanced**
Data Type: **Distribution**
Combine Charts: **No**
Formulas Used: **COUNTIFS, &**

One of the most basic ways to visualize a distribution of data, the histogram is a type of bar chart that presents the frequency of data across distinct intervals (called bins), which sum to the total distribution. The visualization itself is simple: each bar shows the number of observations within each interval, which we can count and plot as columns. We can calculate the bins for a histogram in Excel a number of ways, which I detail after the graph tutorial.

Histograms can help show where values are concentrated within a distribution, where extreme values are, and whether there are gaps or other unusual values. Histograms do not need to be bar charts—line charts and area charts are also viable substitutes. With any type of histogram, careful decisions about color, font, and lines can help the reader better understand the data.

DOI: 10.1201/9781003321552-26

For this tutorial, we are using data on the weight of all National Hockey League (NHL) goalies in the 1980s and 2010s. If you're not a hockey fan, don't worry; this tutorial will clearly show how goalies have gotten bigger (uh, fatter?) over the past several decades.

In newer versions of Excel, the histogram is a built-in graph type, so you don't necessarily need to use this tutorial. But if you want some more flexibility or you want to layer two distributions together, this tutorial will be useful. The default graph can also calculate the bins for you.

To use the default histogram, we can select the data in cells A1:A177 and insert the Histogram just like any other chart type in the *Insert* tab (Figure 24.1).

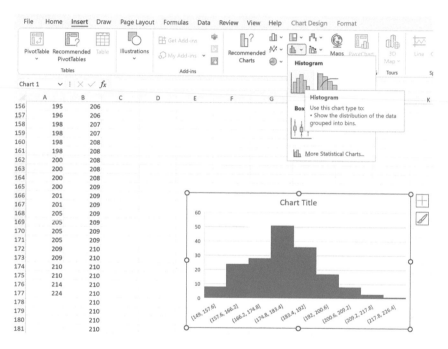

FIGURE 24.1

From here, we can change the number and width of the bins by right-clicking on the bars in the chart and selecting the *Format Data Series* option (Figure 24.2).

No matter what data we choose, Excel assumes the data are from the same series or distribution. In other words, we can't create a single graph that compares the two distributions like we want. Instead, we need to do a little more work to overlay two (or more) histograms.

Before we make our dual histogram, we need to put the raw data into bins. For this example, we are going to use five-pound increments, starting at 150

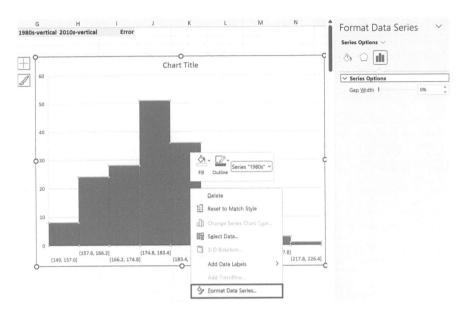

FIGURE 24.2

pounds. I've set up the bins starting in cell C2. In column D, we'll pull data from the 1980s using the following COUNTIFS formula:

```
–COUNTIFS(A:A,">"&$C2,A:A,"<="&$C3)
```

Remember, a COUNTIFS formula lets us make multiple comparisons within the same formula (see page 61). The first comparison includes two arguments: in the first argument (blue), we compare all values in column A (A:A) to anything *greater than* the value in cell C2 (as indicated by the greater than sign in quotation marks joined with the cell C2 reference). The second argument (orange) compares all values in column A (A:A) to values that are *less than or equal to* the value in $C3.

Using the dollar sign absolute reference indicator lets us copy and paste the formula down the 1980s column and into the 2010s column without having to make any additional changes. The formula in cell E2 for the 2010s series is

```
=COUNTIFS(B:B,">"&$C2,B:B,"<="&$C3)
```

Notice the data column moved over to column B (B:B), but the category comparison stayed the same ($C2 and $C3).

We now have counts of the number of goalies in each weight bin and are ready to make the graph. We'll make two versions: one that uses a pair of area charts and another that uses pair of column charts.

Overlaid Area Charts

1. Select the data in cells C1:E22 and insert an *Area Chart*. Depending on how the data line up, only a little bit—or none—of the other series may show up (Figure 24.3).

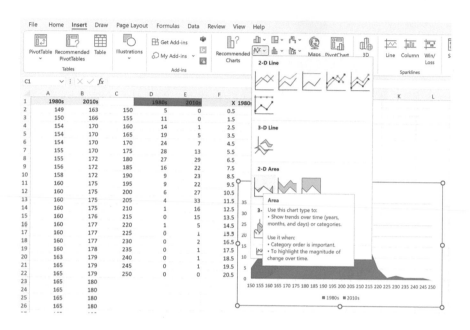

FIGURE 24.3

2. Change the color transparency of both series: right-click > *Format Data Series* > *Fill* > *Solid fill* and move the *Transparency* slider to a higher percentage. I often find something in the 30%–50% range works well (Figure 24.4). In cases where we want to emphasize one distribution over another, we could leave that series with less or no transparency.

3. We can add a border around the top of the chart in two ways. The simplest way is to select the series and add a border in the *Format Data Series* > *Border* > *Solid line* menu. The challenge with this approach is the border will be added around *the entire* series—not just the top but the sides and bottom as well. I've made the border extra thick in the example in Figure 24.5 so you can see that it shows up along the bottom and the sides of the area chart.

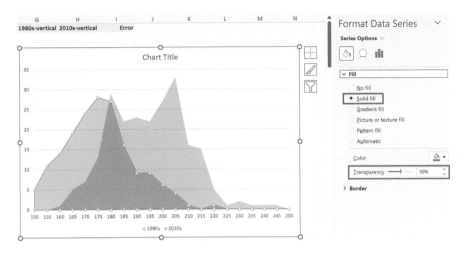

FIGURE 24.4

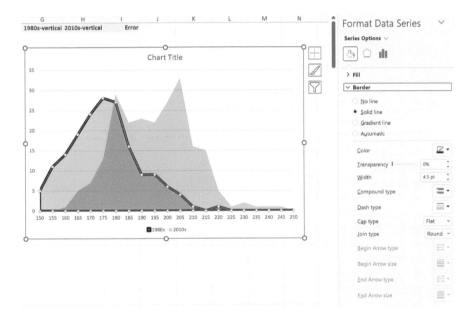

FIGURE 24.5

4. A better way, although it takes a bit more effort, is to add a line chart equal to the series we used to create the area chart. We don't need to create a new data series; we just need to add the same series again. Right-click on the chart, click on *Select Data > Add*, and add the same data series (cells D2:D22 and cells E2:E22). Because these new series have a solid fill by default, we won't be able to see the first two series we started with (Figure 24.6).

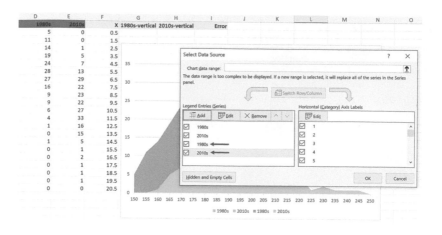

FIGURE 24.6

5. Select one of the new series, which are now on top, and use the *Chart Design > Change Chart Type > Combo* option (or, on Macs, select that series and go to the *Change Chart Type* menu) to change the two new series to basic *Line* charts (Figure 24.7).

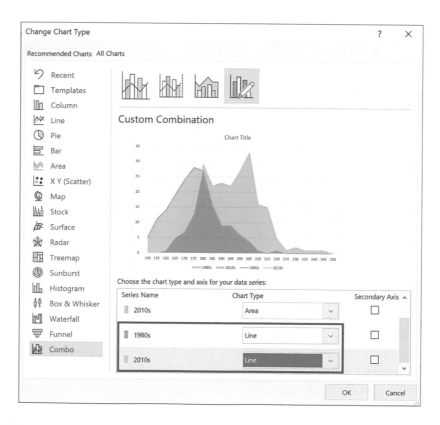

FIGURE 24.7

6. We can change the color of these line charts to match the colors of the area charts (here, blue and orange) in the *Format Data Series > Border > Solid Line* menu. Make sure to change the color of the line chart, not the area chart (use the *Format > Current Selection* dropdown tab to be sure!) (Figure 24.8).

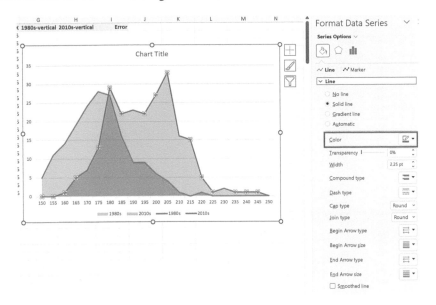

FIGURE 24.8

7. Finally, we can use the *Format Axis > Axis position > On tick marks* option to get the series to start at the left edge of the x-axis. We can finalize by formatting the labels, adding a title, and whatever other changes we want to make (Figure 24.9).

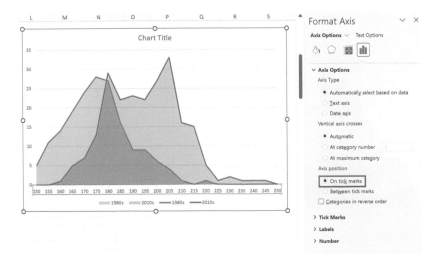

FIGURE 24.9

Setting

Making

Moving

Overlaid Bar Charts

1. This approach will be largely similar to the area chart version, but we will add scatterplots to define the border instead of a separate line chart. To begin, select the data in cells C1:E22 and insert a *Clustered Column Chart* (Figure 24.10).

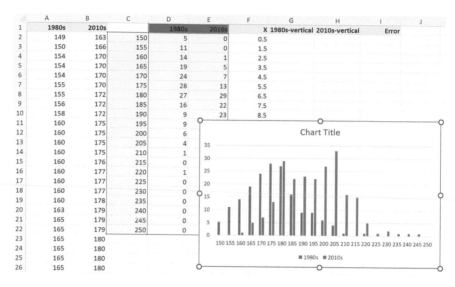

FIGURE 24.10

2. We want the bars for each bin to abut, so select either series, right-click, and select the *Format Data Series* option. In the *Series Options* menu, change the *Series Overlap* to 100% and the *Gap Width* to 0% (Figure 24.11).

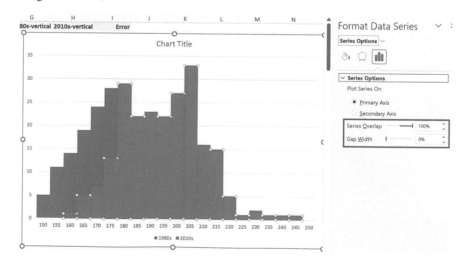

FIGURE 24.11

3. As before, change the color transparency of both series: right-click > *Format Data Series* > *Fill* > *Solid fill* and move the *Transparency* slider to a higher percentage. Again, I often find something in the 30%–50% range works well (Figure 24.12).

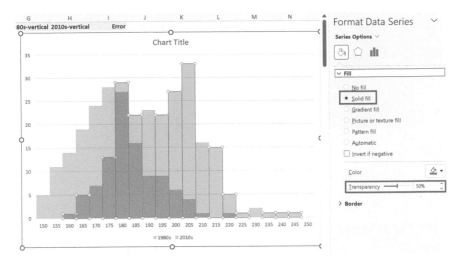

FIGURE 24.12

4. Adding the border is a little more involved with this approach. We could add a border around the bars again (right-click > *Format Data Series* > *Border* > *Solid line*), but it looks somewhat cluttered and can be hard to read. More importantly, it looks like a stacked column chart, which is not what we want (Figure 24.13).

5. We can't add a line here like we did for the area chart either because each bin requires two points—one for the left corner of the column and one for the right corner. The line chart needs to "step" from one bar to the next, which we can't do even if we added two points for each bin (Figure 24.14).

6. Adding scatterplots—with vertical and horizontal error bars—keeps the number of observations in our data the same and enables us to simulate this step effect. For each series, we are going to create an x- and y-value pair with the x-values in increments of 0.5 (to hit the corners of each bar) and the y-values equal to the data value. We will create a series for the vertical error bars equal to the difference in the values between each pair of bars (the step). The horizontal error bars will all be the same width (in this case, one), so we'll have a horizontal error bar series for each histogram.

Setting

Making

Moving

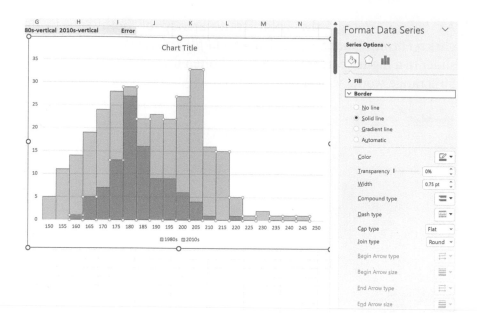

FIGURE 24.13

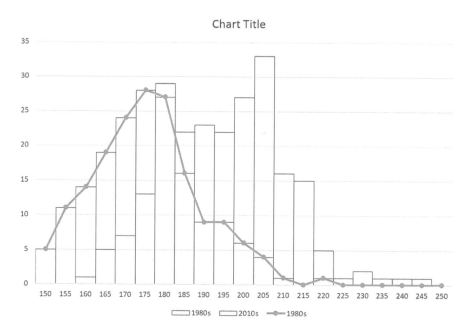

FIGURE 24.14

We can use the following to add the data in columns F:H:

1. **Column F.** Type 0.5 in cell F2, and then =F2+1 in cell F3 to get 1.5. Copy and paste down the column. Remember, Excel views the width of each bar as one, so if we start at 0.5 and add 1, the error bar extends to the left and right edge of each bar.

2. **Column G.** Type =D2, the first value in the *1980s* series, in cell G2. Type =D3-D2 in cell G3, which gives us the difference between the first two rows. Copy and paste this formula down the column to calculate the differences, which serves as the vertical error bars for the *1980s* series (Figure 24.15 and Table 24.1).

3. **Column H.** Follow the same process in column H for the *2010s* series. Type =E2 in cell H2 and =E3-E2 in cell H3. Copy and paste this formula down the column to create the vertical error bars data for the *2010s* series.

| G3 | ⌄ | ⋮ | ✕ ✓ *fx* | =D3-D2 |

FIGURE 24.15

TABLE 24.1

	A	B	C	D	E	F	G	H	I
	1980s	2010s		1980s	2010s	X	1980s-Vertical	2010s-Vertical	Error
1	149	163	150	5	0	0.5	5	0	1
2	150	166	155	11	0	1.5	6	0	1
3	154	170	160	14	1	2.5	3	1	1
4	154	170	165	19	5	3.5	5	4	1
5	154	170	170	24	7	4.5	5	2	1
6	155	170	175	28	13	5.5	4	6	1
7	155	172	180	27	29	6.5	-1	16	1
8	156	172	185	16	22	7.5	-11	-7	1
9	158	172	190	9	23	8.5	-7	1	1
10	160	175	195	9	22	9.5	0	-1	1
11	160	175	200	6	27	10.5	-3	5	1
12	160	175	205	4	33	11.5	-2	6	1
13	160	175	210	1	16	12.5	-3	-17	1
14	160	176	215	0	15	13.5	-1	-1	1

Setting

Making

Moving

7. These two series for each distribution—equal to the height of the bars (y-values) and 0.5 to start, then ticking up by 0.5 (x-values)—give us the inputs for the scatterplot. Right-click on the chart, *Select Data* > *Add* to insert the *1980s* series again (cells D2:D22), and press OK. Excel, of course, will add this new series as a bar chart that will sit on top of the other series (Figure 24.16).

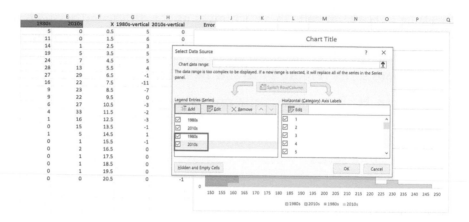

FIGURE 24.16

8. Select the new series and change it to a *Scatter* chart using the *Chart Design* > *Change Chart Type* > *Combo* option (Figure 24.17).

9. Right-click in the chart, *Select Data* > *1980s [the new one]* > *Edit*, and input the x-values (cells F2:F22). In this menu, we can also add the second scatterplot series (*2010s*) for the other distribution—cells F2:F22 for the x-values and cells E2:E22 for the y-values. Enter the appropriate data references and click OK twice (Figure 24.18).

10. We now have dots at the top-left corner of every bar. To set borders along the top and left edge of the bars, we need to add error bars. Select one of the scatterplot series and go to *Chart Design* > *Add Chart Element* > *Error Bars* > *Error Bar Options*. Remember, Excel adds vertical and horizontal error bars to scatterplots, and we will use and format both.

For the horizontal error bars (check for the correct error bar formatting menu!), we make three changes:

a. Change *Direction* to *Plus*.

b. Change *End Style* to *No Cap*.

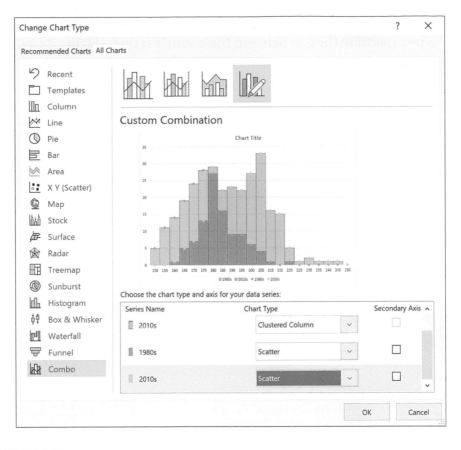

FIGURE 24.17

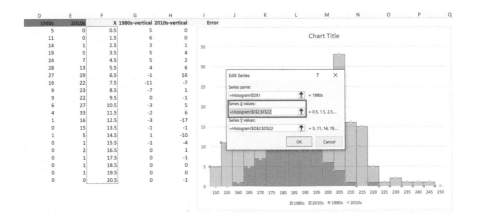

FIGURE 24.18

c. Select the *Error Amount > Fixed Value* option and enter a "1" in the box (because the gap between the x-values is one) (Figure 24.19).

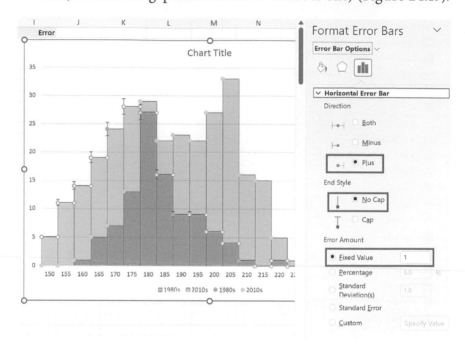

FIGURE 24.19

We are going to make similar changes for the vertical error bars:

a. Change *Direction* to *Minus*.

b. Change *End Style* to *No Cap*.

c. Select the *Error Amount > Custom > Specify Value > Negative Error Value* box and enter the appropriate vertical error bar series (cells G2:G22 for the *1980s* series and cells H2:H22 for the *2010s* series) (Figure 24.20).

11. Now, repeat the same set of steps for the *2010s* series. Once that's done, we can do a bit of styling:

a. Hide the markers: select and right-click > *Format Data Series > Marker > Marker Options > None*.

b. Change the color and thickness of the error bars.

c. Style the bars, error lines, and axes (Figure 24.21).

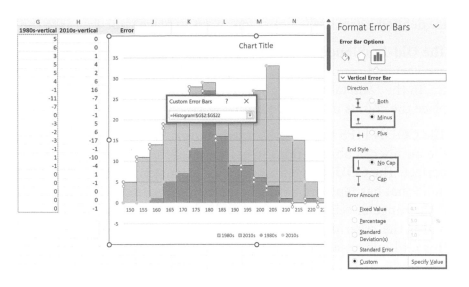

FIGURE 24.20

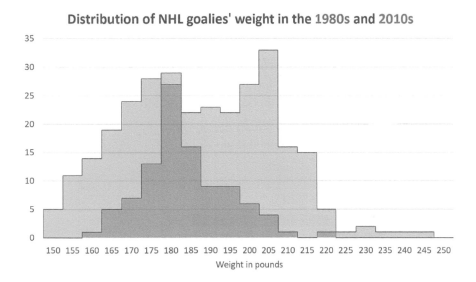

Distribution of NHL goalies' weight in the 1980s and 2010s

Weight in pounds

FIGURE 24.21

How Do You Find the Correct Width of the Bins?

One important caveat to this tutorial is how to determine the widths of the histogram bins. The statistical background behind choosing an optimal bin width is beyond the scope of this book, but the built-in Excel histogram offers one way to define the bins or at least get a sense of what they should be. If you want to communicate the distribution of your data, you can choose the smallest number of bins that conveys your message.

Once defined, there are (at least) four ways to place your data into the bins.

1. **The Old-Fashioned, Manual Way.** If you don't have a lot of data, you can sort and count the data. For ease, I sort the data (use the *Sort* button in the *Data* tab) and highlight the groups so it's easier to see. I then place the counts in a new column.

2. **The COUNTIFS Formula (as used above).** All we're doing is counting the number of observations in each bin, so the COUNTIFS formula is perfect. The COUNTIFS formula is an extension of the COUNTIF formula that has repeated pairs of arguments: the first is the *range*, which is the range of cells you want to apply the criteria against, and the second is the *criteria*, which is the thing you want to count. You can do this multiple times to count across multiple criteria.

3. **Use the FREQUENCY Array.** Arrays have very nice properties in Excel, but they can be challenging to work with and are too advanced for this book. To use arrays, you need to enter the formula—which has two arguments, the range and the bin value—and hit CTRL+SHIFT+ENTER. The array will fill down the column.

4. **Use the Analysis ToolPak.** This add-in is a hidden feature in Excel, so you need to activate it first. Go to the *Options* menu in the *File* dropdown menu and in the *Add-Ins* option on the left side, select "Analysis ToolPak" and press OK (Figure 24.22).

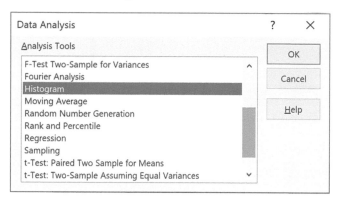

FIGURE 24.22

You will now have a *Data Analysis* button in your *Data* tab. Select the button and select the *Histogram* option. In the new menu, you can type in your *Input Range:* (that's the data), the *Bin Range:* (those are bins), and the *Output Range:* (where you want the results to go). Excel fills in the *Frequency* in that column. (You'll see that the ToolPak offers lots of other fun functionalities, but I won't cover those here.)

Quick Instructions

Method #1: Overlaid Area Charts

1. Arrange data and formulas

2. Select cells C1:E22 and insert an *Area* chart

3. Change the color transparency of both series: right-click > *Format Data Series* > *Fill* > *Solid fill* > *Transparency*

4. Add borders (two series):

   a. Right-click > *Select Data* > *Add* > *Series Name: 1980s (cell D1); Series values: D2:D22* and *Series Name: 2010s (cell E1); Series values: E2:E22*

   b. Change series to line charts:

      i. **On PCs**: select each series > *Chart Design* > *Change Chart Type* > *Combo* > drop-down menu for each series > *Line*

      ii. **On Macs**: select each series > *Chart Design* > *Change Chart Type* > *Line*

Method #2: Overlaid Bar Charts

1. Arrange data and formulas

2. Select cells C1:E22 and insert a *Clustered Column* chart

3. Align the bars: right-click on either set > *Format Data Series* > *Series Options* > *Series Overlap* to 100% and *Gap Width* to 0%

4. Change the color transparency of both series: right-click > *Format Data Series* > *Fill* > *Solid fill* > *Transparency*

5. Add scatterplots for borders: right-click > *Select Data* > *Add* > *Series Name: 1980s (cell D1)* and *Series values: D2:D22*

6. Change the new *1980s* series to a scatterplot:

   a. **On PCs**: select new *1980s* series > *Chart Design* > *Change Chart Type* > *Combo* > *1980s* > *Scatter*

   b. **On Macs**: select new *1980s* series > *Chart Design* > *Change Chart Type* > *Scatter*

Setting

Making

Moving

7. Insert x-values: right-click > *Select Data* > *1980s [the bottom one]* > *X Values: F2:F22*

8. Add other series: right-click > *Select Data* > *Add* > *Series Name (cell E1): 2010s; X Values: F2:F22*; and *Y values: E2:E22*

9. Add borders using the scatterplots: select > *Chart Design* > *Add Chart Element* > *Error Bars* > *Error Bar Options*

10. Format horizontal error bars: select > right-click > *Format Error Bars* >

    a. Set *Direction* to *Plus*

    b. Set *End Style* to *No Cap*

    c. Set *Error Amount* > *Fixed Value* > 1

11. Format vertical error bars: select > right-click > *Format Error Bars* >

    a. Set *Direction* to *Minus*

    b. Set *End Style* to *No Cap*

    c. Set *Error Amount* > *Custom* > *Specify Value* > *Negative Error Value* > *1980s series: G2:G22* and *2010s series: H2:H22*

12. Hide markers for both series: right-click on each > *Format Data Series* > *Marker* > *Marker Options* > *None*

Setting

Making

Moving

Chapter **25**

Marimekko Chart

Marimekko Chart
Level: **Advanced**
Data Type: **Categorical**
Combine Charts: **Yes**
Formulas Used: **IF, INT, VLOOKUP, SUM**

The Marimekko chart is a bar chart that encodes two variables: one along the height of the vertical axis and another along the width of the columns. They are often used to show a two-way, part-to-whole relationship. I like to think of Marimekko charts as an alternative to a scatterplot with the data summing to 100% along both axes.

There's no way to make Excel change the width of individual columns in a column chart, so this tutorial approaches building a Marimekko chart by creating a column chart with 100 columns and repeating values as necessary. We'll group the data to make it easier to color each series separately instead of having to select and recolor each of the 100 columns. This process will require working with a number of formulas, but it will be more flexible in the end.

The data for this example consists of the share of people living on less than $30 per day in ten countries around the world, and each individual country's

DOI: 10.1201/9781003321552-27

share of the 10 countries' total population. We'll put the poverty metric along the y-axis and the population shares along the x-axis.

The raw data are shown in cells A5:C14, and the rest of the worksheet is constructed to build the graph, with much of it repeating so we can use multiple VLOOKUP formulas. I've included all of the data and calculations in the practice file, so if you aren't interested in setting up the data—and there's a lot of it!—skip right to the graph building section. This version of the Marimekko uses rounded data values, but if your data have decimals, simply multiply everything by 10 or 100 and use 1,000 or 10,000 columns in the chart (Figure 25.1). (Jorge Camões (2020) has a different solution to building this chart, but I find the data preparation steps to be more complicated than these.)

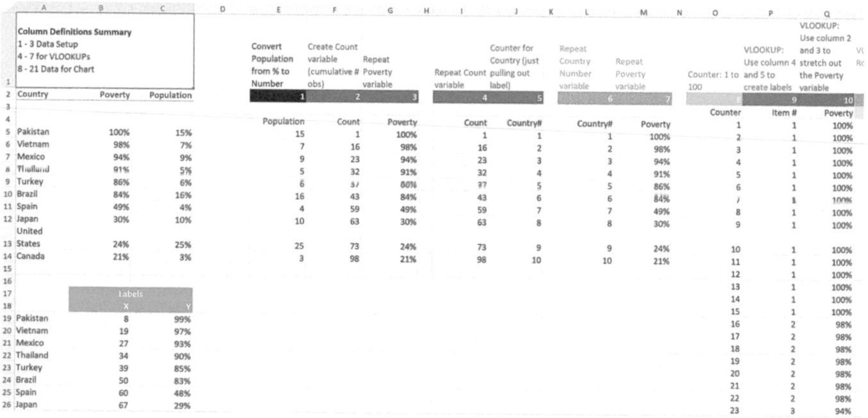

FIGURE 25.1

Setting Up the Data

Column E. Create a new column for the *Population* series but change it from a percentage to an integer. We can copy and paste the original data and change the format of the new cells (select the cells and right-click or use the CTRL+1 keyboard shortcut), or we can use a formula [E5=C5*100] so the data can be easily updated (Figure 25.2).

Column F. Create a *Count* variable that denotes the cumulative count of each item. We'll start with 1, which is typed in cell F5. A simple formula [F6=F5+E5, F7=F6+E6, …] sets the number of cells for each value down the column. The first item is represented by the 1st through 15th columns, the second item starts with the 16th column, and so on (Figure 25.3).

Column G. Repeat the *Poverty* series. Again, the formula [G5=B5] will make it easier to update if the data change. (We repeat a few series to make it easier to use the VLOOKUP formulas next.)

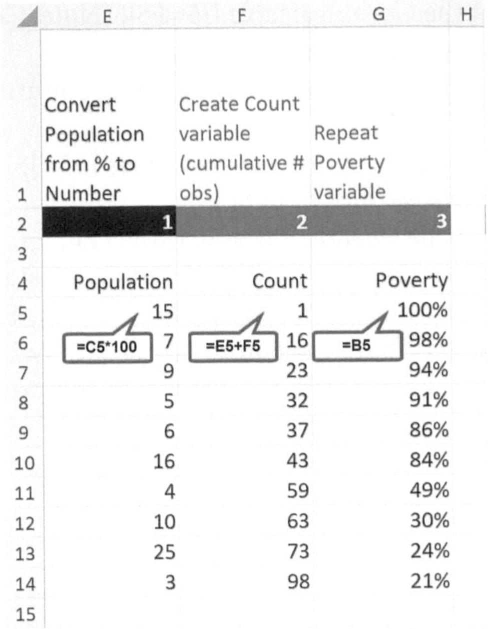

	E	F	G	H
1	Convert Population from % to Number	Create Count variable (cumulative # obs)	Repeat Poverty variable	
2	**1**	**2**	**3**	
3				
4	Population	Count	Poverty	
5	15	1	100%	
6	=C5*100 7	=E5+F5 16	=B5 98%	
7	9	23	94%	
8	5	32	91%	
9	6	37	86%	
10	16	43	84%	
11	4	59	49%	
12	10	63	30%	
13	25	73	24%	
14	3	98	21%	
15				

FIGURE 25.2

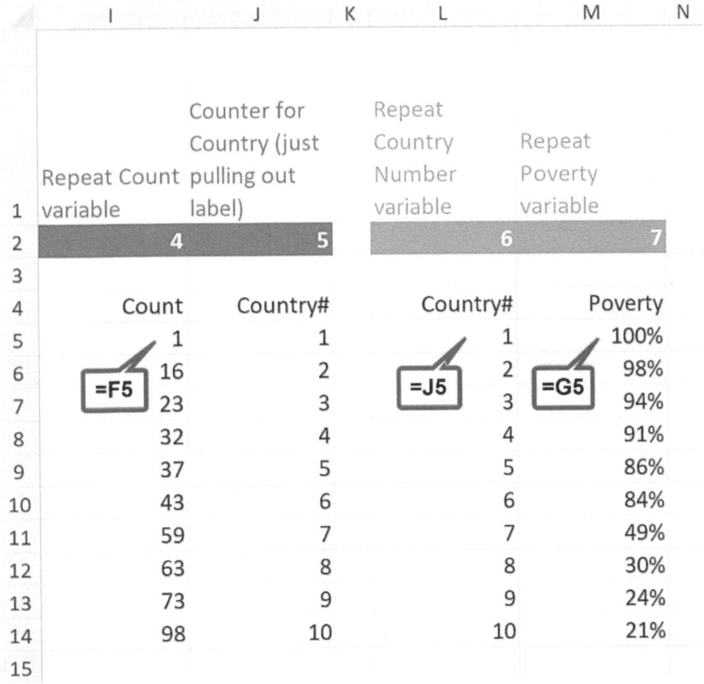

	I	J	K	L	M	N
1	Repeat Count variable	Counter for Country (just pulling out label)		Repeat Country Number variable	Repeat Poverty variable	
2	**4**	**5**		**6**	**7**	
3						
4	Count	Country#		Country#	Poverty	
5	1	1		1	100%	
6	=F5 16	2		=J5 2	=G5 98%	
7	23	3		3	94%	
8	32	4		4	91%	
9	37	5		5	86%	
10	43	6		6	84%	
11	59	7		7	49%	
12	63	8		8	30%	
13	73	9		9	24%	
14	98	10		10	21%	
15						

FIGURE 25.3

Setting

Making

Moving

Column I. Repeat the *Count* variable [I5=F5]. (Note: Column H is left blank as a visual cue to separate the groups of data.)

Column J. Add a simple *Country Number* here, counting up from 1 to 10 so we can label the countries later.

Column L. Repeat the *Country Number* series [L5=J5]. (Note: Column K is left blank to separate the groups of data.)

Column M. Repeat the *Poverty* variable [M5=G5].

Column O. Now, we can set up the columns that start to build the chart (Figure 25.4). The first column counts from 1 to 100. Each value (row) will become a bar in the bar chart—the number of bars will sum to 100 (%) and the value (height) of the bars will correspond to the poverty rate. There's no need to type this manually. Instead, type a "1" in cell O4 then add the formula [O5=O4+1] in the cell below and drag it down to row 103.

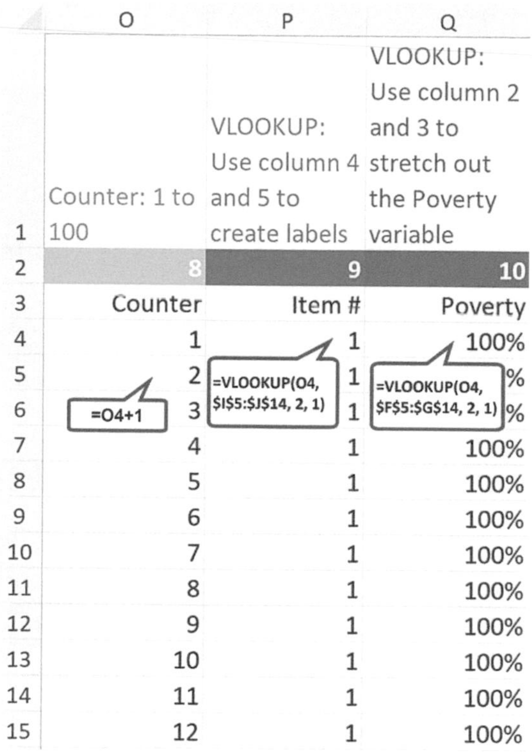

Setting

Making

Moving

	O	P	Q
			VLOOKUP: Use column 2 and 3 to stretch out the Poverty variable
	Counter: 1 to 100	VLOOKUP: Use column 4 and 5 to create labels	
1			
2		8	9	10
3	Counter	Item #	Poverty
4	1	1	100%
5	2	=VLOOKUP(O4, $I$5:$J$14, 2, 1)	1	=VLOOKUP(O4, $F$5:$G$14, 2, 1) %
6	=O4+1 3	1	%
7	4	1	100%
8	5	1	100%
9	6	1	100%
10	7	1	100%
11	8	1	100%
12	9	1	100%
13	10	1	100%
14	11	1	100%
15	12	1	100%

FIGURE 25.4

Column P. This series denotes the number of bars for each country and corresponds to each country's assigned number that we created in column J. We use a VLOOKUP formula to enter the data for the chart. In cell P4, we use

=VLOOKUP(O4, $I$5:$J$14, 2, 1) and drag it down to row 103. Here's how this VLOOKUP formula works:

=VLOOKUP(O4,

This cell is what we want to look up. We are going to match each entry in this *Counter* series to another look-up table to pull out the corresponding number for each country.

$I$5:$J$14

Here, we query the data we created earlier, consisting of the *Count* and *Country Number* data in columns I and J. VLOOKUP matches the first argument in the VLOOKUP formula to the first column in the I:J table, which is why we ordered the first few columns the way we did (Figure 25.3). (The dollar signs ($) are the *absolute references* that allow us to copy and paste this formula without changing the cell references.)

2

This number corresponds to the column number we want to extract, so it refers to the *Country Number* data in column J.

1

This number is the "range_lookup" value and tells Excel we want an "approximate match" of the value in cell O4 instead of an "exact match." *This part of the formula is key for this exercise.* The approximate match compares the specified cell (O4) to the lookup values in column I. If the value in cell O4 is greater than or equal to the first lookup value and less than the second lookup value, the formula will pull the first value from the *Counter* series (column J) into column P. If the value of the specified cell is greater than or equal to the second lookup value and less than the third lookup value, the formula will pull the second value from the *Counter* series (column J) into column P. This process will occur for each value in column O and generate a series of repeated numbers that correspond to each country number in column J and matches the population share for each country. Thus, the first 15 values in column P will equal 1, corresponding to Pakistan. On the 16th entry, the values will equal 2 for Vietnam. And so on.

In sum, this VLOOKUP queries the *Counter* series and pulls out the *Country Number* from column J to create a designation for each country in the chart.

Setting

Making

Moving

Column Q. Here, we pull in the data value that will become the height of the bars in the chart. In cell Q4, we use another VLOOKUP formula and drag it down to row 103: =VLOOKUP(O4, $F$5:$G$14, 2, 1). This VLOOKUP works in the same way as the formula in column P and queries column F to extract the *Poverty* rate series in column G.

COLUMNS R:AA. We're going to create ten different data series—one for each country—so we can add them all to one chart and color each by grabbing the entire group. The numbers at the top of the series (in row 2) are important here and correspond to each *Country Number*. This formula is a little complicated, but once it's inserted into the first column, we can just drag it horizontally and vertically (Figure 25.5).

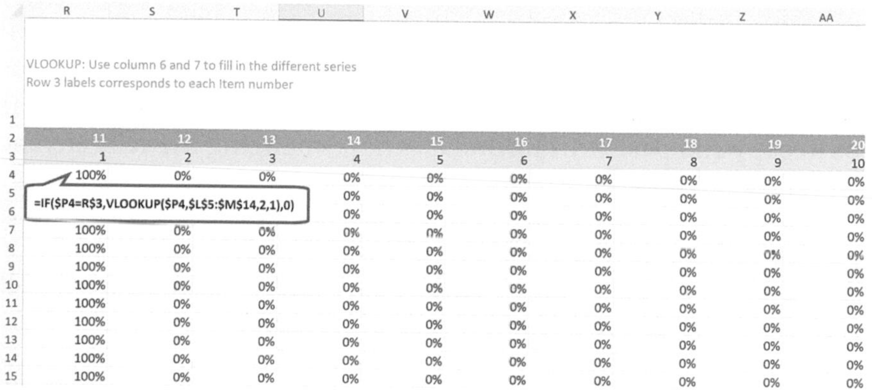

	R	S	T	U	V	W	X	Y	Z	AA
	VLOOKUP: Use column 6 and 7 to fill in the different series									
	Row 3 labels corresponds to each Item number									
1										
2	11	12	13	14	15	16	17	18	19	20
3	1	2	3	4	5	6	7	8	9	10
4	100%	0%	0%	0%	0%	0%	0%	0%	0%	0%
5	=IF($P4=R$3,VLOOKUP($P4,$L$5:$M$14,2,1),0)			0%	0%	0%	0%	0%	0%	0%
6				0%	0%	0%	0%	0%	0%	0%
7	100%	0%	0%	0%	0%	0%	0%	0%	0%	0%
8	100%	0%	0%	0%	0%	0%	0%	0%	0%	0%
9	100%	0%	0%	0%	0%	0%	0%	0%	0%	0%
10	100%	0%	0%	0%	0%	0%	0%	0%	0%	0%
11	100%	0%	0%	0%	0%	0%	0%	0%	0%	0%
12	100%	0%	0%	0%	0%	0%	0%	0%	0%	0%
13	100%	0%	0%	0%	0%	0%	0%	0%	0%	0%
14	100%	0%	0%	0%	0%	0%	0%	0%	0%	0%
15	100%	0%	0%	0%	0%	0%	0%	0%	0%	0%

FIGURE 25.5

In cell R4, we have =IF($P4=R$3,VLOOKUP($P4,$L$5:$M$14,2,1), 0) Let's break it down again:

$$=IF(\$P4=R\$3, \quad VLOOKUP(\$P4,\$L\$5:\$M\$14,2,1), \quad 0)$$

$$=IF(\$P4=R\$3,$$

To start, the IF statement evaluates the first argument, here $P4=R$3. We're simply comparing the *Country Number* entered in the second row to how many times each item number will repeat in column P. Notice the strategic use of the absolute/relative reference "$" symbol. With these references, we can move the formula across the columns and down the rows without having to make any further edits.

$$VLOOKUP(\$P4,\$L\$5:\$M\$14,2,1),$$

If the first argument in the IF formula is *True*, the VLOOKUP formula is evaluated and placed in the cell. Here, the first argument ($P4) looks up the *Country Number* from column P in the last set of data placed in columns L and M ($L$5:$M$14). The third argument in the VLOOKUP (2) looks in the second column (M). The final piece of the VLOOKUP (1) specifies an approximate match. The VLOOKUP formula pulls out the *Poverty rate* percentage, which we will plot along the vertical dimension.

0)

If the first argument in the IF formula is *False*, the formula places a 0 in the cell. For the first country (column R), the first 15 rows fill with 100% and the remainder fills with 0%. For the second country, the first 15 rows are set to 0%, the next seven rows are 98%, and the remaining 72 rows are 0%.

Dragging this formula across and down will give us blocks of numbers that repeat the *Population* values corresponding to their shares of the total.

Column AB. In this graph, we'll place x-axis labels at every 10% increment. To do so, we'll create a custom x-axis series to add to the chart. Here's the formula:

```
=IF(INT(O5/10)*10=O5,O5/100,"")
```

This formula uses the INT function to round the number down to the nearest integer. If we divide the *Counter* series (in column O) by 10 and round down to the nearest integer [INT(O5/10)] then multiply by 10, we get whole numbers. If those whole numbers are equal increments of 10 (which works because we divided by 10 in the INT formula), we set the cell value to that percentage. If not, the formula returns an empty cell, denoted by the " " in the IF statement. If we enter this formula in cell AB4 and drag it down the column, we only see "10%," "20%," "30%," etc. show up in the cells (Figure 25.6).

Creating the Chart

1. We can create a bar chart using the data in columns R4:AA103. To close the gaps between the bars, right-click and select *Format Data Series > Series Overlap* to 0% and *Gap Width* to 100% (Figure 25.7).

2. With our data set up, let's change the color of each country by selecting it on the chart and using the *Format Data Series > Fill > Solid Fill* menu (Figure 25.8).

Setting

Making

Moving

	Y	Z	AA	AB
1				Formula off column 8
2	**18**	**19**	**20**	**21**
3	8	9	10	X axis Labels
4	0%	0%	0%	
5	0%		=IF(INT(O4/10)*10=O4,O4/100," ")	
6	0%			
7	0%	0%	0%	
8	0%	0%	0%	
9	0%	0%	0%	
10	0%	0%	0%	
11	0%	0%	0%	
12	0%	0%	0%	
13	0%	0%	0%	10%
14	0%	0%	0%	
15	0%	0%	0%	
16	0%	0%	0%	
17	0%	0%	0%	
18	0%	0%	0%	
19	0%	0%	0%	
20	0%	0%	0%	
21	0%	0%	0%	
22	0%	0%	0%	
23	0%	0%	0%	20%
24	0%	0%	0%	

FIGURE 25.6

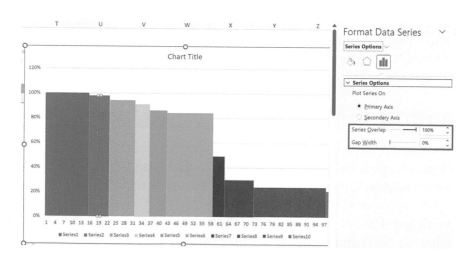

FIGURE 25.7

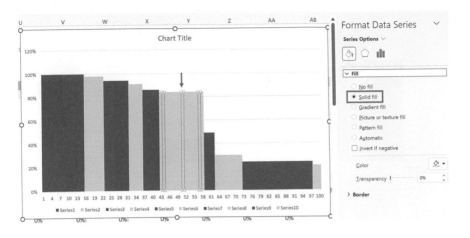

FIGURE 25.8

3. To add the x-axis labels, right-click on the chart, choose *Select Data* > *Horizontal (Category) Axis Labels:* and insert cells AB4:AB103 in the box. Click OK (Figure 25.9).

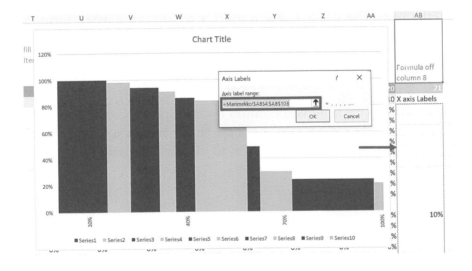

FIGURE 25.9

4. Return to the chart and format the x-axis by right-clicking (or CTRL+1). Change *Format Axis* > *Tick Marks* > *Interval between marks* from 1 to 10. We also need to select *Format Axis* > *Labels* > *Interval between labels* > *Specify interval unit* option and set it equal to 1 (though Excel should have filled in a "1" already) (Figure 25.10).

Setting

Making

Moving

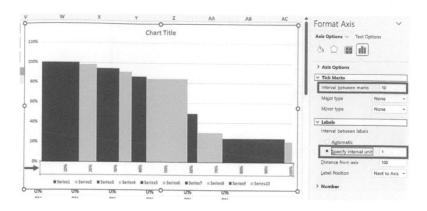

FIGURE 25.10

5. We can add country labels to this chart in a few ways, with or without the x-axis labels. Both methods add a scatterplot on top of the bar chart.

   a. **Place Labels above the Columns.** We can place horizontally oriented labels above the bars. The scatterplot data for this approach are shown in cells A17:C28 where the y-values are equal to the *Poverty* estimate minus 0.01, which moves them a little closer to the tops of the bars. The x-values use a slightly more complicated formula to convert the percentages to numbers and center them within each band of bars. The formula in cell B21 for Mexico, for example, is:

$$=(SUM(\$C\$5:C6)+C7/2)*100$$

This formula adds the values for the first two countries and half of the value for Mexico. Because those entries are percentages, I multiply by 100 to convert them to integers (Figure 25.11).

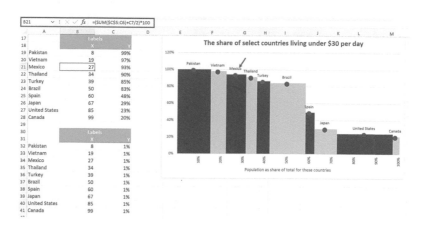

FIGURE 25.11

Once the *Scatter* chart is added—right click, *Select Data > Add*, then *Chart Design > Change Chart Type > Combo*. Now, we add data labels to each point (right-click and select *Add Data Labels*). Select the labels to format: *Format Data Labels > Value From Cells >* insert cells A19:A28 in the box. Position the labels above the dots with *Format Data Labels > Label Position > Above*. Finally, hide the markers in the *Format Data Series > Marker > Marker Options > None* menu. I've left the markers on in Figure 25.12 so you can see them.

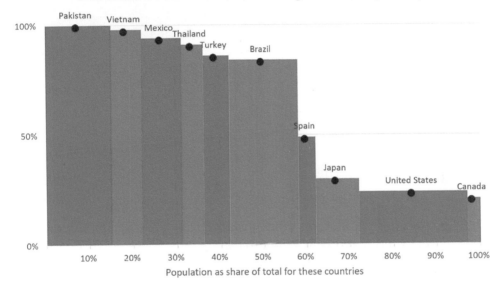

The share of select countries living under $30 per day

FIGURE 25.12

We can adjust the labels manually, either by moving the text boxes or adjusting the formula slightly.

b. **Place Labels in the Columns.** We could alternatively place vertically oriented labels inside the bars. The scatterplot data for this approach are shown in cells A30:C51 where the y-values are equal to 1%—placing them just above the x-axis—and the x-values are calculated the same way as before. The process is the same as above: add the new data, convert to a scatterplot, add and format data labels, and hide the markers (Figure 25.13).

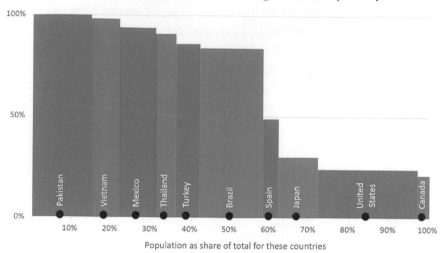

The share of select countries living under $30 per day

Population as share of total for these countries

FIGURE 25.13

Quick Instructions

1. Arrange data and formulas

2. Select cells R4:AA103 and insert a *Clustered Column* chart

3. Align the bars: right-click > *Format Data Series* > *Series Options* > *Series Overlap* to 100% and *Gap Width* to 0%

4. Format the x-axis:

   a. Right-click > *Format   Axis* > *Tick   Marks* > *Interval   between marks* > 10

   b. Right-click > *Format Axis* > *Labels* > *Interval between labels* > 1

5. Edit x-axis labels: right-click > *Select Data* > *Horizontal (Category) axis labels:* > *AB4:AB103*

6. Edit range of vertical axis: right-click > *Format Axis* > *Bounds* > 0 for *Minimum* and 1 for *Maximum*

7. Add data labels with a scatterplot in cells A17:C41, see full tutorial for details

Chapter 26

Cycle Plot

Cycle Plot
Level: **Advanced**
Data Type: **Time**
Combine Charts: **Yes**
Formulas Used: **IF, AVERAGEIF, TEXT**

William Cleveland and Irma Terpenning introduced the cycle plot in a 1982 paper, *Graphic Methods for Seasonal Adjustment*, in which they proposed a method to visualize seasonal patterns in data, such as monthly industrial production and telephone installations from Bell Labs. At its core, the cycle plot reshapes a standard line chart. Instead of showing monthly data in a standard format, a cycle plot shows annual data *within* each month—that is, data from the first year to the last year for January, again for February, and so on.

Creating a cycle plot largely entails formatting the data by month-year instead of the more standard year-month. Typically, cycle plots also include the monthly average and may have a bit of separation between each month. These aspects add some complexity to building the chart but also provide more information and clarity for the reader.

For this tutorial, we will use data on the monthly average extent of sea ice in the northern hemisphere from 1979 to 2020 (Figure 26.1).

DOI: 10.1201/9781003321552-28

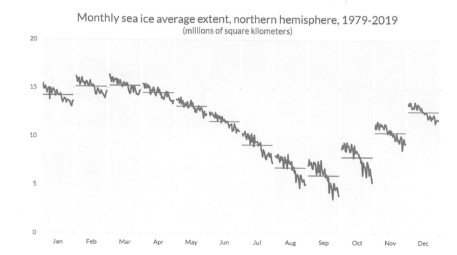

Monthly sea ice average extent, northern hemisphere, 1979-2019
(millions of square kilometers)

FIGURE 26.1

1. Arrange the data *annually* within each *month* and add three extra years as placeholders for the white space between each month. Because we have data from January 1979 through December 2020, we can add rows for each month in 2021, 2022, and 2023 at the bottom of the dataset. Sort (*Data > Sort*) by *Month* and *Year* (the data in the Excel sheet is already sorted) (Figure 26.2).

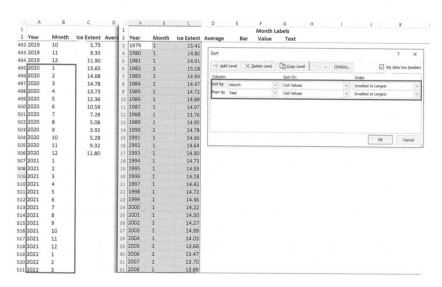

FIGURE 26.2

2. We can use an AVERAGEIF formula to create the average for each month in column D. Because the placeholder rows for 2021, 2022, and 2023 are included in the data but shouldn't be included in the average, we need to use an IF statement with the AVERAGEIF formula:

```
=IF(A3<=2020,AVERAGEIF($B$3:$B$542,B3,$C$3:$C$542),
                      NA())
```

Here, the monthly average of the *Ice Extent* data in column C is only calculated for years up to and including 2020. For years after 2020, a #N/A will appear in the cell (Figure 26.3).

SUM			f_x	=IF(A3<=2020,AVERAGEIF($B$3:$B$542,B3,$C$3:$C$542),NA())				
	A	B	C	D	E	F	G	H
1						Month Labels		
2	Year	Month	Ice Extent	Average	Bar	Value	Text	
3	1979	1	15.41	NA())	20			
4	1980	1	14.86	14.2	20			
5	1981	1	14.91	14.2	20			
6	1982	1	15.18	14.2	20			
7	1983	1	14.94	14.2	20			
8	1984	1	14.47	14.2	20			
9	1985	1	14.72	14.2	20			
10	1986	1	14.89	14.2	20			
11	1987	1	14.97	14.2	20			
12	1988	1	13.76	14.2	20			
13	1989	1	14.95	14.2	20			
14	1990	1	14.78	14.2	20			
15	1991	1	14.36	14.2	20			
16	1992	1	14.64	14.2	20			
17	1993	1	14.90	14.2	20			
18	1994	1	14.73	14.2	20			
19	1995	1	14.59	14.2	20			
20	1996	1	14.18	14.2	20			
21	1997	1	14.42	14.2	20			
22	1998	1	14.72	14.2	20			
23	1999	1	14.36	14.2	20			
24	2000	1	14.22	14.2	20			
25	2001	1	14.20	14.2	20			
26	2002	1	14.27	14.2	20			
27	2003	1	14.39	14.2	20			
28	2004	1	14.03	14.2	20			
29	2005	1	13.66	14.2	20			
30	2006	1	13.47	14.2	20			
31	2007	1	13.70	14.2	20			
32	2008	1	13.89	14.2	20			

FIGURE 26.3

3. We also need a data series for the gray background in the chart. We calculate it in a similar way (column E), using a simpler IF statement: =IF(A3<=2020, 20, NA()). Here again, if the year is before 2021, the data value is set to 20; otherwise, it's set to missing or #N/A. I chose 20 because it's larger than all of our data values and still provides some padding for the top of the chart.

4. Finally, we need a data series to add the month labels at the bottom of the chart. We're going to place these labels in the middle of each band, which is the year 2000. Another IF statement makes this easy: =IF(A3=2000, 0, NA()). This formula gives us a zero when the year is 2000 and a #N/A otherwise.

In the neighboring *Text* series in column G, another IF will give us the abbreviation for each month: =IF(A3=2000, TEXT(B3*29,"mmm"), NA()). It's a bit of a complex formula, so let's break it down:

- A3=2000. This argument sets the condition of the IF formula. We are only going to add month labels in the rows where the year is 2000.

- TEXT(B3*29,"mmm"). The TEXT function converts numbers to text, and in this scenario, we use it to convert a date to a three-letter month abbreviation. The first part of the formula obtains the date by multiplying the month number (cell B3) by 29. This multiplication will sync up with the appropriate month. For January, 1*29 is the 29th day of the year, January 29th. Easy. For February, 2*29 is 58, indicating the 58th day of the year, February 27th. For June, 6*29 is 174, indicating the 174th day of the year or June 23rd. And so on. The second part of the formula sets the format for the date in the first argument: a three-letter abbreviation for the month. For February, Excel sees the number 58 in the first part of the formula, evaluates it as a date (February 27), and formats that date as a three-letter month abbreviation, which it knows as "Feb."

- NA(). The last argument says if the value is not the year 2000, put an NA() (rendered as #N/A) in the cell, which, as we've seen before, Excel will ignore when we plot it in the chart (Figure 26.4).

5. With these four series, we can insert a standard *Line* chart using cells C3:F542, which gets us close to a finished product (Figure 26.5).

6. We can change the *Bar* series to a *Clustered Column* chart (the #N/A values for 2021, 2022, and 2023 end up as blank spaces): select the *Bar* series > *Chart Design* > *Change Chart Type* > *Combo*. Select the vertical bars to format: *Format Data Series* > *Gap Width* to 0%. Change the color to a light gray in the *Fill* > *Solid Fill* menu (Figure 26.6).

7. We can add the month labels using the *Value* series in cells G3:G542. First, select the default x-axis labels and delete. We can't see the line in the *Value* series because the data values are equal to zero, and we've

SUM ⌄ : ✕ ✓ *fx* =IF(A3=2000, TEXT(B3*29,"mmm"), NA())

	A	B	C	D	E	F	G
1						Month Labels	
2	Year	Month	Ice Extent	Average	Bar	Value	Text
3	1979	1	15.41	14.2	20	#N/A	NA()
4	1980	1	14.86	14.2	20	#N/A	#N/A
5	1981	1	14.91	14.2	20	#N/A	#N/A
6	1982	1	15.18	14.2	20	#N/A	#N/A
7	1983	1	14.94	14.2	20	#N/A	#N/A
8	1984	1	14.47	14.2	20	#N/A	#N/A
9	1985	1	14.72	14.2	20	#N/A	#N/A
10	1986	1	14.89	14.2	20	#N/A	#N/A
11	1987	1	14.97	14.2	20	#N/A	#N/A
12	1988	1	13.76	14.2	20	#N/A	#N/A
13	1989	1	14.95	14.2	20	#N/A	#N/A
14	1990	1	14.78	14.2	20	#N/A	#N/A
15	1991	1	14.36	14.2	20	#N/A	#N/A
16	1992	1	14.64	14.2	20	#N/A	#N/A
17	1993	1	14.90	14.2	20	#N/A	#N/A
18	1994	1	14.73	14.2	20	#N/A	#N/A
19	1995	1	14.59	14.2	20	#N/A	#N/A
20	1996	1	14.18	14.2	20	#N/A	#N/A
21	1997	1	14.42	14.2	20	#N/A	#N/A
22	1998	1	14.72	14.2	20	#N/A	#N/A
23	1999	1	14.36	14.2	20	#N/A	#N/A
24	2000	1	14.22	14.2	20	0	Jan
25	2001	1	14.20	14.2	20	#N/A	#N/A
26	2002	1	14.27	14.2	20	#N/A	#N/A
27	2003	1	14.39	14.2	20	#N/A	#N/A
28	2004	1	14.03	14.2	20	#N/A	#N/A
29	2005	1	13.66	14.2	20	#N/A	#N/A
30	2006	1	13.47	14.2	20	#N/A	#N/A
31	2007	1	13.70	14.2	20	#N/A	#N/A
32	2008	1	13.89	14.2	20	#N/A	#N/A

FIGURE 26.4

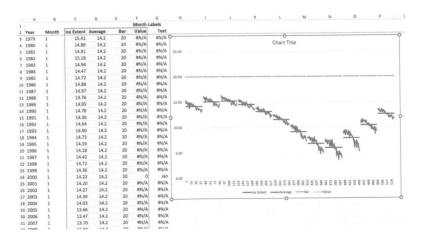

FIGURE 26.5

Setting

Making

Moving

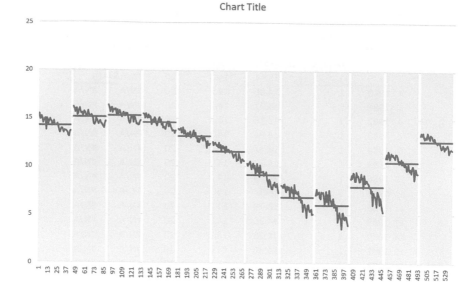

FIGURE 26.6

inserted a line chart with no markers. But we can select the series using *Format > Current Selection > Value* before going to the *Chart Design* tab to use *Chart Design > Add Chart Element > Data Labels > Below* to add the data labels, which we initially see as zeros (Figure 26.7).

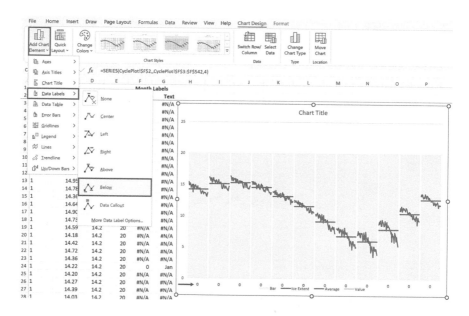

FIGURE 26.7

We can modify the labels by selecting and right-clicking to get to the *Format Data Labels* menu. Here, we select the *Value from Cells* option, reference the data in column G (cells G3:G542), and click OK. If we unselect the *Value* option, we are left with the month abbreviations in the middle of each gray band of bars (Figures 26.8 and 26.9).

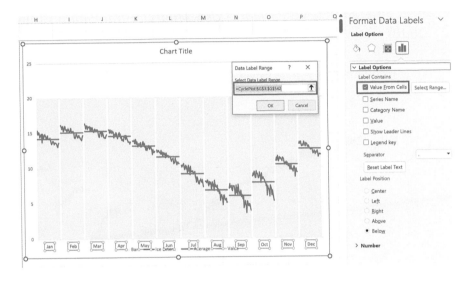

FIGURE 26.8

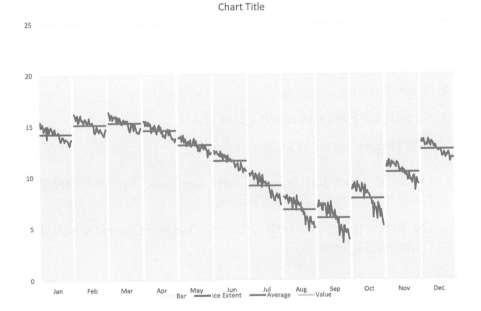

FIGURE 26.9

Setting

Making

Moving

8. Just a little cleanup to do:

- Delete the legend and edit the title.

- Change the color and thickness of the lines.

- As always, Excel doesn't allow us to plot the data to the top of the y-axis, so we need to change the dimensions of the y-axis to go from 0 to 20 (right-click > *Format Axis* > *Minimum/Maximum*) (Figure 26.10).

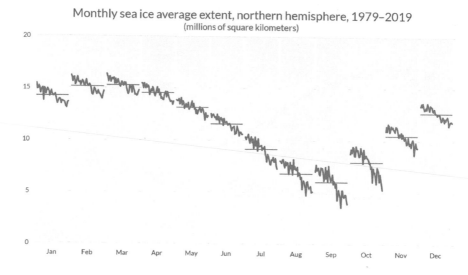

FIGURE 26.10

Quick Instructions

1. Arrange data and formulas

2. Select cells C2:F542 and insert a *Line* chart

3. Change the *Bar* series to a column chart:

   a. On PCs: select *Bar* series > *Chart Design* > *Change Chart Type* > *Combo* > *Bar* > *Clustered Column*

   b. On Macs: select *Bar* series > *Chart Design* > *Change Chart Type* > *Clustered Column*

4. Select *Bar* series > *Format Data Series* > *Series Options* > *Gap Width* to 0%

5. Delete horizontal axis

6. Add month labels: select *Value* series in the *Format > Current Selection* menu. Then, *Chart Design > Add Chart Element > Data Labels > Below*

7. Format month labels: right-click on labels *> Format Data Labels > Value from Cells > cells G3:G542* (and uncheck the *Value* box)

8. Edit range of vertical axis: right-click *> Format Axis > Bounds > 0* for *Minimum* and 20 for *Maximum*

Setting

Making

Moving

Chapter 27

Strip Chart

Strip Chart
Level: **Intermediate**
Data Type: **Distribution**
Combine Charts: **No**
Formulas Used: **None**

At a basic level, a strip chart is just a scatterplot with the x-values encoding the data and the y-values organizing the data in rows. Strip charts are useful when you want to show the data distribution as actual data points rather than as bars.

For this example, we are going to use the average weekly temperature for Chicago, Los Angeles, and Washington, DC, in 2021.

1. Select cells B2:C54 and insert a *Scatter* chart. The temperature data for each city should be in the "X" column while the "Y" column is a separate integer for each: 1 for Los Angeles, 2 for Chicago, and 3 for Washington, DC (Figure 27.1).

DOI: 10.1201/9781003321552-29

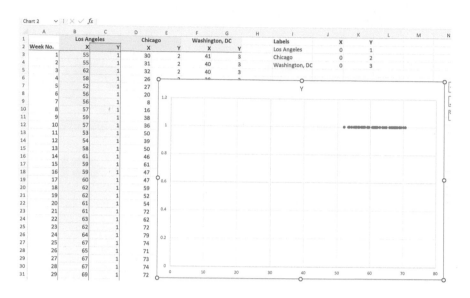

FIGURE 27.1

2. Add the data for Chicago and Washington, DC: right-click > *Select Data* > *Add*. For Chicago, the three cell references are: *Series Name* in cell D1, *X Values:* in cells D3:D54, and *Y Values:* in cells E3:E54. For Washington, DC, the three cell references are: *Series Name* in cell F1, *X Values:* in cells F3:F54, and *Y Values:* in cells G3:G54. We can also change the *Series Name* for Los Angeles to reference cell B1. To be clear, we could select all of the data (cells B3:G54) and insert a single scatter-plot. In that case, Excel would generate five separate scatterplot series with the first series (cells B3:B54) as the x values for all five series, so we would still need to do some editing (Figure 27.2).

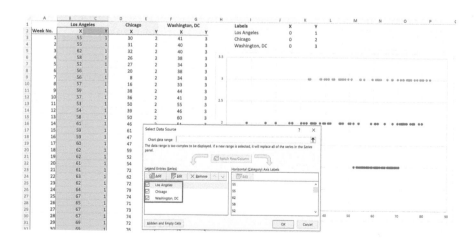

FIGURE 27.2

3. We're well on our way. Let's insert labels for each city along the y-axis and clean it up. To add the labels, add another scatterplot series: right-click > *Select Data* > *Add.* Insert cell I1 for the *Series Name* ("Labels"), cells J2:J4 for the *X Values*, and cells K2:K4 for the *Y Values* (Figure 27.3).

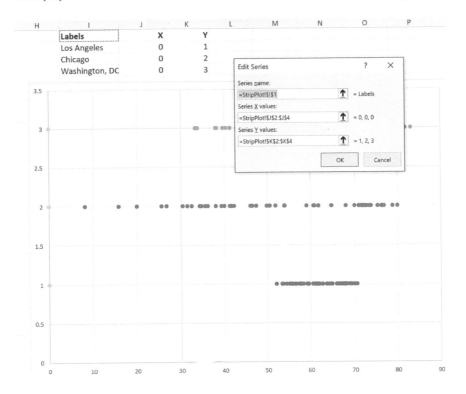

FIGURE 27.3

4. To add the labels, we will right-click on the *Labels* series and select *Add Data Labels.* Next, right-click on the labels, *Format Data Labels* > *Value from Cells* > insert cells I2:I4, and click OK. Uncheck the *Y Value* box and set the *Label Position* to the *Left* (Figure 27.4).

5. Let's clean it up a little bit.

a. Change the y-axis dimensions to center the dots in the space: right-click on the y-axis > *Format Axis* > set the *Minimum* to 0 and the *Maximum* to 4. We can style the graph by adjusting the numbers used for each series and the increments of the gridlines.

b. Remove the y-axis labels: *Format Axis* > *Labels* > *Label Position* > *None.*

c. Select the *Plot Area* and slide the left edge to the right slightly.

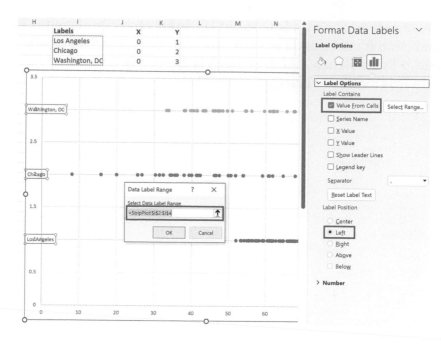

FIGURE 27.4

d. Hide the markers for the *Labels* series by right-clicking > *Format Data Series > Marker > Marker Options > None* (Figure 27.5).

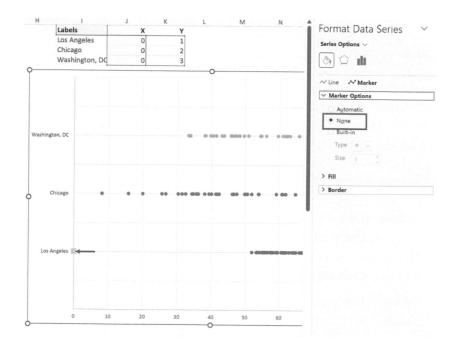

FIGURE 27.5

6. Let's style the dots by making them a little bigger and making the fill color transparent. We need to do this step separately for each series.

   a. Select the dots, right-click > *Format Data Series* > *Marker* > *Marker Options* > *Built-In* > change the size to 10.

   b. Change the fill color: right-click > *Format Data Series* > *Fill* > *Solid Fill* > set *Transparency* to 40%.

   c. Change the border color: right-click > *Format Data Series* > *Border* > *Solid line* > set *Transparency* to 40%.

7. Finally, let's edit the horizontal axis labels to include the degree symbol. Right-click on the horizontal axis: *Format Axis* > *Number* > *Custom* and enter #"°F";# "°F";0"°F" in the *Format Code* box (*Type* on Macs). This code will add the piece in quotation marks (°F) after any number. (You can find the degree symbol in the *Insert* > *Object* menu) (Figure 27.6).

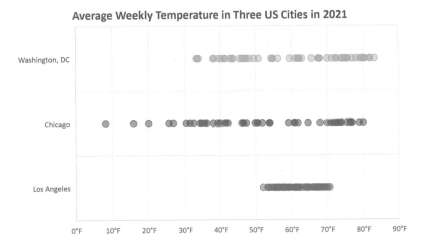

FIGURE 27.6

Quick Instructions

1. Select cells B2:C54 and insert a *Scatter* chart

2. Add data for Chicago and Washington, DC: right-click > *Select Data* > *Add* >

   a. *Series Name: Chicago (cell D1); X values: D3:D54; and Y values: E3:E54*

   b. *Series Name: Washington, DC (cell F1); X values: F3:F54; and Y values: G3:G54*

Setting

Making

Moving

3. Fix *Los Angeles* series name label: right-click > *Select Data* > *Y* > *Edit* > *Series Name: Los Angeles (cell B1)*

4. Add series for labels: right-click > *Select Data* > *Add* > *Series Name: Labels (Cell I1)*; *X values: J2:J4*; and *Y values: K2:K4*

5. Add labels: right-click on *Labels* series > *Add Data Labels*

6. Format labels: right-click > *Format Data Labels* >

   a. *Value from Cells* > *I2:I4*

   b. Uncheck the *Y Value* box

   c. *Label Position* > *Left*

7. Adjust *Plot Area* to fit labels by selecting the left edge and moving it to the right

8. Hide markers: right-click on *Labels* series > *Format Data Series* > *Marker* > *Marker Options* > *None*

9. Format the horizontal axis labels: right-click > *Format Axis* > *Number* > *Custom* > *Format Code* > #"°F";# "°F";0"°F" [for the degree symbol: *Insert* > *Symbols* menu]

10. Delete the vertical axis

Chapter 28

Raincloud Plot

Raincloud Plot
Level: **Advanced**
Data Type: **Distribution**
Combine Charts: **Yes**
Formulas Used: **WEEKNUM, AVERAGEIF, PERCENTILE, COUNTIF, IF**

Visualizing the uncertainty of distributions within a data visualization poses a big challenge. Many people are not familiar with statistics and distributions, and the mathematical concept of uncertainty can be difficult to understand. Visualizing distributions and uncertainty requires more significant annotation to help explain not only how to read the graph, but also what is being graphed.

We can help people better understand the data distribution by *showing them the data*. In this example, we will use the same weekly average temperature data for Los Angeles, Chicago, and Washington, DC, from the last chapter, to create a raincloud plot, which combines a box-and-whisker plot with individual data points as circles.

DOI: 10.1201/9781003321552-30

The raincloud plot consists of three different elements:

1. A stacked column chart for the box,

2. A scatterplot for the whiskers, and

3. A scatterplot for the data points.

As usual, I try to set up my Excel file so this graph can be more easily replicated with other data later. It takes a little longer to build the initial chart, but this extra effort pays off through future time saved.

Before we get to the chart, we need to set up the data. I've done most of it in the Excel file already, so you can read the following to understand the method or skip to the next section (step number 4) to learn how to build the chart.

1. We'll start with the completely raw data (Figure 28.1). For each city, the first two columns are the average temperature for each day in 2021. The next three columns (headers are highlighted in yellow) organize the data and consist of three separate formulas:

   a. **Week Count (Column C).** We're going to narrow the data to average weekly temperature, so this column uses the built-in WEEKNUM Excel formula, which returns the week number of a specific date. When we insert the formula =WEEKNUM(A3,2) in cell C3, we get "1" for the first week of the year.

   b. **Week# (Column D).** Because we want weekly data, we're going to set up a simple counter for the weeks of the year from 1 to 52, which we type in manually.

   c. **Avg (Column E).** We want the average temperature for each week, so we use the AVERAGEIF formula to look in columns C and D. That formula is:

   =AVERAGEIF($C$3:$C$367,D3,$B$3:$B$367)

   As we've seen before, the first argument ($C$3:$C$367) looks for the range of cells to average across, in this case the *Week Count*. The second argument (D3) defines the *criteria* for which cells are averaged, the numbers 1–52. The last argument ($B$3:$B$367) indicates the series over which we will calculate the average, in this case *Temp. Avg.* So, we use the 52 weekly data points in columns E, K, and Q rather than the 365 daily values in columns B, H, and N.

Los Angeles

Date	Temp. Avg.	Week Count	Week#	Avg
1/1/2021	57	1	1	55
1/2/2021	54	1	2	55
1/3/2021	54	1	3	62
1/4/2021	54	2	4	58
1/5/2021	54	2	5	52
1/6/2021	54	2	6	56
1/7/2021	55	2	7	56
1/8/2021	52	2	8	57
1/9/2021	59	2	9	59
1/10/2021	60	2	10	57
1/11/2021	58	3	11	53
1/12/2021	59	3	12	54
1/13/2021	58	3	13	58
1/14/2021	60	3	14	61
1/15/2021	66	3	15	59
1/16/2021	67	3	16	59
1/17/2021	67	3	17	60
1/18/2021	63	4	18	62
1/19/2021	59	4	19	62
1/20/2021	65	4	20	61
1/21/2021	63	4	21	61
1/22/2021	57	4	22	63
1/23/2021	54	4	23	62
1/24/2021	49	4	24	64
1/25/2021	52	5	25	67
1/26/2021	49	5	26	65
1/27/2021	51	5	27	67
1/28/2021	53	5	28	67
1/29/2021	53	5	29	69

Chicago

Date	Temp. Avg.	Week Count	Week#	Avg
1/1/2021	27	1	1	30
1/2/2021	32	1	2	31
1/3/2021	32	1	3	32
1/4/2021	27	2	4	26
1/5/2021	31	2	5	27
1/6/2021	33	2	6	20
1/7/2021	35	2	7	8
1/8/2021	34	2	8	16
1/9/2021	31	2	9	38
1/10/2021	29	2	10	36
1/11/2021	25	3	11	50
1/12/2021	31	3	12	39
1/13/2021	35	3	13	50
1/14/2021	36	3	14	46
1/15/2021	35	3	15	61
1/16/2021	33	3	16	47
1/17/2021	32	3	17	47
1/18/2021	28	4	18	59
1/19/2021	24	4	19	52
1/20/2021	23	4	20	54
1/21/2021	34	4	21	72
1/22/2021	23	4	22	62
1/23/2021	17	4	23	72
1/24/2021	30	4	24	79
1/25/2021	31	5	25	74
1/26/2021	31	5	26	71
1/27/2021	24	5	27	73
1/28/2021	17	5	28	74
1/29/2021	22	5	29	72

Washington, DC

Date	Temp. Avg.	Week Count	Week#	Avg
1/1/2021	39	1	1	41
1/2/2021	43	1	2	40
1/3/2021	42	1	3	40
1/4/2021	40	2	4	38
1/5/2021	42	2	5	34
1/6/2021	41	2	6	38
1/7/2021	40	2	7	34
1/8/2021	37	2	8	33
1/9/2021	37	2	9	44
1/10/2021	41	2	10	41
1/11/2021	37	3	11	55
1/12/2021	38	3	12	46
1/13/2021	39	3	13	60
1/14/2021	42	3	14	51
1/15/2021	43	3	15	63
1/16/2021	44	3	16	56
1/17/2021	40	3	17	55
1/18/2021	41	4	18	66
1/19/2021	41	4	19	62
1/20/2021	40	4	20	62
1/21/2021	38	4	21	72
1/22/2021	42	4	22	68
1/23/2021	36	4	23	72
1/24/2021	30	4	24	77
1/25/2021	37	5	25	76
1/26/2021	34	5	26	74
1/27/2021	39	5	27	79
1/28/2021	35	5	28	80
1/29/2021	29	5	29	83

FIGURE 28.1

2. With our weekly data set up, we need to do some calculations for each of our three cities, which are found in columns S:V (Figure 28.2).

a. **Percentiles**. We can calculate five percentile points (10th, 25th, 50th, 75th, and 90th) for Los Angeles from the data directly in Excel with the formula =PERCENTILE($E:$E, $S3) in cell T3. This formula looks in the data column for Los Angeles (column E) for the 10th percentile point specified in cell S3 as 0.10.

b. **Bar**. In this section, we pull out the percentiles and generate differences we need to create the box. The bottom of the box in this chart will show the 25th percentile, the middle will show the median (50th percentile), and the top will show the 75th percentile. The formulas in these cells (T11:V13) reference the cells above and calculate the differences. The formula in cell T12, for example, is T5–T4, the difference between the 50th and 25th percentiles.

c. **Whiskers**. To add the whiskers to the right and left edge of the boxes, we need to add a scatterplot point at the 50th percentile and a horizontal error bar that extends to the 10th and 90th percentiles. The scatterplots require x-values, which are pulled from the *Percentiles* section above, and y-values, which we set as decimals to position at the bottom of the bar chart. The values for the error bars are calculated as differences between the 90th and 50th percentiles (*PosError*) and the 50th and 10th percentiles (*NegError*).

Setting

Making

Moving

	S	T	U	V
1		**Percentiles**		
2		**Los Angeles**	**Chicago**	**Washington, DC**
3	0.10	55	30	40
4	0.25	58	39	46
5	0.50	62	53	62
6	0.75	67	72	74
7	0.90	68	76	80
8				
9		**Bar**		
10		**Los Angeles**	**Chicago**	**Washington, DC**
11	Fill	58	39	46
12	Bottom	4	14	16
13	Top	5	19	13
14				
15		**Whiskers**		
16		**Los Angeles**	**Chicago**	**Washington, DC**
17	X	62	53	62
18	Y	4.7	2.7	0.7
19	PosError	6	23	18
20	NegError	6	22	22

FIGURE 28.2

3. Lastly, we need to ready the actual data points to be plotted as scatterplots, done separately for each city. In this section of the worksheet (columns X:AI), there are four data series for each city (Figure 28.3). Essentially, we are grouping observations with the same value and setting up a way to stack them in the chart. Let's go through the data for Los Angeles as an example.

   a. **X-value**. In column X, we can paste the original (weekly) average temperature data as values (not formulas) by copying the data in column E and using the *Paste Special > Paste Values* option. After the data are pasted, sort them from lowest to highest.

   b. **Y-value**. In column Y, we use a formula to identify the first occurrence of each data "group" to plot them together along the x-axis. In other words, we want to identify the first occurrence of 52 degrees, 53 degrees, 54 degrees, and so on. To do so, we use a COUNTIF formula =COUNTIF($X$3:X3,X3). When copied-and-pasted (or dragged) down the column, this formula counts the number of occurrences in each cell from the top of the column (because $X$3 is locked) to that cell position. I've layered on some default *Conditional Formatting* to highlight the first occurrences (when the cell value is equal to one) as well.

	X	Y	Z	AA	AB	AC	AD	AE	AF	AG	AH	AI
		LA-Dots				Chicago-Dots				DC-Dots		
	X-value	Y-value	Y-position	Scalars	X-value	Y-value	Y-position	Scalars	X-value	Y-value	Y-position	Scalars
3	52	1.0	0.550	0.550	8	1.0	2.550	2.550	33	1.0	4.550	4.550
4	53	1.0	0.550	0.130	16	1.0	2.550	0.130	34	1.0	4.550	0.130
5	54	1.0	0.550		20	1.0	2.550		34	2.0	4.420	
6	54	2.0	0.420		26	1.0	2.550		38	1.0	4.550	
7	55	1.0	0.550		27	1.0	2.550		38	2.0	4.420	
8	55	2.0	0.420		30	1.0	2.550		40	1.0	4.550	
9	56	1.0	0.550		31	1.0	2.550		40	2.0	4.420	
10	56	2.0	0.420		32	1.0	2.550		41	1.0	4.550	
11	56	3.0	0.290		34	1.0	2.550		41	2.0	4.420	
12	57	1.0	0.550		35	1.0	2.550		43	1.0	4.550	
13	57	2.0	0.420		36	1.0	2.550		43	2.0	4.420	
14	57	3.0	0.290		36	2.0	2.420		44	1.0	4.550	
15	58	1.0	0.550		38	1.0	2.550		46	1.0	4.550	
16	58	2.0	0.420		39	1.0	2.550		46	2.0	4.420	
17	58	3.0	0.290		40	1.0	2.550		47	1.0	4.550	
18	59	1.0	0.550		41	1.0	2.550		47	2.0	4.420	
19	59	2.0	0.420		42	1.0	2.550		48	1.0	4.550	
20	59	3.0	0.290		42	2.0	2.420		50	1.0	4.550	
21	59	4.0	0.160		46	1.0	2.550		51	1.0	4.550	
22	60	1.0	0.550		47	1.0	2.550		54	1.0	4.550	
23	61	1.0	0.550		47	2.0	2.420		55	1.0	4.550	
24	61	2.0	0.420		47	3.0	2.290		55	2.0	4.420	
25	61	3.0	0.290		50	1.0	2.550		56	1.0	4.550	
26	61	4.0	0.160		50	2.0	2.420		60	1.0	4.550	
27	61	5.0	0.030		51	1.0	2.550		61	1.0	4.550	
28	62	1.0	0.550		52	1.0	2.550		62	1.0	4.550	
29	62	2.0	0.420		54	1.0	2.550		62	2.0	4.420	
30	62	3.0	0.290		54	2.0	2.420		62	3.0	4.290	
31	62	4.0	0.160		59	1.0	2.550		63	1.0	4.550	
32	63	1.0	0.550		61	1.0	2.550		66	1.0	4.550	

FIGURE 28.3

Setting

Making

Moving

c. **Y-position**. With the ordering done, we need to set up the y-position for each point. Again, we want to stack the points, so for any repeated temperatures, we need to set up different y-values. Take the formula in cell Z6, the second occurrence of 54 degrees in Los Angeles as an example:

$$=IF(Y6=1,\$AA\$3,Z5-\$AA\$4)$$

It's an IF statement where the first argument evaluates whether the value in the neighboring cell Y6 is equal to 1, which would indicate it is either the first or only occurrence of that value. If the evaluation is true, the second argument of the formula ($AA$3) points to a specific value, here specified as 0.550 in a bold, red font.

If the value is *not* equal to one, the formula specifies Z5-$AA$4. This formula subtracts a fixed number (0.130 in cell AA4) from the number above that cell (here, 0.550). Thus, the first occurrence of the temperature sits at a y-position of 0.550, and the second occurrence of that same temperature sits below the first at a y-position of 0.420 (=0.550—0.130). (As in previous tutorials, numbers other than 0.130 could work as well, but this value worked well for this chart.)

4. Phew! Okay, now that the data are all set up, let's go about (finally!) making the graph. We'll start with the box-and-whisker plot. Select cells S10:V13 and insert a *Stacked Bar Chart*. As before, select the y-axis to flip and arrange: *Format Axis > Axis Options > At maximum category* and *Format Axis > Axis Options > Categories in reverse order* (Figure 28.4).

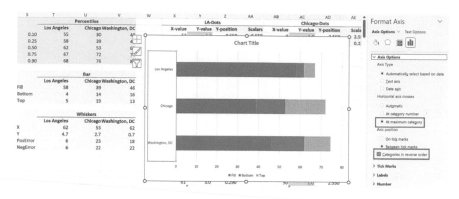

FIGURE 28.4

5. Select the bottom (**blue**) segment and change the fill color: *Format Data Series > Fill > No Color*. For the other two segments, add a border (*Format Data Series > Border > Solid line*), so the median is visible (Figure 28.5).

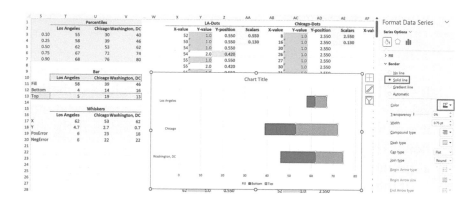

FIGURE 28.5

6. Next, let's add the whiskers. We need to add our first scatterplot then horizontal error bars in both directions. Right-click on the chart and choose *Select Data > Add* to add a new data series with cells T18:V18 for *Y Values:* and cell T15 for the *Series Name*. Click OK (Figure 28.6).

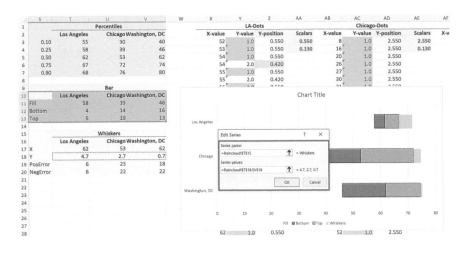

FIGURE 28.6

7. Select the new series and change it to a *Scatter* chart (*Chart Design > Change Chart Type > Combo*). Go back to the chart, right-click, *Select Data > Whiskers > Edit* and insert cells T17:V17 in the *X Values:* box. Again, click OK twice (Figure 28.7).

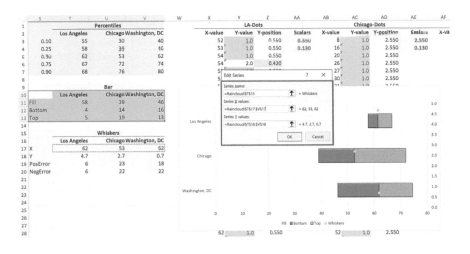

FIGURE 28.7

8. Notice that Excel added a *secondary vertical axis* to this chart. We need to edit that axis so it lines up correctly with the primary axis. In this case, we can extend it from zero to six: select the secondary y-axis > *Format Axis > Axis Options > Minimum/Maximum* (Figure 28.8).

Setting

Making

Moving

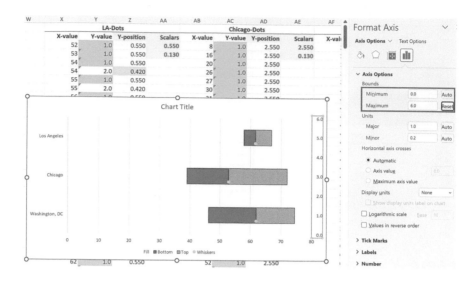

FIGURE 28.8

9. To align those dots with the bottom of the bar, change the *Format Data Series > Gap Width* of the bars to 230%. If we want the bars thicker or thinner, we can change *Gap Width* to something else and adjust the y-position of the *Whisker* series in the spreadsheet (Figure 28.9).

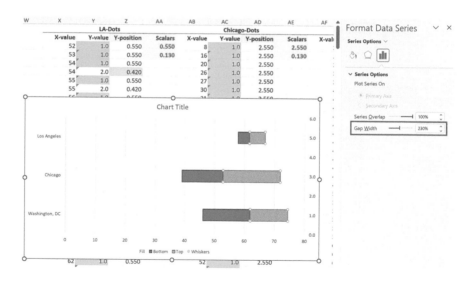

FIGURE 28.9

10. Let's add the whiskers to the dots. Select any of the three dots and add the error bars in the *Chart Design > Add Chart Element > Error Bars > More Error Bars Options* menu (Figure 28.10).

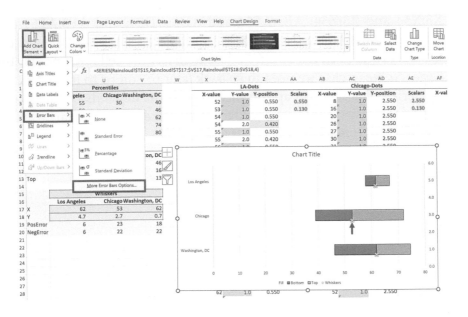

FIGURE 28.10

11. Format the horizontal error bars by selecting them, right-clicking > *Error Amount* > *Custom* > *Specify Value*, and inserting the reference to cells T19:V19 in the *Positive Error* box and cells T20:V20 in the *Negative Error* box. We can select and delete the vertical error bars because we don't need them for this chart (Figure 28.11).

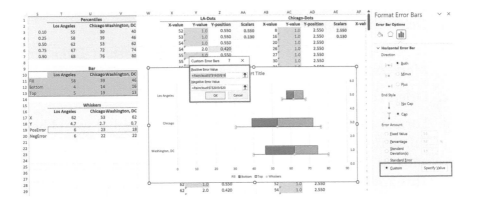

FIGURE 28.11

12. Now, we need the final element: plotting the dots representing the data. Basically, we want to create a unit-histogram of the data points and separate them enough to be visible. We've already done the hard work by preparing the data. Add three new scatterplot series as pairs—cells

X3:X54 and Z3:Z54; AB3:AB54 and AD3:AD54; and AF3:AF54 and AH3:AH54—to the chart one at a time: *Select Data > Add > insert cell references* and click OK twice. Be sure to insert the cell reference for the *Series Name* in case we need to go back later to edit or to format different series. The size and appearance of the dots depends on the size of the overall chart, so we may need to adjust the size of the chart itself (in the *Marker Options* menu area) (Figure 28.12).

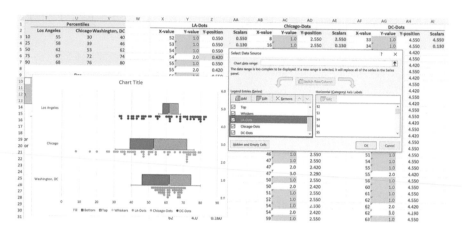

FIGURE 28.12

13. Finally, we can clean the chart up:

a. Delete the secondary y-axis.

b. Hide the markers for the *Whiskers* series (*Format Data Series > Markers > Marker Options > None*).

c. Delete the legend.

d. Format the x-axis labels—adding a degree symbol would be useful, so right-click on the axis *Format Axis > Number > Custom* and enter in the *Format Code* box (*Type* on Macs): #"°F";# "°F";0"°F". This code will add the piece in quotation marks (°F) after any number. (You can find the degree symbol in the *Insert > Object* menu.)

e. We can change the colors of the bars to differentiate each city by clicking twice and changing each segment manually (Figure 28.13).

Setting

Making

Moving

Average Weekly Temperature of Three US Cities in 2021

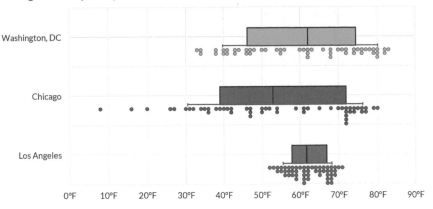

FIGURE 28.13

Quick Instructions

1. Arrange data and formulas

2. Select cells S10:V13 and insert a *Stacked Bar* chart

3. Format vertical axis:

   a. *Format Axis > Axis Options > Categories in reverse order*

   b. *Format Axis > Axis Options > Horizontal axis crosses > At maximum category*

4. Select the bottom (blue) series: right-click > *Format Data Series > Fill > No Fill*

5. Change bar width: right-click on either set of bars > *Format Data Series > Gap Width* to 230%

6. Select the other two series (orange and gray) and add a border: right-click > *Format Data Series > Border > Solid line*

7. Add whiskers series: right-click > *Select Data > Add > Series Name: Whiskers (cell T15)* and *Series values (cells T18:V18)*

8. Change the *Whiskers* series to a scatterplot:

   a. **On PCs**: select *Whiskers* series > *Chart Design > Change Chart Type > Combo > Whiskers > Scatter*

   b. **On Macs**: select *Whiskers* series > *Chart Design > Change Chart Type > Scatter*

Setting

Making

Moving

9. Insert x-values for the *Whiskers* series: right-click > *Select Data* > *Whiskers* > *Edit* > *X Values: T17:V17*

10. Add the actual whiskers: select any of the three dots > *Chart Design* > *Add Chart Element* > *Error Bars* > *More Error Bars Options*

11. Format horizontal error bars: select > right-click > *Format Error Bars* >

   a. Set *Direction* to *Both*

   b. Set *End Style* to *Cap*

   c. Set *Error Amount* > *Custom* > *Specific Value* > *Positive Error: T19:V19* and *Negative Error: T20:V20*

12. Delete vertical error bars

13. Edit secondary vertical axis: right-click on axis > *Format Axis* > *Axis Options* > *Bounds* > set 0 for *Minimum* and 6 for *Maximum*

14. Add three new series for the dots: right-click > *Select Data* > *Add* >

   a. **Series Name**: *LA-Dots (cell X1)*; *X Values: X3:X54*; and *Y Values: Z3:Z54*

   b. **Series Name**: *Chicago-Dots (cell AB1)*; *X Values: AB3:AB54*; and *Y Values: AD3:AD54*

   c. **Series Name**: *DC-Dots (cell AF1)*; *X Values: AF3:AF54*; and *Y Values: AH3:AH54*

   d. **Note**: the size and appearance of dots will depend on the size of the overall chart

15. Hide markers for the *Whiskers* series: right-click > *Format Data Series* > *Marker* > *Marker Options* > *None*

16. Delete legend and secondary vertical axis

Setting

Making

Moving

Chapter 29

Making Better Tables

We close this part of the book by taking a brief look at tables in Excel. Yes, tables are a form of data visualization. A table may be a better way to convey your message than a chart when you need to show your user *specific* values. And just like a chart, a table has a lot of parts, each of which we can modify and style (Figure 29.1).

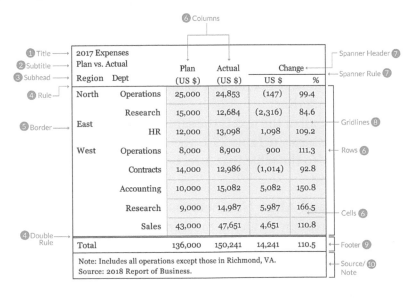

FIGURE 29.1 Source: Jonathan Schwabish, Better Data Visualizations: A Guide for Scholars, Researchers, and Wonks.

DOI: 10.1201/9781003321552-31

Excel is still one of the best tools to create clean, effective tables. We can easily format the cells with borders, fills, different font styles, and more. Excel has a built-in table-formatting menu located next to the *Conditional Formatting* menu. The advantage of the Excel built-in options is that you can easily customize your table with filters and styles like border lines, banded rows or columns, and totals along the rows or columns. These Excel default tables are also accessible for people with disabilities who may need to use a screen reader to navigate from cell to cell (Figure 29.2).

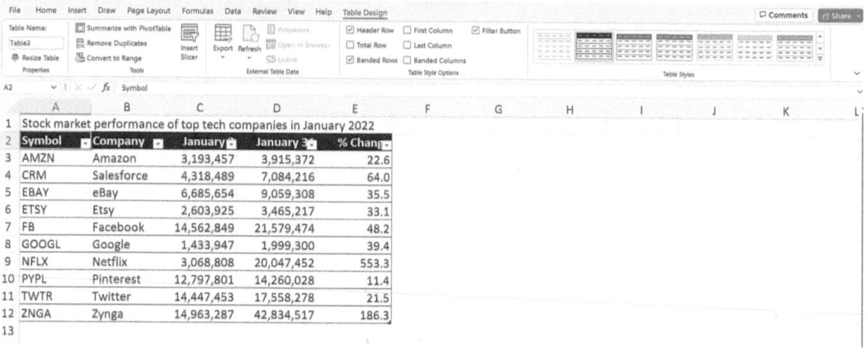

FIGURE 29.2

Generally speaking, there are five guidelines to make better tables in Excel (I discuss more in Chapter 11 of *Better Data Visualizations*).

1. **Offset Headers and Footers from the Body.** Too many people make the text or numbers in their headers and footers the same weight and style as the numbers in the body of the table. To make the table easier to read and to help direct a reader's attention, consider offsetting headers and footers from the body of the table. We can offset headers and footers by making the text boldface or using the *Borders* area of the *Home* tab to add an underline.

   In Table 29.1, all of the text is the same weight, so the table looks like a jumble of numbers. In Table 29.2, the boldface text and lines create a visual hierarchy to the table that directs a reader's eyes. The title is also larger and bolded.

2. **Reduce Digits and Align Numbers and Text.** We can make our data tables easier to read by reducing the number of digits and aligning the text and numbers. There is no "correct" number of digits, but for our table, we don't need the *exact* number of people in each country or the per capita gross domestic product (GDP) number to the pennies. When we reduce the number of digits—such as by showing country populations in millions—we can add a label in the column title or in the table subtitle if there is a single unit for the whole table.

TABLE 29.1 Health and Income of Nations in 2019

Country	Population	GDP per capita (Current US$)	Life Expectancy
Bangladesh	145924795	$1,855.74	72.59 years
Brazil	193886505	$8,897.55	75.88 years
China	1331260000	$10,143.84	76.91 years
Egypt	81134789	$3,019.09	71.99 years
Ethiopia	85233923	$855.76	66.6 years
India	1217726217	$2,100.75	69.66 years
Indonesia	238620554	$4,135.20	71.72 years
Japan	128047000	$40,777.61	84.36 years
Mexico	112463886	$9,950.45	75.05 years
Nigeria	154324939	$2,229.86	54.69 years
Pakistan	175525610	$1,288.56	67.27 years
Philippines	92414161	$3,485.34	71.23 years
Russia	142785349	$11,685.42	73.08 years
United States	306771529	$65,279.53	78.79 years
Vietnam	87092250	$2,715.28	75.4 years
Global Average	314251079	$17,114.17	72.62 years

TABLE 29.2 **Health and Income of Nations in 2019**

Country	Population	GDP per Capita (Current US$)	Life Expectancy
Bangladesh	145924795	$1,855.74	72.59 years
Brazil	193886505	$8,897.55	75.88 years
China	1331260000	$10,143.84	76.91 years
Egypt	81134789	$3,019.09	71.99 years
Ethiopia	85233923	$855.76	66.6 years
India	1217726217	$2,100.75	69.66 years
Indonesia	238620554	$4,135.20	71.72 years
Japan	128047000	$40,777.61	84.36 years
Mexico	112463886	$9,950.45	75.05 years
Nigeria	154324939	$2,229.86	54.69 years
Pakistan	175525610	$1,288.56	67.27 years
Philippines	92414161	$3,485.34	71.23 years
Russia	142785349	$11,685.42	73.08 years
United States	306771529	$65,279.53	78.79 years
Vietnam	87092250	$2,715.28	75.4 years
Global Average	**314251079**	**$17,114.17**	**72.62 years**

Setting

Making

Moving

When it comes to alignment, English speakers are accustomed to reading text left-to-right, so creating a left-aligned grid makes the text easier to read. But for numbers, it's more important to right-align along the decimal or comma. We might need to add some trailing zeros to get the alignment just right, but it makes comparing values that much easier. See how much faster and easier it is to pick out the highest and lowest per capita GDP numbers when they are right-aligned in Table 29.3 rather than centered as in the version in Table 29.2.

TABLE 29.3 **Health and Income of Nations in 2019**

Country	Population (Millions)	GDP per capita (Current US$)	Life Expectancy
Bangladesh	146	$1,856	72.6 years
Brazil	194	$8,898	75.9 years
China	1331	$10,144	76.9 years
Egypt	81	$3,019	72.0 years
Ethiopia	85	$856	66.6 years
India	1218	$2,101	69.7 years
Indonesia	239	$4,135	71.7 years
Japan	128	$40,778	84.4 years
Mexico	112	$9,950	75.1 years
Nigeria	154	$2,230	54.7 years
Pakistan	176	$1,289	67.3 years
Philippines	92	$3,485	71.2 years
Russia	143	$11,685	73.1 years
United States	307	$65,280	78.8 years
Vietnam	87	$2,715	75.4 years
Global Average	**314**	**$17,114**	**72.6 years**

In some cases, we may want to center the numbers in the cell. Maybe the table looks better with the numbers centered and with centered column headers. Or maybe, as in the case with Table 29.4, the cells are shaded to add highlights, but the table looks strange with more space on the left side than the right side of the number. In Table 29.5, we can use the *Indent* button in the *Home* tab to push the numbers toward the center of the cell and still maintain the right-alignment along the comma.

TABLE 29.4 **Health and Income of Nations in 2019**

Country	Population (Millions)	GDP per capita (Current US$)	Life Expectancy
Bangladesh	146	$1,856	72.6 years
Brazil	194	$8,898	75.9 years
China	1331	$10,144	76.9 years
Egypt	81	$3,019	72.0 years
Ethiopia	85	$856	66.6 years
India	1218	$2,101	69.7 years
Indonesia	239	$4,135	71.7 years
Japan	128	$40,778	84.4 years
Mexico	112	$9,950	75.1 years
Nigeria	154	$2,230	54.7 years
Pakistan	176	$1,289	67.3 years
Philippines	92	$3,485	71.2 years
Russia	143	$11,685	73.1 years
United States	307	$65,280	78.8 years
Vietnam	87	$2,715	75.4 years
Global Average	**314**	**$17,114**	**72.6 years**

TABLE 29.5 **Health and Income of Nations in 2019**

Country	Population (Millions)	GDP per capita (Current US$)	Life Expectancy
Bangladesh	146	$1,856	72.6 years
Brazil	194	$8,898	75.9 years
China	1331	$10,144	76.9 years
Egypt	81	$3,019	72.0 years
Ethiopia	85	$856	66.6 years
India	1218	$2,101	69.7 years
Indonesia	239	$4,135	71.7 years
Japan	128	$40,778	84.4 years
Mexico	112	$9,950	75.1 years
Nigeria	154	$2,230	54.7 years
Pakistan	176	$1,289	67.3 years
Philippines	92	$3,485	71.2 years
Russia	143	$11,685	73.1 years
United States	307	$65,280	78.8 years
Vietnam	87	$2,715	75.4 years
Global Average	**314**	**$17,114**	**72.6 years**

Setting

Making

Moving

3. Resize Columns and Rows. We can double right-click on the column and row separators in Excel to automatically resize the columns according to the maximum width or height in that column or row. In Table 29.6, Excel has stretched out the first column because the title of the chart is in cell A1. But we can resize the columns to tighten up the table, let the column headers wrap on two lines, and place the numbers closer to the country labels in the first column as in Table 29.7. There is no perfect column width or row height—my strategy is to find the maximum width that makes the column with the longest cell contents look good and match the others to that value.

TABLE 29.6 Health and Income of Nations in 2019

Country	Population (Millions)	GDP per capita (Current US$)	Life Expectancy
Bangladesh	146	$1,856	72.6 years
Brazil	194	$8,898	75.9 years
China	1331	$10,144	76.9 years
Egypt	81	$3,019	72.0 years
Ethiopia	85	$856	66.6 years
India	1218	$2,101	69.7 years
Indonesia	239	$4,135	71.7 years
Japan	128	$40,778	84.4 years
Mexico	112	$9,950	75.1 years
Nigeria	154	$2,230	54.7 years
Pakistan	176	$1,289	67.3 years
Philippines	92	$3,485	71.2 years
Russia	143	$11,685	73.1 years
United States	307	$65,280	78.8 years
Vietnam	87	$2,715	75.4 years
Global Average	**314**	**$17,114**	**72.6 years**

4. Remove Unit Repetition. Our table is coming along nicely now. Lastly, we want to remove repeated units throughout the table. We've kept the dollar sign in the GDP per capita column in this example, but it's clear these are in dollars from the column subtitle. I would remove the dollar signs from the values here, but in other cases, I might leave the symbol in the first and last rows. Repeating the word "years" in the final column is also unnecessary and clutters the table. Instead, we can add a subtitle or label in the column header (Table 29.8).

TABLE 29.7 Health and Income of Nations in 2019

Country	Population (Millions)	GDP per capita (Current US$)	Life Expectancy
Bangladesh	146	$1,856	72.6 years
Brazil	194	$8,898	75.9 years
China	1331	$10,144	76.9 years
Egypt	81	$3,019	72.0 years
Ethiopia	85	$856	66.6 years
India	1218	$2,101	69.7 years
Indonesia	239	$4,135	71.7 years
Japan	128	$40,778	84.4 years
Mexico	112	$9,950	75.1 years
Nigeria	154	$2,230	54.7 years
Pakistan	176	$1,289	67.3 years
Philippines	92	$3,485	71.2 years
Russia	143	$11,685	73.1 years
United States	307	$65,280	78.8 years
Vietnam	87	$2,715	75.4 years
Global Average	314	$17,114	72.6 years

TABLE 29.8 Health and Income of Nations in 2019

Country	Population (Millions)	GDP per capita (Current US$)	Life Expectancy (Years)
Bangladesh	146	1,856	72.6
Brazil	194	8,898	75.9
China	1331	10,144	76.9
Egypt	81	3,019	72.0
Ethiopia	85	856	66.6
India	1218	2,101	69.7
Indonesia	239	4,135	71.7
Japan	128	40,778	84.4
Mexico	112	9,950	75.1
Nigeria	154	2,230	54.7
Pakistan	176	1,289	67.3
Philippines	92	3,485	71.2
Russia	143	11,685	73.1
United States	307	65,280	78.8
Vietnam	87	2,715	75.4
Global Average	314	17,114	72.6

Setting

Making

Moving

5. **Add Visuals When Appropriate.** In general, tables are intended to enable exploration of the detailed data values. But in some case, we may want to make our tables more visual and draw attention to certain numbers, values, or outliers. It's relatively easy to add visuals to our tables in Excel by using the *Conditional Formatting* menu options. The table in Figure 29.3 is not necessarily one I would use, but it demonstrates the visual elements that we can add in Excel.

a. Create a bar chart in the *Home > Conditional Formatting > Data Bars* menu.

b. Add icons by using the Wingdings 3 font and color the values using the *Conditional Formatting > Highlight Cells Rules > Equal To* option.

c. Highlight the top five values using the *Conditional Formatting > Top/ Bottom Rules > Top 10 Items* option.

Health and income of nations in 2019

Country	Population (millions)		GDP per capita (current US$)		Life Expectancy (years)
China	1331		10,144	▼	76.9
India	1218		2,101	▼	69.7
United States	307		65,280	▲	78.8
Indonesia	239		4,135	▼	71.7
Brazil	194		8,898	▼	75.9
Pakistan	176		1,289	▼	67.3
Nigeria	154		2,230	▼	54.7
Bangladesh	146		1,856	▼	72.6
Russia	143		11,685	▼	73.1
Japan	128		40,778	▲	84.4
Mexico	112		9,950	▼	75.1
Philippines	92		3,485	▼	71.2
Vietnam	87		2,715	▼	75.4
Ethiopia	85		856	▼	66.6
Egypt	81		3,019	▼	72.0
Global Average	314		17,114		72.6

FIGURE 29.3

Many who publish data tables fail to recognize that people read them like they read graphs, charts, and diagrams. The use of color, font size, thickness, alignment, and other aspects can help or hinder a reader's ability to process and absorb the information. Just like you would in your graphs, consider how you can use these strategies to make a reader's experience better.

Moving Visuals Out of Excel

30

Exporting Graphs from Excel

Excel does not have a built-in image-exporting feature, so preparing a high-resolution Excel chart for sharing as an image file or posting to the web requires a separate process. In my experience, many people export their graphs using screenshots, which often ends up looking blurry and pixelated, especially compared with the surrounding text. Screenshots are less consistent because the quality depends on the monitor (Figure 30.1).

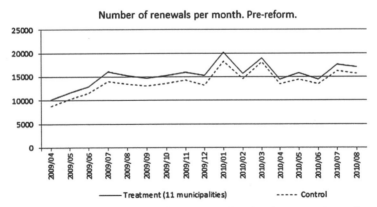

Number of renewals per month. Pre-reform.

──── Treatment (11 municipalities)   ----- Control

Note: Pre-treatment graph for the 11 (out of 16) locations where the reform was implemented post-September 2010.
Source: DETRAN.

FIGURE 30.1 Source: Figure 3 in Fredriksson, Anders. "One Stop Shops for Public Services: Evidence from Citizen Service Centers in Brazil." Journal of Policy Analysis and Management 39.4 (2020): 1133–1165.

DOI: 10.1201/9781003321552-33

There are better ways to obtain high-quality images of our Excel graphs. I've identified five common ways to convert an Excel graph to an image below.

1. **Use PowerPoint.** We can copy the graph from Excel and paste it into PowerPoint as an Excel object (not an image). In PowerPoint, we can size the slides to specific dimensions and export the modified image directly. On PCs, we can get the slide/image out of PowerPoint in two ways. One, use the standard *Save As* command in the *File* menu. Two, right-click on the graph and select the *Save As a Picture* option. I find that this second method creates higher-quality images. For Macs, only the first method works.

2. **Use VBA Code.** It's possible to build an exporting engine in Excel using VBA code. I've tested that approach, but the quality of the final images isn't that high, likely because the image resolution depends on the quality of the screen.

3. **Save As a PDF.** If we want to stay in Excel, we can save the graph as a PDF file (through the *Save As* menu), then crop the image in Adobe and export it to your preferred format (JPEG, PNG, or TIFF). I tested a few options here, but image quality wasn't high enough to warrant the lengthy process.

4. **Use Preview (Macs only).** On Macs, we can copy the graph from Excel (CMD+C), open the Preview tool, and create a new document (CMD+N). This process will load the copied graph from Excel directly into Preview. In Preview, we can select *Save* and change the file format to PNG. In the save window, we can change the dots per linear inch (DPI) to whatever we want (300 pixels works well). Of all the methods I tested, this one provided the highest quality image and is what I use in my daily work.

5. **Take a Screenshot.** Probably the option of last resort is to take a screenshot of the graph. Screenshots on Macs are better than those on PCs because Mac screens have higher resolutions. But the image size may vary depending on where the user places their cursor. Third-party tools like Snagit or Screencast-o-matic can help create high-resolution images without relying on your computer's built-in screenshot capabilities, but consistent image sizes are an issue if you need to select the area of the screen to capture.

For testing, I used a graph on my Macbook Pro and my Asus (PC) laptop, both of which run Office 365. In addition to my subjective grading of the image quality, I documented the image size and dimensions (in pixels), which can give a more objective measure of quality (Table 30.1).

Setting

Making

Moving

TABLE 30.1

Operating System	Method	File Format	Image Size (KB)	Width (Pixels)	Height (Pixels)	Area (Pixels)	Reason to Use or Reject
Mac	Export as GIF from PPT	GIF	48	1,000	797	797,000	Lower resolution
Mac	Right-click and Save As Picture	GIF	20	587	468	274,716	OK resolution; Mac only
PC	Save As GIF from PPT	GIF	25	705	589	415,245	Lower resolution
PC	Copy from Excel to PPT; right-click in PPT and Save As GIF	GIF	21	704	588	413,952	Lower resolution
Mac	Screenshot	JPG	280	1,782	1,382	2,462,724	Lower resolution
Mac	Save As JPEG from PPT	JPG	116	1,000	797	797,000	Lower resolution
Mac	Right-click and Save As Picture	JPG	56	587	468	274,716	OK resolution; Mac only
PC	Save As PDF and export as JPEG	JPG	79	734	613	449,942	Too many steps
PC	Save As JPEG from PPT	JPG	77	705	589	415,245	Lower resolution
PC	Copy from Excel to PPT; right-click in PPT and Save As JPEG	JPG	158	1,102	919	1,012,738	About the same as PNG
PC	Save as PDF	PDF	63	N/A	N/A	N/A	Does not work on websites
Mac	Copy from Excel and Paste in Preview; Save As PNG	PNG	303	2,445	1,950	4,767,750	Recommended Mac approach
Mac	Create PNG from PPT	PNG	123	1,000	797	797,000	Lower resolution
Mac	Right-click and Save As Picture	PNG	50	587	468	274,716	OK resolution; Mac only
PC	Save As PDF and export as PNG	PNG	33	1,468	1,226	1,799,768	Too many steps
PC	Save As PNG from PPT	PNG	42	705	589	415,245	Lower resolution
PC	Copy from Excel to PPT; right-click in PPT and Save As PNG	PNG	85	1,101	919	1,011,819	Recommended PC approach
PC	Screenshot (WIN+Shift+S)	PNG	56	865	726	627,990	Lower resolution
Mac	Save As TIF from PPT	TIF	2400	1,000	797	797,000	File too large
PC	Save As TIF from PPT	TIF	69	705	589	415,245	Lower resolution
PC	Copy from Excel to PPT; right-click in PPT and Save As TIF	TIF	185	1,101	919	1,011,819	Same as PNG, but larger file size

Moving   Making   Setting

Of course, size matters here. If you only need thumbnail images, the loss of resolution in any of these methods probably won't matter. But if you want a large image, the method may have a big impact on the image resolution. If you look carefully, you can see the differences in clarity between these two images (especially the *Source* line) in Figures 30.2 and 30.3.

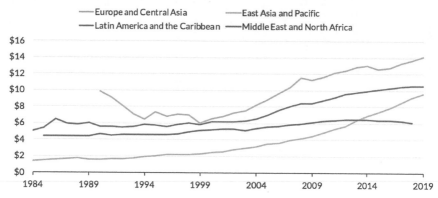

Daily Median Income, 1984 to 2019

Source: Our World In Data, PovCal (2021).
Note: Median incomes or expenditures are derived from household surveys. Some countries conduct surveys that ask for the household's income, while others ask for the household's expenditure. It is adjusted for price changes over time (inflation) and for price differences between countries – it is expressed in international-$.

FIGURE 30.2

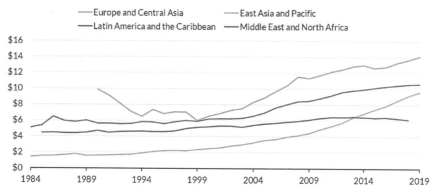

Daily Median Income, 1984 to 2019

Source: Our World In Data, PovCal (2021).
Note: Median incomes or expenditures are derived from household surveys. Some countries conduct surveys that ask for the household's income, while others ask for the household's expenditure. It is adjusted for price changes over time (inflation) and for price differences between countries – it is expressed in international-$.

FIGURE 30.3 *Top image uses the Excel-to-Preview method on a Mac, and the bottom image is a standard screenshot on a PC.*

Zooming into the titles of these images and taking a screenshot make the comparison even clearer (Figure 30.4).

Daily Median Income, 1984 to 2019

*Using Excel-to-
Preview on a Mac*

—— Europe and Central Asia
—— Latin America and the Caribbean

Daily Median Income, 1984 to 2019

*Using a standard
screenshot on a PC*

—— Europe and Central Asia
—— Latin America and the Caribbean

FIGURE 30.4

For reports—in many cases, created by writing text in Microsoft Word and pasting in graphs from Excel—the same procedures work, but you don't need to worry about creating a standalone image. In these cases, you can paste the Excel graph into Word (or PowerPoint) directly. It often carries the entire workbook with it, which I dislike because it can increase the file size and may contain all of your underlying data, causing potentially security issues (see Paradi, 2014). You could also paste the graph as a picture (in the *Paste Special* menu). I recommend the *Enhanced Metafile* option for PC users and the *PDF* option for Mac users. But if you make any changes to the graph in Excel, you will need to re-import the image to the other program (Figure 30.5).

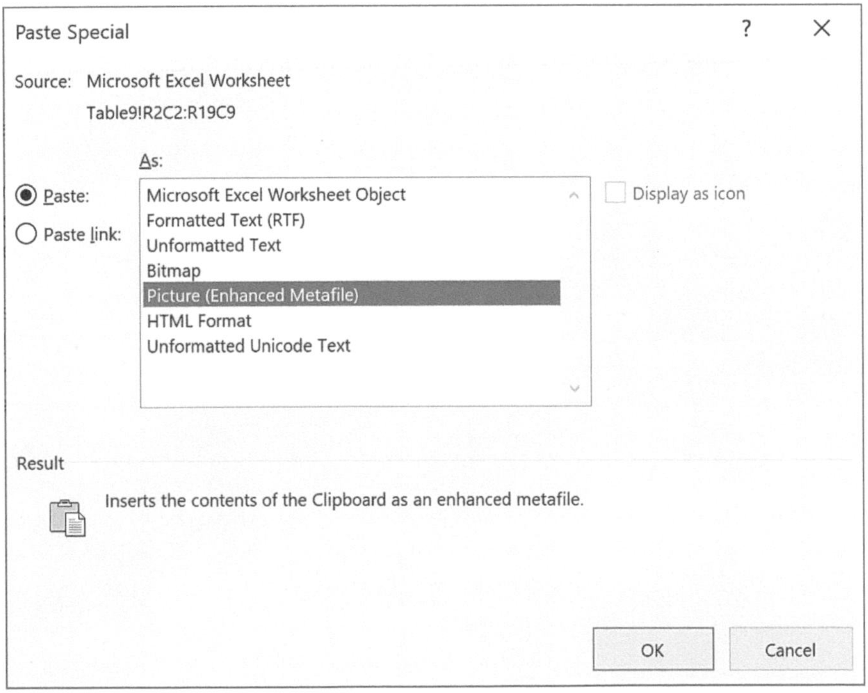

Setting

Making

Moving

Paste Special   ?   ×

Source: Microsoft Excel Worksheet
         Table9!R2C2:R19C9

                As:
○ Paste: ┌─────────────────────────────────┐   ☐ Display as icon
○ Paste link: │ Microsoft Excel Worksheet Object ∧ │
             │ Formatted Text (RTF)   │
             │ Unformatted Text   │
             │ Bitmap   │
             │ Picture (Enhanced Metafile)   │
             │ HTML Format   │
             │ Unformatted Unicode Text   │
             │   │
             │   ∨ │
             └─────────────────────────────────┘

Result
  📋   Inserts the contents of the Clipboard as an enhanced metafile.

                                          OK   Cancel

FIGURE 30.5

To create standalone images (without using a separate third-party tool), I recommend different solutions for PC and Mac users:

- **PC Users.** Copy the graph in Excel (CTRL+C) and paste into PowerPoint as a Microsoft Excel object. (The PowerPoint slide size should be set to match the size of the graph using the *Slide Size* option in the *Chart Design* tab.) From there, right-click on the slide, select "Save As Picture," and use the PNG file format option.

- **Mac Users.** Copy the graph in Excel (CMD+C), open a new file in Preview (CMD+N), and save as a PNG image (changing the resolution to 300 DPI). This process ensures consistent image size and image quality.

These approaches have three major advantages:

1. The images are high quality and the same file type (PNG).

2. The images are the same size.

3. The steps are relatively simple.

Creating high-quality images of Excel graphs outside Excel is admittedly a challenge. But we can overcome it by understanding what the computer can and cannot do. The options listed here offer a viable path for creating high-resolution Excel graphs.

Setting

Making

Moving

31

Redesigns and Examples

By this point, your Excel skills have hopefully advanced at least one rung, if not several, on the Excel skills ladder. You've learned numerous graphs using a variety of methods, formulas, and formatting options. As you further develop your abilities in Excel, you'll find more places where you can improve your productivity and use the tool to create even better data visualizations.

In this chapter, we'll cover a variety of ways to build on the basic graphs from the tutorials by remaking or redesigning graphs people have made in other tools. I won't explain step-by-step how to make these graphs. Instead, I want to demonstrate how the basic strategies we've learned can be extended and modified to make more data visualizations.

The changes here are not the only ways to create these graphs or even the best ways to visualize the data, but each example uses tools and techniques you have learned throughout the book.

How Did America Vote?

In early 2022, data visualization creator Erin Davis posted a tile grid map of the US on Twitter that garnered nearly 40,000 likes in less than a week. In her original map, each state tile was an area chart with three series showing how many people were born in that state, in another state, or outside of the US from 1850 to 2020. Later, Erin wrote a blog post about how to create the map in the R programming language, but this time used voting results data in presidential elections from 1976 to 2020 (Figure 31.1).

DOI: 10.1201/9781003321552-34

Erin
@erindataviz   •••

Rather pleased with this map

5:56 PM · Feb 2, 2022 · Twitter Web App

4,542 Retweets   **1,054** Quote Tweets   **39.3K** Likes

FIGURE 31.1   *Source: Erin Davis, Twitter, February 2, 2022.*

I thought Erin's examples provided a good opportunity to expand upon the slope chart tile grid map we created in Chapter 23. Instead of 2 years in each state, how could we extend it to include 12 observations and change the graph from a slope chart (line chart) to an area chart (Figure 31.2)?

The process of creating this graph turned out to be more of an organizational challenge than a data visualization challenge. Just like the tile grid map we created in Chapter 23, this map consists of a series of area charts that stretch across the country. Scatterplots with error bars break the area charts and generate the vertical dividing lines. Another scatterplot adds the state abbreviation labels.

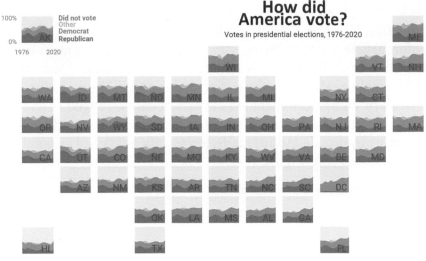

FIGURE 31.2

The resulting spreadsheet is large, to put it mildly. With four data series for each state, plus a series to serve as the horizontal breaks, *multiplied by* 12 years of data, plus another row to serve as the vertical break, we end up with a data table that is 40 columns wide and 143 rows long or 5,720 cells. And that's just for the map (Figure 31.3)!

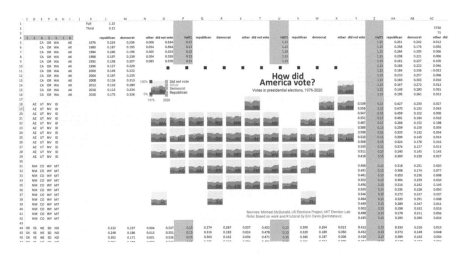

FIGURE 31.3

Decline in Auto Fatalities in the US

In spring 2021, Nicholas Kristof and Bill Marsh of the *New York Times* wrote an opinion article about reducing gun violence and gun control laws in the US. They compared the legislative efforts around gun control with the battles around automobile safety over the last several decades. The resulting chart was not particularly complex. It included 71 years of data arranged as a vertical bar chart, with the first and last bars in red and the bars in the middle in shades of tan alternating by decade. Additionally, ten specific years had annotations with numbers and some text (Figure 31.4).

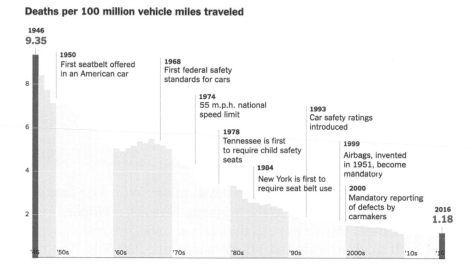

FIGURE 31.4   Source: Bill March, © 2021 The New York Times Company.

Could this graph be created in Excel without drawing a bunch of lines and adding text boxes? Turns out, the answer is yes—with some thoughtfully combined bar charts and scatterplots (Figure 31.5).

Although the graph itself is relatively simple, incorporating all the annotations and labels with data is more difficult. We have three bar charts for the main graph—one for the two red bars, one for the light-tan-colored decades, and another for the dark-tan-colored decades. We can layer on a series of scatterplots to add specially positioned y-axis labels (the red squares at the bottom); white gridlines on top of the bars (the black squares on the left); placeholders for the text labels (the blue boxes); and years (the green labels). Some special character breaks make the labels (see the two cells under the "Label Text" cell in the bottom-right of Figure 31.6) wrap on multiple lines rather than fitting them manually by playing around with the label boxes.

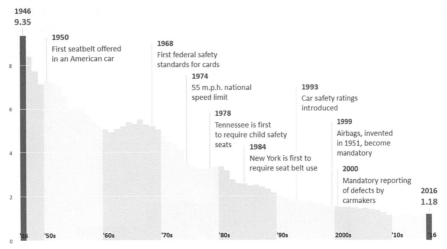

FIGURE 31.5

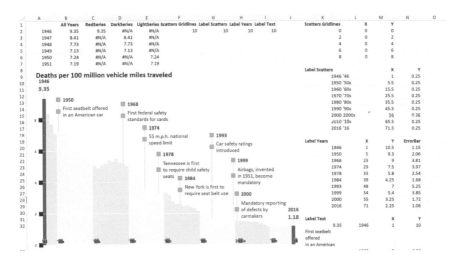

FIGURE 31.6

Setting

Making

Moving

Distribution of Poverty
Across the Country

In Chapter 24, we walked through several ways to layer two distributions together on the same graph. But what about the distribution of geographic data? For many people, creating a map is the standard approach to plotting geographic data, but if you are not trying to tell an inherently geographic story, a map may not be the best visualization.

If we focus on the distribution of data, we could create a histogram or a similar kind of graph. Take the 2020 state-level poverty rate. We could create a standard histogram with a series of six bars, which gives us a general sense of the data. But maybe we could give readers a bit more detail (Figure 31.7)?

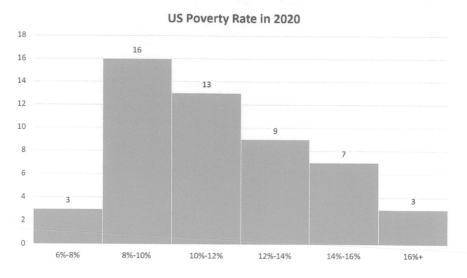

FIGURE 31.7

Here, we replace the abstract bar shapes with the name of each state, colored by region of the country. This version combines a histogram and a map, in that it enables us to see the distribution of the data and the geographic patterns (Figure 31.8).

US Poverty Rate in 2020

■ Midwest   ▪ Northeast   ■ South   ▪ West

16 states		**9 states**		
Illinois				
Wisconsin	**13 states**			
Nebraska	Missouri			
Minnesota	North Dakota			
Iowa	Michigan	**9 states**		
Kansas	South Dakota			
Maine	Pennsylvania	Indiana	**7 states**	
New Jersey	Connecticut	Ohio		
Massachusetts	New York	Florida	Texas	
Vermont	Delaware	Georgia	Kentucky	
Rhode Island	Maryland	South Carolina	Arkansas	**3 states**
3 states	Washington	Tennessee	West Virginia	
New Hampshire	Idaho	North Carolina	Alabama	District of Columbia
Virginia	Colorado	Nevada	Oklahoma	Mississippi
Utah	Oregon	Alaska	Louisiana	New Mexico
6%–8%	8%–10%	10%–12%	12%–14%	14%–16%	16%+

FIGURE 31.8

Again, to create this visualization we combine a bar chart—which helps align the stacks of labels and the x-axis labels—and scatterplots. It requires a bit of clever organizing and IF statements to create separate series for each of the four regions (with "NAs" so as to not over-plot the chart). We also use a few scatterplots to add the column headers and the legend (Figure 31.9).

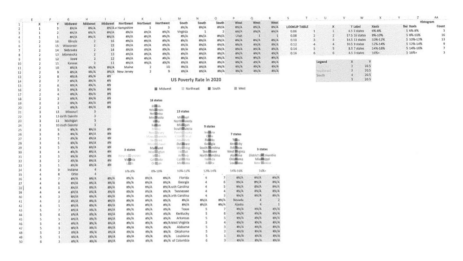

FIGURE 31.9

When Do Public Schools Start in the Morning?

In this example, our data show the average start time of public schools for every US state during the 2017–2018 school year. Like the state-level poverty data, these data may not be best represented by a map. Instead, why don't we use a clock? In Figure 31.10, we can see that, on average, public schools in North Carolina and South Carolina start at 8:00 am (blue labels at the top of the image) and public schools in Washington, DC, and Alaska start at 8:30 am (blue labels at the very bottom of the image).

Let's remember the philosophy of creating effective visualizations in Excel: we need lines, bars, or circles plotted in an X-Y space. Well, at its core, a clock-face is just that—a series of dots or markers around the circumference of a circle, which we can create with a bit of trigonometry (prepare to do some Googling!). Once we figure out how to place the 60 markers around the circle to mark minutes and hours, finishing the graph is a matter of making slightly larger circles to place the labels for each state abbreviation. I find a little color-coding in my worksheets helps organize the data for when I need to update later (Figure 31.11).

Setting

Making

Moving

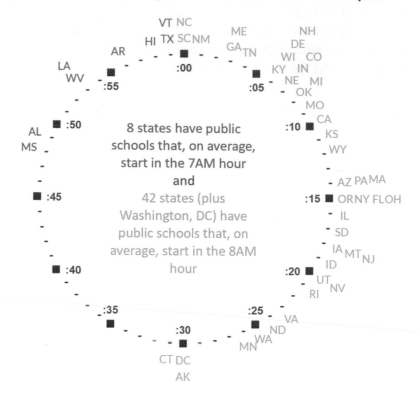

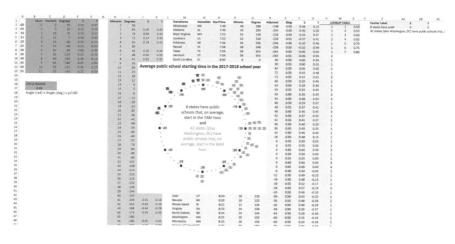

FIGURE 31.10   *Source: Jonathan Schwabish. "The Practice of Visual Data Communication: What Works." Psychological Science in the Public Interest 22.3 (2021a): 97–109.*

FIGURE 31.11

How Many Different Ways Can You Label a Dot Plot?

We created dot plots in Chapter 18, but we didn't focus too much on the different ways we can label the dots and lines in the chart. In the fall of 2021, Will Chase, a data journalist at Axios, published a dot plot that showed the time it took for seven major social media platforms to go from launch to one billion active users (Figure 31.12).

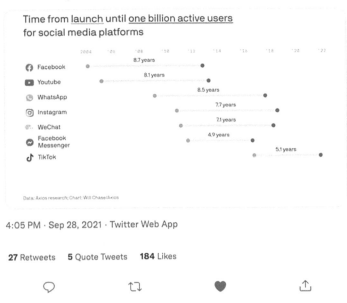

FIGURE 31.12   *Source: Will Chase, Twitter, September 28, 2021.*

Will's approach raises the question: how can we create this dot plot in Excel and what are the various ways we can add the labels in our dot plots? The process for creating the dot plot in Excel is still the same—use scatterplots to place the data, then use additional scatterplot series to position the labels. As always, the placement of the labels depends on the content and the overall shape of the data. In this case, the labels can go next to, above, or to the left of the dots. If we had more data, the best approach might be clearer (Figures 31.13–31.16).

Setting

Making

Moving

Time from launch until one billion active users for social media platforms

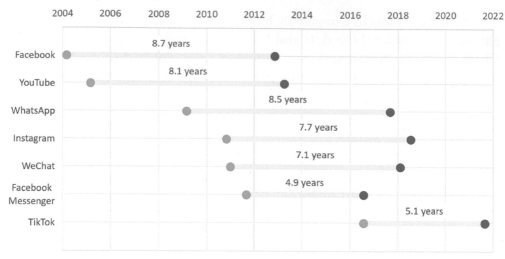

FIGURE 31.13

Time from launch until one billion active users for social media platforms

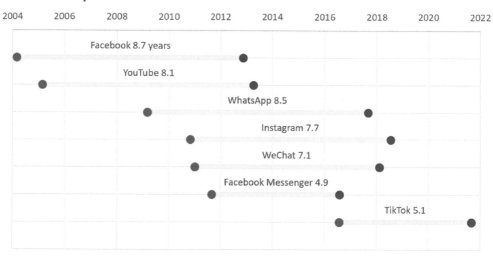

FIGURE 31.14

Time from launch until one billion active users for social media platforms

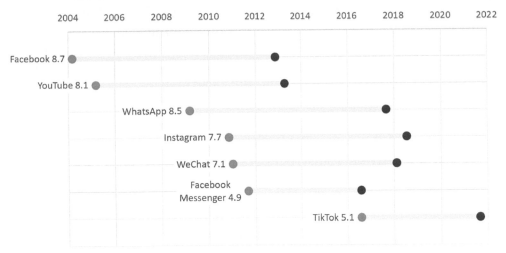

FIGURE 31.15

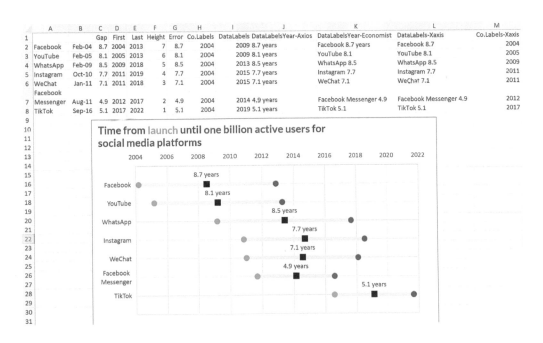

FIGURE 31.16

Setting

Making

Moving

Juvenile Arrests in Pittsburgh

In late 2020, a research team at the University of Pittsburgh, the American Civil Liberties Union of Pennsylvania, and Gwen's Girls, Inc. (a Pittsburgh-based organization that strives to empower girls and young women) reached out to me about helping with data visualizations for their final report. Their research centered on juvenile justice reforms in Pittsburgh and Allegheny County, and the over-referral of Black youth to juvenile justice.

In one of their graphs, the team looked at the breakdown of youth arrests across race (Black and white), gender (boys and girls), and police department (City Police and Pittsburgh Public Schools Police). The text that surrounded the image told a striking story, but not so much the graph (Figure 31.17).

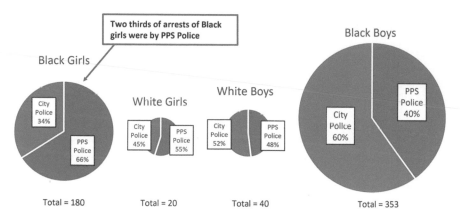

2019 Pittsburgh Juvenile Arrests by Police Type

FIGURE 31.17

Although I'm not a data practitioner who refuses to use pie charts, these charts are difficult to read and ask the reader to compare not just the two slices but also the size of the circles, which makes comprehension difficult.

Instead, I thought a mosaic chart might work better. A mosaic chart is like a stacked bar chart where the lengths of the bars represent one variable and the widths represent another variable. They are similar to the Marimekko chart we created in Chapter 25, but both the vertical and horizontal dimensions sum to a total (Figure 31.18).

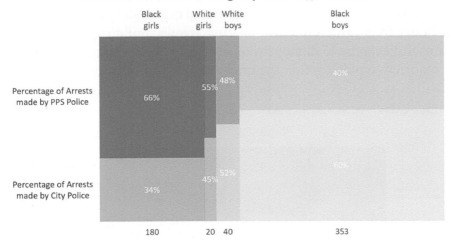

FIGURE 31.18

I created my version in Excel by aligning the four data points into eight different series (one for each gender-race group) and inserted them into a stacked bar chart. I added three separate scatterplots to help with the labels along the top edge, bottom edge, and left edge. I incorporated a final scatterplot series to add the number labels in the middle of each rectangle (Figure 31.19).

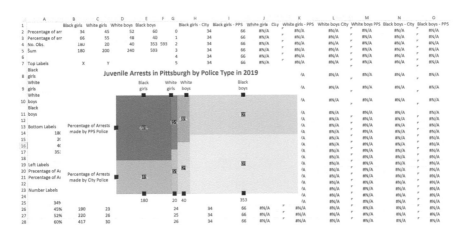

FIGURE 31.19

Although this graph got the team closer to what they wanted, they went back to their design team to incorporate additional explanatory text and annotation, some better fonts, and some nice-looking arrows. Building the chart in Excel was a useful exercise to demonstrate what could be built, but additional tools were required to pull together the final visualization (Figure 31.20).

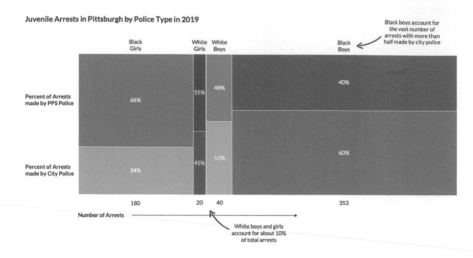

FIGURE 31.20 *Source: Elliott, Kathy, Sara Goodkind, Ghadah Makoshi, and Jeff Shook. 2020. "Understanding and addressing institutionalized inequity: Disrupting pathways to juvenile justice for Black youth in Allegheny County."*

Chapter 32

Conclusion

It's possible you never opened Excel before reading this book. Or maybe you've made countless graphs, charts, and tables in the tool. Wherever you fall in that spectrum of experience and expertise, I hope you have learned ways to improve how you create data visualizations in Excel. Whether it's using basic formulas like IF, COUNT, and VLOOKUP to format your data, combining different chart types, or inserting and aligning labels and markers, I hope you feel you have moved up a level in your Excel knowledge.

Of course, this book doesn't cover *everything* about using Microsoft Excel. We didn't talk about formula arrays or table names, the Visual Basic for Applications (VBA) programming language, PowerQuery, or data analysis tools. There are numerous other books, blog posts, and courses that you can use to learn more about these, and I have listed some of my personal favorites in Appendix 3.

You might also be inspired by this book to try other data visualization tools. Maybe you'd like to try dashboarding tools like Tableau or PowerBI, programming languages like D3 or R, or browser-based tools like Datawrapper or Flourish. The point of this book is not to argue that Excel is any better than any of those tools, rather it's a tool with features you might love and features you might hate. But in the end, it's just a tool.

DOI: 10.1201/9781003321552-35

As you go forward with your data visualization creation process, seek inspiration from freelancers, media organizations, and others. When you find a visual that inspires you, consider if it consists of lines, bars, or circles and if it lives in an X-Y space. If so, you might find that Excel—with a little tweaking and tricking—can be the right tool for you.

Setting

Making

Moving

Appendix 1

Color Tools

This list compiles some of the online color tools that can be used to build color palettes and test for accessibility. I maintain a longer list on my website at https://policyviz.com/resources/color-tools/.

Adobe Color. Color is a service of Adobe Creative Cloud that allows you to generate themes to directly pipe into design tools like Photoshop and Illustrator. It's the all-around color palette generator with essentially unlimited options. Adobe has a relatively new tool called Leonardo that goes even deeper into color codes, accessibility design, and more.

Color Brewer. Designed primarily for making maps, Color Brewer has a finite set of color palettes available but enables the user to filter by number of data series, data type, and other attributes.

Color Contrast Checker. Developed by Mari Johannessen, this contrast checker (https://marijohannessen.github.io/color-contrast-checker/) works similarly to the WebAIM tool below—simply type in your color HEX codes, and it gives you a color contrast score based the Web Content Accessibility Guidelines international standards.

Color Oracle. Color Oracle is a free program that simulates color vision deficiencies directly on your computer. It's a lightweight tool that runs on PC and Mac computers.

Coolors. Create, save, and share color palettes, or use the Coolors library to choose another palette. The color palette generator is a bit less robust than the Adobe Color tool, which makes it easier to use for non-designers.

Paletton. A growing source of information about color theory, color perception, color vision, and color combinations. Users can create custom color palettes and check them against an example, as well as use their color vision deficiency tool.

Sim Daltonism. Another program that simulates colors as they are perceived with various types of color vision deficiencies. This program is available on Macs only and can be downloaded through the App Store.

WebAIM Color Contrast Checker. I use this tool for all my color contrast checking needs. Insert the HEX color codes of the foreground and background colors and the site will tell you whether the combination passes contrast ratios as defined by the Web Content Accessibility Guidelines international standards.

Data Visualization Tools

Although this book focuses exclusively on Excel, there are a myriad of data visualization tools that can enable you to make different kinds of visuals. I've listed the ones that I see as the most popular tools and that I regularly use in my work. Just like Excel, these are all tools, so you should pick one that best meets your needs.

Dashboarding Tools

We can define a dashboard in many ways, but I prefer the definition from *The Big Book of Dashboards* by Steve Wexler, Jeffrey Shaffer, and Andy Cotgreave: "A dashboard is a visual display of data used to monitor conditions and/or facilitate understanding." By that definition, a dashboard does not need to be interactive nor does it need to have multiple views of the data, although they tend to have both. You can create some level of interactivity and align different charts in Excel, but you're probably better off using one of the other tools currently on the market.

- **Google Data Studio.** One of the more underused dashboarding tools available, Google Data Studio integrates directly into the Google ecosystem, including Google Sheets, Google Analytics, Google Ads, and more. There are many other data connections available for the tool, and its data visualization library is growing. It's free to use (unless you need a larger enterprise solution), but the data you plug into it will live online, which might be a problem if you have secure or private data.

- **PowerBI.** PowerBI's usage has grown recently, likely for two reasons. First, it's directly connected to the Microsoft Office suite, which means it's easy for many people to drop right into their existing workflow. Second, it's cheap compared with many other tools, especially because most people and organizations already have the Microsoft Office suite. At the time of this writing, the basic PowerBI Pro package is $9.99 per user per month but comes free with Microsoft Office 365 (although it's not currently available on Macs). That being said, I don't think the PowerBI visualizations look as glossy as those created in Tableau, but if you want to use it to create a collaborative data workspace, maybe that doesn't matter.

- **Tableau.** Probably the most popular dashboarding tool in the data visualization field is Tableau. Tableau includes many good features, such as the ability to quickly change between visualizations and a growing suite of data cleaning and reshaping tools. As an introductory user, I personally find the claim from users that you just "drop in your data and make a bunch of visualizations" not so true—your data need to be in the right format to make your visualizations. Pricing probably prevents more Tableau usage—licenses for the desktop version are $70 per user per month.

Browser-Based Tools

Some of the most interesting movement in the area of data visualization tools has occurred over the past several years with browser-based tools. Creating relatively easy-to-use, drag-and-drop-type tools in the cloud enables more sharing and collaboration capabilities, as well as the ability to create interactive visualizations that can be embedded on any website. But these tools are difficult to expand past what's in the existing menus. It's also true that your data are loaded into the cloud instead of sitting on your desktop, which introduces all sorts of considerations around data privacy and security.

There are three browser-based tools that I particularly like:

- **Datawrapper.** Now a team of around 20 people based mostly in Germany, Datawrapper was originally founded by Mirko Lorenz, Gregor Aisch, and David Kokkelink. The beta version launched in 2012 and quickly hit 10 million chart views about a year later. Since then, Datawrapper has become immensely popular among people creating interactive data visualizations, especially in smaller newsrooms. They have a somewhat limited set of visualizations in the library and focus on the more standard visualization types, but their table templates are probably the best you'll find among this set of tools. The pricing model is basically free to any individual but jumps up to $599/month for teams or if you want to include custom branding and specific exporting options.

- **Flourish.** Launched in 2018, Flourish is an online data visualization tool that enables users to create highly stylized, interactive visualizations, often with animation, without needing to know any code. I like that Flourish seems to keep up with the data visualization field and incorporates new visualization types and methods quickly. They have a wide range of visualizations available, including some not-so-standard charts and maps. In early 2022, Flourish announced its acquisition by the online design tool Canva. Soon after, it became free for most individual use cases (including working privately, which previously required a subscription). Business and enterprise versions are available with extra features such as custom branding, team administration, and more.

- **RAWGraphs.** RAWGraphs started in 2013 as an open-source project from a team based in Milan, Italy. The first iteration of RAWGraphs focused on some standard graphs plus some harder to make ones, like streamgraphs and Sankey diagrams. For a while, the tool sat there without much enhancement, but recently, a group of developers started adding a larger set of graphs. It's also completely free, and you can download the code from the site to run an instance of RAWGraphs directly on your own machine, which makes it somewhat more flexible (i.e., hackable) than Datawrapper and Flourish. Of course, you need coding knowledge to make your desired hacks.

Programming Languages

Some people argue that everyone should learn to code. I think that's a worthy idea—there are lots of things to learn just from understanding how to think through code—but I also think that not everyone has the time or inclination to code. That being said, conducting data analysis and data visualization with code has a lot of advantages, namely that it is more reproducible and often more accurate than point-and-click-type tools.

There are three primary coding languages used for data visualizations:

- **D3**. D3 is an open source JavaScript library for manipulating objects based on data and was developed by Mike Bostock along with Jeff Heer and Vadim Ogievetsky at Stanford University in the early 2010s. Most of the interactive data visualizations we currently see on the web are run on D3. Bostock opened his new company Observable in 2016, which fosters collaboration through code. Unlike D3, Observable has a pricing model for teams and organizations, but it enables more and better collaboration, code sharing, and transparent design than standard coding languages. Observable can also be used with any tool or coding language.

- **R.** For data visualization, R is especially useful because it can be combined with R's existing statistical analysis capabilities. The data visualization engine in R, ggplot, was developed by Hadley Wickham and is based on the Grammar of Graphics, which was originally conceptualized by Leland Wilkinson (2013). To my mind, the biggest advantage of this approach is that you can easily layer graph encodings together, making the coding process easier and more replicable.

- **Python.** I've never coded in Python, so I can't say much about its ease of use or effectiveness. A lot of people like Python, especially for its ability to facilitate web scraping. The biggest benefit I hear from Python users is the language offers the ability to easily build notebooks, specifically in Jupyter, which is a web-based application that can show code and text.

Design Tools

As mentioned, I do a lot of my data visualization work in Excel, but there are times when I need to add more customization, pull multiple (static) graphs together in a single view, or make a custom slide deck or infographic. Over the past few years, a growing number of browser-based graphic design tools have helped democratize the graphic design space (which can be good and bad). Although having more accessible tools probably bugs a lot of graphic designers, I'm all for tools that make it easier for me to create and lay out different graphic objects. That being said, if I'm creating a really polished-looking visualization—especially if it's for a print project—I'm more likely to reach out to a professional graphic designer.

There are four tools in particular worth knowing about: Adobe Illustrator, Canva, Figma, and PowerPoint.

- **Adobe Creative Suite.** The best infographics and graphic design work will likely be made in a custom graphic design tool like Adobe

Illustrator. But Illustrator is not easy to use and requires a lot of practice. The data visualization tool in Illustrator is pretty terrible—as a novice user, I could never understand why I needed to delink the graph from the data to properly style and format it. Pricing is also a consideration, though it's more affordable now in the subscription model than it was a few years ago. The entire Adobe Creative Suite goes for $52.99/month, and Illustrator on its own goes for $20.99/month.

- **Canva.** Of all the browser-based graphic design tools (and there are many), I like Canva the best. It has a really nice user interface, a good library of photographs (though the icon library is just okay), and the ability to create and save styles and formats. Canva also allows users to easily create social media posts for different platforms with the click of a "resize" button. The free version of Canva is good but limited in the various libraries. The Pro version is $12.99/month for five different users. If you are an educator (with a.edu email address), you can get a large discount as well. As noted above, Canva acquired Flourish in early 2022, so it will be interesting to see how both tools evolve over time.

- **Figma.** With the increased power and speed of internet browsers, Figma facilitates a level of online collaboration between designers and teams that was previously difficult to achieve. At its core, Figma helps people create website wireframes and test user experiences, but people are using the tool for all kinds of graphic design tasks. As an admittedly novice Adobe Illustrator user, I find Figma easier to use—but again, I'm not a professional designer, so I'm probably not the best judge. Figma has three pricing levels: a free version, a $12 per person per month option, and an up to $45 per person per month option for larger teams.

- **PowerPoint.** It won't surprise you that I use Microsoft PowerPoint for a lot of my design work. PowerPoint syncs directly with Excel and almost everybody has it. A PowerPoint slide is a blank template, which I can modify and edit to the needed size and shape. Sure, it has some weird things that I don't like—bad defaults and ugly templates—but I can override them. For many of my audiences, what I can do in PowerPoint is largely sufficient.

Additional Excel Resources

This book is not going to teach you *everything* you need to know about Excel. We didn't cover coding in the VBA (Visual Basic for Applications) language, Pivot Tables, Power Query, dashboards, or more advanced formulas. But there are a lot of different websites, videos, books, and other training materials available. Here are some of my favorite sites:

- **Chandoo.org.** Includes a variety of Excel lessons, especially for formulas, Excel dashboards, and PowerBI.

- **Contextures.com.** An all-around Excel site with a long, alphabetical list of Excel tutorials that includes videos, workbooks, and step-by-step instructions.

- **ExcelCampus.com.** One of the better sites to learn VBA—the video courses are fantastic and walk you through the process of creating your own Excel macros.

- **ExcelJet.net.** A large resource of free and paid video courses including formulas, conditional formatting, and much more. It also has a great Excel keyboard shortcut reference sheet that I regularly recommend.

- **Mr. Excel (mrexcel.com).** Classic, incredible site to learn all about Excel. Mr. Excel features a whole range of learning materials from blogs to books to videos.

- **MyOnlineTrainingHub.com.** Terrific collection of courses and webinars on learning a whole suite of Excel skills including Power Query, Pivot Tables, and PowerBI.

- **PeltierTech.com.** A great blog with (free!) step-by-step instructions on how to create data visualizations in Excel and additional content on macros and VBA.

- **Xelplus.com.** A great site to learn more about Excel spreadsheets and formulas, and it features one of the better YouTube Excel playlists out there.

- **Wisevis.com.** A helpful site to learn more about data visualization in Excel and is maintained by the author of the book *Data at Work: Best Practices for Creating Effective Charts and Information Graphics in Microsoft Excel* (Camões, 2016).

Quick Instructions List

These Quick Instructions are provided as an abbreviated set instruction to build each graph in this book. These instructions don't always exactly line up with the numbered steps in the full tutorials and use more shorthand than the full descriptions. If you just need a quick refresher or reminder for a certain graph, these instructions may be what you need.

Sparklines

1. *Insert* > *Sparklines* > *Line*

2. Enter the data range (H3:AA12) in the top box and the placement range (F3:F12) in the bottom box

Heatmap

1. Select data (either entire data table or each column individually)

2. *Home* > *Conditional Formatting* > *Color Scales* > *More Rules*

3. Set *Minimum* and *Maximum* colors

4. Hide numbers: right-click > *Format Cells* > *Number* > *Custom* > type three semicolons (;;;) into the *Type* box

Stripe Chart

1. Select cells A3:FP3

2. *Home > Conditional Formatting > Color Scales > More Rules > Format Style > 3-Color Scale*

3. Set *Minimum* color to blue and *Maximum* color to red

4. Change *Midpoint* value to *Number,* type zero (0) in the box, and change color to white

5. Hide numbers: right-click *> Format Cells > Number > Custom >* type three semicolons (;;;) into the *Type* box

6. Select columns A to FP and change column width

7. Select row number three and make it taller

8. To add or adjust year labels, see full tutorial

Waffle Chart

1. Arrange data and formulas

2. Select cells R3:AA12

3. *Home > Conditional Formatting > Highlight Cells Rules > Equal To*

4. Type one (1) in the box and set fill color in the drop-down menu: *Custom Format > Fill*

5. Repeat for each number (1, 2, 3, and 4)

6. Hide numbers: right-click *> Format Cells > Number > Custom >* type three semicolons (;;;) into the *Type* box

7. Add borders: *Home > Borders* (in *Font* area) *> All Borders*

Gantt Chart

Method #1: Conditional Formatting

1. Arrange data and formulas

2. Select cells F3:CD12

3. Home *>* Conditional Formatting *>* Highlight Cells Rules *>* Equal To

4. Type one (1) in menu box

5. Set the style (e.g., fill color) for the cells: Custom Format > Fill

6. Hide numbers: right-click > Format Cells > Number > Custom > type three semicolons (;;;) into the Type box

7. Select columns F to CD and change column width

8. Resize rows to correspond to number of Lifetime Goals (see cells CG17:CH27)

9. To add or adjust year labels, see full tutorial

Method #2: Stacked Bar Chart

1. Arrange data and formulas

2. Select cells A1:D11 and insert a Stacked Bar Chart

3. Format vertical axis:

   - Right-click > Format Axis > Axis Options > Categories in reverse order

   - Right-click > Format Axis > Axis Options > Horizontal axis crosses > At maximum category

4. Add labels:

   - Right-click on the *First Year* series > *Add Data Labels*

   - Right-click on the *Last Year* series > *Add Data Labels*

5. Format labels:

   - Right-click on labels for *First Year* series > *Format Data Labels* > *Label Position* > *Inside End*

   - Right-click on labels for *Last Year* series > *Format Data Labels* > *Label Position* > *Inside Base*

6. Edit range of horizontal axis: right-click > *Format Axis* > *Bounds* > 1940 for *Minimum* and 2021 for *Maximum*

7. Remove fill color of *First Year* series and *Last Year* series: right-click > *Format Data Series* > *Fill* > *No Fill*

8. Delete legend and adjust *Plot Area* to fit all labels by dragging the right edge of the *Plot Area* to the left

Comparing Values with Two Graph Types

Vertical Layout

1. Select cells A1:C11 and insert a *Clustered Column* chart

2. Change the *Supplemental Poverty Rate* series to a *Line with Markers*:

   a. On PCs: select Supplemental Poverty Rate series Chart Design > Change Chart Type > Combo > Supplemental Poverty Rate > Line with Markers

   b. On Macs: select Supplemental Poverty Rate series > Chart Design > Change Chart Type > Line with Markers

3. Select line for Supplemental Poverty Rate series:

   a. Right-click > Format Data Series > Line > No Line

   b. Right-click > *Format Data Series > Marker >* format as needed

Horizontal Layout

1. Arrange data and formulas

2. Select cells A1:C11 and insert a Clustered Bar chart

3. Format vertical axis:

   a. Right-click > Format Axis > Axis Options > Categories in reverse order

   b. Right-click > Format Axis > Axis Options > Horizontal axis crosses > At maximum category

4. Change the Supplemental Poverty Rate series to a scatterplot:

   a. On PCs: select Supplemental Poverty Rate series Chart Design > Change Chart Type > Combo > Supplemental Poverty Rate > Scatter

   b. On Macs: select Supplemental Poverty Rate series > Chart Design > Change Chart Type > Scatter

5. Insert the correct cell references for the Supplemental Poverty Rate series: right-click > Select Data > Supplemental Poverty Rate > Edit > X Values: C2:C11 and Y Values: D2:D11

6. Delete secondary vertical axis

Broken Stacked Bars

1. Select cells A8:I12 and insert a *Stacked Bar* chart

2. Switch order of the chart: *Chart Design > Switch Row/Column*

3. Format vertical axis:

   a. Right-click > Format Axis > Axis Options > Categories in reverse order

   b. Right-click > *Format Axis > Axis Options > Horizontal axis crosses > At maximum category*

4. Change color of each Filler series: right-click on each > Format Data Series > Fill > No Fill

5. Edit range of horizontal axis: right-click > Format Axis > Bounds > 0 for Minimum and 200 for Maximum

6. Edit horizontal axis units: right-click > Format Axis > Units > 50 for Major

7. Delete the four Filler series labels in legend: click on legend > click on each Filler label > delete

8. Delete the horizontal axis

Diverging Bar Chart

1. Select cells A7:G11 and insert a Stacked Bar chart

2. Switch order of the chart: Chart Design > Switch Row/Column

3. Format vertical axis:

   a. Right-click > Format Axis > Axis Options > Categories in reverse order

    b. Right-click > Format Axis > Axis Options > Horizontal axis crosses > At maximum category

    c. Right-click > Format Axis > Labels > Low

    d. Right-click > Format Axis > Line > Solid line

4. Delete the legend entries for the Strongly disagree and Somewhat disagree categories, and change the colors of the other Strongly disagree and Somewhat disagree categories.

    Format x-axis labels: right-click > *Format Axis* > *Number* > *Custom* > insert #,###;#,###;0 into *Format Code* box.

Block Shading (same frequency)

1. Select cells B1:D182 and insert a Line chart

2. Change the Recession series to a Clustered Column chart:

    a. On PCs: select Recession series > Chart Design > Change Chart Type > Combo > Recession > Clustered Column

    b. On Macs: select Recession series > Chart Design > Change Chart Type > Clustered Column

3. Select Recession series > right-click > Format Data Series > Series Options > Gap Width to 0%

4. Change vertical axis dimensions: right-click > Format Axis > Axis Options > 0 for Minimum and 16 for Maximum

Block Shading (different frequencies)

1. Select cells A1:B16 and insert a Line chart

2. Add Recession data: right-click > Select Data > Add > Series Name: Recession (cell E1) and Y Values: E2:E169

3. Select Recession series > right-click > Format Data Series > Series Options > Plot Series On > Secondary Axis

4. Change the Recession series to Clustered Column chart:

a. On PCs: select Recession series > Chart Design > Change Chart Type > Combo > Recession > Clustered Column

b. On Macs: select Recession series > Chart Design > Change Chart Type > Clustered Column

5. Turn on secondary horizontal axis: select chart > Chart Design > Add Chart Element > Axes > Secondary Horizontal

6. Change the dimensions of the secondary vertical axis (on the right): right-click > Format Axis > Axis Options > 1 for Minimum and 2 for Maximum

7. Select Recession series > right-click > Format Data Series > Series Options > Gap Width to 0%

8. Format secondary horizontal and secondary vertical axis:

a. Format Axis > Line color > No line

b. Format Axis > Tick Marks > None

c. Format Axis > Labels > Label Position > None

9. Adjust primary horizontal axis tick marks: right-click > Format Axis > Axis Options > Axis position > On tick marks

Mark an Event with a Line

Method #1

1. Arrange data and formulas

2. Select cells B1:D91 and insert a *Line with Markers* chart

3. Add an *Error Bar* to the orange dot (the *First McDonald's restaurant opens* series in column D): select dot > *Chart Design > Add Chart Element > Error Bars > More Error Bars Options*

4. Format error bar: select > right-click > *Format Error Bars >*

a. Set Direction to Minus

b. Set End Style to No Cap

c. Set Error Amount > Percentage > 100%

5. Select scatterplot marker, right-click, and Add Data Label

6. Hide markers for both series: right-click on each > Format Data Series > Marker > Marker Options > None

7. Change vertical axis dimensions: right-click > Format Axis > Axis Options > 0 for Minimum and 100 for Maximum

8. To add or adjust year labels, see full tutorial

Method #2

1. Arrange data and formulas

2. Select cells B1:C91 and insert a Line chart

3. Add a new series: right-click > Select Data > Add > Series Name: First McDonald's restaurant opens (cell H2) and Series Values: I4

4. Change the new series to a scatterplot:

   a. On PCs: select McDonald's series (use the Format > Current Selection menu) Chart Design > Change Chart Type > Combo > McDonald's > Scatter

   b. On Macs: select McDonald's series (use the Format > Current Selection menu) > Chart Design > Change Chart Type > Scatter

5. Assign the x-value: right-click > Select Data > First McDonald's restaurant opens > Edit > Series X Values: H4

6. Add error bars to scatterplot point: select dot > Chart Design > Add Chart Element > Error Bars > More Error Bars Options

7. Format vertical error bar: select > right-click > Format Error Bars >

   a. Set Direction to Minus

   b. Set End Style to No Cap

   c. Set Error Amount > Percentage > 100%

8. Delete horizontal error bars

9. Select scatterplot marker, right-click, and Add Data Label

10. Hide scatterplot point: right-click > Format Data Series > Marker > Marker Options > None

11. Change vertical axis dimensions: right-click > Format Axis > Axis Options > 0 for Minimum and 100 for Maximum

12. To add or adjust year labels, see full tutorial

Dot Plot

1. Select cells A1:C8 and insert a Scatter chart

2. Edit both series:

    a. Right-click > Select Data > 2000 > Edit > Series Name: 2017 (cell D1); X values: D2:D8; and Y values: B2:B8

    b. Right-click > Select Data > Height > Edit > Series Name: 2000 (cell C1); X values: C2:C8; and Y values: B2:B8

3. Add error bars to the 2017 series: select series > Chart Design > Add Chart Element > Error Bars > More Error Bars Options

4. Format horizontal error bars: select > right-click > Format Error Bars >

    a. Set Direction to Minus

    b. Set End Style to No Cap

    c. Set Error Amount > Custom > Specify Values > Negative Error Value > cells E2:E8

5. Delete vertical error bars

6. Add labels or modify lines to arrows, see full tutorial for more details and options

Slope Chart

Method #1

1. Select cells A2:C9 and insert a Line with Markers chart

2. Switch order of the chart: Chart Design > Switch Row/Column

3. Select one line, right-click, and Add Data Labels

4. Select left data label only, right-click, select Format Data Label, and make three changes:

   a. Label contains > Series Name and Value

   b. Change Separator to Space

   c. Change Label Position to Left

5. Repeat data labeling and formatting steps (3 and 4) for each series

6. Delete legend, vertical axis, and horizontal gridlines

7. Format horizontal axis: right-click > Format Axis > Axis Options > Axis position > On tick marks

8. Adjust Plot Area by selecting the left edge and moving it to the right to fit labels

Method #2

1. Arrange data and formulas

2. Select cells A2:C9 and insert a Line with Markers chart

3. Switch order of the chart: Chart Design > Switch Row/Column

4. Add scatterplot for left labels: right-click > Select Data > Add > Series Name: Left Labels (cell D1) and Series values: E3:E9

5. Change the Left Labels series to a scatterplot:

   a. On PCs: select Left Labels series > Chart Design > Change Chart Type > Combo > Left Labels > Scatter

   b. On Macs: select Left Labels series > Chart Design > Change Chart Type > Scatter

6. Add x-values to Left Labels series: right-click > Select Data > Left Labels > Edit > X values: D3:D9

7. Add Right Labels series: right-click > Select Data > Add > Series Name: Right Labels (cell G1); X values: G3:G9; and Y values: H3:H9

8. Add and format labels to the Left Labels series:

   a. Right-click > Add Data Labels

   b. Select data labels > right-click > Format Data Labels and make two changes:

      i. Label contains > Value from Cells > F3:F9 (and uncheck the box next to Y Value)

      ii. Change Label Position to Left

9. Add labels to the Right Labels series: right-click > Add Data Labels

10. Format horizontal axis: right-click > Format Axis > Axis Options > Axis position > On tick marks

11. Adjust Plot Area by selecting the left edge and moving it to the right to fit labels

12. Delete legend, vertical axis, and horizontal gridlines

Overlaid Gridlines

1. Select cells A2:B9 and insert a Clustered Column chart

2. Right-click > Select Data > Add > Series Name: Scatter-Overlaid (cell C1) and Series values: D3:D12

3. Change the Scatter-Overlaid series to a scatterplot:

   a. On PCs: select Scatter-Overlaid series > Chart Design > Change Chart Type > Combo > Scatter-Overlaid > Scatter

   b. On Macs: select Scatter-Overlaid series > Chart Design > Change Chart Type > Scatter

4. Add x-values to Scatter-Overlaid series: right-click > Select Data > Scatter-Overlaid > Edit > X values: cells C3:C12

5. Add error bars to the Scatter-Overlaid series: select > Chart Design > Add Chart Element > Error Bars > More Error Bars Options

6. Format horizontal error bars: select > right-click > Format Error Bars >

   a. Set Direction to Both

   b. Set End Style to No Cap

   c. Set Error Amount > Fixed Value > 3.5

   d. Set color: Line > Solid Line > Color > change to white

7. Delete vertical error bars

8. Delete existing gridlines

9. Hide Scatter-Overlaid markers: right-click > Format Data Series > Marker > Marker Options > None

10. Edit vertical axis limits: right-click > Format Axis > Axis Options > 0 for Minimum and 20 for Maximum

11. If keeping the vertical axis, adjust the labels to match new gridlines: right-click > Format Axis > Bounds > Units > Major > 2

Lollipop

1. Select cells A1:B8 and insert a Clustered Bar chart

2. Format vertical axis:

   a. Format Axis > Axis Options > Categories in reverse order

   b. Format Axis > Axis Options > Horizontal axis crosses > At maximum category

3. Select bars and add error bars: Chart Design > Add Chart Element > Error Bars > More Error Bars Options

4. Format error bars: select > right-click > Format Error Bars >

   a. Set Direction to Minus

   b. Set End Style to No Cap

   c. Set Error Amount > Percentage > 100%

5. More error bar formatting (paint can icon):

   a. Change Begin Arrow Type to circle

   b. Change Begin Arrow Size to the largest size

6. Change color of the bars: right-click > *Format Data Series > Fill > No Fill*

Bullet Chart

1. Arrange data and formulas

2. Select cells A38:F44 and insert a Stacked Column chart

3. Switch order of the chart: Chart Design > Switch Row/Column

4. Move Best and Average series to the secondary axis: right-click on each > Format Data Series > Secondary Axis

5. Change width of Average series: right-click > Format Data Series > Series Options > Gap Width to 400%

6. Change the Best series to a scatterplot:

   a. On PCs: select Best series > Chart Design > Change Chart Type > Combo > Best > Scatter

   b. On Macs: select Best series > Chart Design > Change Chart Type > Scatter

7. Format scatterplot point (Best series) to a line:

   a. Method #1. Change marker format: right-click > Format Data Series > Marker > Marker Options > Built-In > select dash shape and adjust size

   b. Method #2. Add error bar: select dots > Chart Design > Add Chart Element > Error Bars > More Error Bars Options. Format the horizontal error bars:
   Set Direction to Both
   Set End Style to No Cap
   Set Fixed value to 0.2

   c. Hide *Best* marker: right-click > *Format Data Series > Marker > Marker Style > None*

   d. Delete vertical error bars (may need to use the *Format > Current Selection* menu)

8. Edit ranges of both the primary and secondary vertical axis:

   a. Right-click > Format Axis > Bounds > 0 for Minimum and 2,000 for Maximum

   b. Right-click > Format Axis > Bounds > Units > Major > 500

Tile Grid Map

Map #1: Default Map

1. Select cells A1:B52 and insert Maps in the Insert tab

2. Right-click > Format Data Series to modify colors, projection, labels, and more

Map #2: Single Values with Continuous Legend

1. Arrange data, formulas, and tiles

2. Select cells B4:L13

3. Set tile colors: Home > Conditional Formatting > Color Scales > More Rules

4. Set Minimum and Maximum colors

5. Set text colors: Home > Conditional Formatting > Highlight Cells Rules > Greater Than > 0.40 > Custom Format > Font > Color > white

Map #3: Single Values with Discrete Legend

1. Arrange data, formulas, and tiles

2. Select cells B5:L12

3. Set tile colors for first category: Home > Conditional Formatting > Highlight Cells Rules > Equal To > 1 > Custom Format > Fill > Background color

4. Repeat for other categories

5. Set text colors: Home > Conditional Formatting > Highlight Cells Rules > Greater Than > 0.40 > Custom Format > Font > Color > white

Map #4: Multiple Values

1. Arrange data and formulas

2. Select cells T4:AJ32 and insert a Line with Markers chart

3. Add error bars to the Vertical series (dots along the top): Chart Design > Add Chart Element > Error Bars > More Error Bars Options

4. Format error bars: select > right-click > Format Error Bars >

   a. Set Direction to Minus

   b. Set End Style to No Cap

   c. Set Error Amount > Percentage > 100%

   d. Set color: Line > Solid Line > white

   e. Increase line width: Line > Width

5. Add *State Names* series for state abbreviation labels: right-click > *Select Data* > *Add* > Series Name: State Names (cell G1) and Series values: H4:H54

6. Change the State Names series to a scatterplot:

   a. On PCs: select State Names series > Chart Design > Change Chart Type > Combo > State Names > Scatter

   b. On Macs: select State Names series > Chart Design > Change Chart Type > Scatter

7. Insert x-values: right-click > Select Data > State Names > X Values: H4:H54

8. Add and format data labels:

   a. Right-click on the State Names series > Add Data Labels

   b. Right-click on labels > Format Data Labels > Value From Cells > B4:B54 (and uncheck the box next to Y Value)

   c. Right-click on labels > Format Data Labels > Label Position > Center

9. Hide scatterplot markers for labels (Vertical and State Names series): right-click on each > Format Data Series > Marker > Marker Options > None

10. Edit range of vertical axis: right-click > Format Axis > Bounds > 0 for Minimum and 8 for Maximum

11. Delete legend, horizontal axis, and vertical axis

Histogram

Method #1: Overlaid Area Charts

1. Arrange data and formulas

2. Select cells C1:E22 and insert an Area chart

3. Change the color transparency of both series: right-click > Format Data Series > Fill > Solid fill > Transparency

4. Add borders (two series):

   a. Right-click > Select Data > Add > Series Name: 1980s (cell D1); Series values: D2:D22 and Series Name: 2010s (cell E1); Series values: E2:E22

   b. Change series to line charts:

On PCs: select each series > *Chart Design* > *Change Chart Type* > *Combo* > drop-down menu for each series > *Line*

On Macs: select each series > *Chart Design* > *Change Chart Type* > *Line*

Method #2: Overlaid Bar Charts

1. Arrange data and formulas

2. Select cells C1:E22 and insert a Clustered Column chart

3. Align the bars: right-click on either set > Format Data Series > Series Options > Series Overlap to 100% and Gap Width to 0%

4. Change the color transparency of both series: right-click > Format Data Series > Fill > Solid fill > Transparency

5. Add scatterplots for borders: right-click > Select Data > Add > Series Name: 1980s (cell D1) and Series values: D2:D22

6. Change the new 1980s series to a scatterplot:

   a. On PCs: select new 1980s series > Chart Design > Change Chart Type > Combo > 1980s > Scatter

   b. On Macs: select new 1980s series > Chart Design > Change Chart Type > Scatter

7. Insert x-values: right-click > Select Data > 1980s [the bottom one] > X Values: F2:F22

8. Add other series: right-click > Select Data > Add > Series Name (cell E1): 2010s; X Values: F2:F22; and Y values: E2:E22

9. Add borders using the scatterplots: select > Chart Design > Add Chart Element > Error Bars > Error Bar Options

10. Format horizontal error bars: select > right-click > Format Error Bars >

   a. Set *Direction* to *Plus*

   b. Set *End Style* to *No Cap*

   c. Set *Error Amount > Fixed Value > 1*

11. Format vertical error bars: select > right-click > Format Error Bars >

   a. Set *Direction* to *Minus*

   b. Set *End Style* to *No Cap*

   c. Set *Error Amount > Custom > Specify Value > Negative Error Value > 1980s series: G2:G22* and *2010s series: H2:H22*

12. Hide markers for both series: right-click on each > Format Data Series > Marker > Marker Options > None

Marimekko

1. Arrange data and formulas

2. Select cells R4:AA103 and insert a Clustered Column chart

3. Align the bars: right-click > Format Data Series > Series Options > Series Overlap to 100% and Gap Width to 0%

4. Format the x-axis:

5. Right-click > Format Axis > Tick Marks > Interval between marks > 10

6. Right-click > Format Axis > Labels > Interval between labels > 1

7. Edit x-axis labels: right-click > Select Data > Horizontal (Category) axis labels: > AB4:AB103

8. Edit range of vertical axis: right-click > Format Axis > Bounds > 0 for Minimum and 1 for Maximum

9. Add data labels with a scatterplot in cells A17:C41, see full tutorial for details

Cycle Plot

1. Arrange data and formulas

2. Select cells C2:F542 and insert a Line chart

3. Change the Bar series to a column chart:

   a. On PCs: select *Bar* series > *Chart Design* > *Change Chart Type* > *Combo* > *Bar* > *Clustered Column*

   b. On Macs: select *Bar* series > *Chart Design* > *Change Chart Type* > *Clustered Column*

4. Select Bar series > Format Data Series > Series Options > Gap Width to 0%

5. Delete horizontal axis

6. Add month labels: select Value series in the Format > Current Selection menu. Then, Chart Design > Add Chart Element > Data Labels > Below

7. Format month labels: right-click on labels > Format Data Labels > Value from Cells > cells G3:G542 (and uncheck the Value box)

8. Edit range of vertical axis: right-click > Format Axis > Bounds > 0 for Minimum and 20 for Maximum

Strip Chart

1. Select cells B2:C54 and insert a Scatter chart

2. Add data for Chicago and Washington, DC: right-click > Select Data > Add >

   a. *Series Name: Chicago (cell D1); X values: D3:D54;* and *Y values: E3:E54*

   b. *Series Name: Washington, DC (cell F1); X values: F3:F54;* and *Y values: G3:G54*

3. Fix Los Angeles series name label: right-click > Select Data > Y > Edit > Series Name: Los Angeles (cell B1)

4. Add series for labels: right-click > Select Data > Add > Series Name: Labels (Cell I1); X values: J2:J4; and Y values: K2:K4

5. Add labels: right-click on Labels series > Add Data Labels

6. Format labels: right-click > Format Data Labels >

   a. *Value from Cells > I2:I4*

   b. Uncheck the *Y Value* box

   c. *Label Position > Left*

7. Adjust Plot Area by selecting the left edge and moving it to the right to fit labels

8. Hide markers: right-click on Labels series > Format Data Series > Marker > Marker Options > None

9. Format the horizontal axis labels: right-click > Format Axis > Number > Custom > Format Code > #"°F";# "°F";0"°F" [for the degree symbol: Insert > Symbols menu]

10. Delete the vertical axis

Raincloud Plot

1. Arrange data and formulas

2. Select cells S10:V13 and insert a Stacked Bar chart

3. Format vertical axis:

   a. *Format Axis > Axis Options > Categories in reverse order*

   b. *Format Axis > Axis Options > Horizontal axis crosses > At maximum category*

4. Select the bottom (blue) series: right-click > Format Data Series > Fill > No Fill

5. Change bar width: right-click on either set of bars > Format Data Series > Gap Width to 230%

6. Select the other two series (orange and gray) and add a border: right-click > Format Data Series > Border > Solid line

7. Add whiskers series: right-click > Select Data > Add > Series Name: Whiskers (cell T15) and Series values (cells T18:V18)

8. Change the Whiskers series to a scatterplot:

   a. On PCs: select *Whiskers* series > *Chart Design* > *Change Chart Type* > *Combo* > *Whiskers* > *Scatter*

   b. On Macs: select *Whiskers* series > *Chart Design* > *Change Chart Type* > *Scatter*

9. Insert x-values for the Whiskers series: right-click > Select Data > Whiskers > Edit > X Values: T17:V17

10. Add the actual whiskers: select any of the three dots > Chart Design > Add Chart Element > Error Bars > More Error Bars Options

11. Format horizontal error bars: select > right-click > Format Error Bars >

    a. Set *Direction* to *Both*

    b. Set *End Style* to *Cap*

    c. Set *Error Amount* > *Custom* > *Specific Value* > *Positive Error: T19:V19* and *Negative Error: T20:V20*

12. Delete vertical error bars

13. Edit secondary vertical axis: right-click on axis > Format Axis > Axis Options > Bounds > set 0 for Minimum and 6 for Maximum

14. Add three new series for the dots: right-click > Select Data > Add >

    a. *Series Name: LA-Dots (cell X1); X Values: X3:X54; and Y Values: Z3:Z54*

    b. *Series Name: Chicago-Dots (cell AB1); X Values: AB3:AB54; and Y Values: AD3:AD54*

    c. *Series Name: DC-Dots (cell AF1); X Values: AF3:AF54; and Y Values: AH3:AH54*

    d. Note: the size and appearance of dots will depend on the size of the overall chart

15. Hide markers for the Whiskers series: right-click > Format Data Series > Marker > Marker Options > None

16. Delete legend and secondary vertical axis

References

For references to specific data used in this book, please see the Excel files available at https://policyviz.com/pv_books/data-visualization-in-excel-a-guide-for-beginners-intermediates-and-wonks/ and https://www.routledge.com/Data-Visualization-in-Excel-A-Guide-for-Beginners-Intermediates-and-Wonks/Schwabish/p/book/9781032343266.

Bruns, Dave. "Excel custom number formats." ExcelJet (blog), https://exceljet.net/custom-number-formats.

Bump, Philip. 2021. "The two halves of the pandemic." *Washington Post*, December 1, 2021, https://www.washingtonpost.com/politics/2021/12/01/two-halves-pandemic/.

Camões, Jorge. 2016. Data at work: Best practices for creating effective charts and information graphics in Microsoft Excel. New Riders.

Camões, Jorge. 2020. "How to make Marimekko charts in excel." Blog post, Flowing Data. https://flowingdata.com/2020/11/12/how-to-make-marimekko-charts-in-excel/.

Cesal, Amy. 2020. "Writing alt text for data visualization." Nightingale blog. https://medium.com/nightingale/writing-alt-text-for-data-visualization-2a218ef43f81.

Cleveland, William S., and Irma J. Terpenning. 1982. "Graphical methods for seasonal adjustment." *Journal of the American Statistical Association* 77(377): 52–62.

Elliott, Kathy, Sara Goodkind, Ghadah Makoshi, and Jeff Shook. 2020. *Understanding and Addressing Institutionalized Inequity: Disrupting Pathways to Juvenile Justice for Black Youth in Allegheny County*. Pittsburgh, PA: Black Girls Equity Alliance. https://www.gwensgirls.org/wp-content/uploads/2020/09/20-011-BGEA_JuvenileJustice-BlackYouth_v4.pdf.

Fredriksson, Anders. 2020. "One stop shops for public services: Evidence from Citizen Service Centers in Brazil." *Journal of Policy Analysis and Management* 39(4): 1133–1165.

Gates Foundation. 2021. "Maternal mortality," The Goalkeepers. https://www.gatesfoundation. org/goalkeepers/report/2021-report/progress-indicators/maternal-mortality/.

Haveman, Robert and Jonathan Schwabish. March 1999. "Macroeconomic performance and the poverty rate: A return to normalcy?" IRP Discussion Paper No. 1187–99.

Hawkins, Ed. 2018. ShowYourStripes.com. https://showyourstripes.info/.

Paradi, Dave. 2014. "2 Big mistakes professionals make using excel data in PowerPoint." Slideshare. https://www.slideshare.net/thinkoutsidetheslide/2-big-mistakes-professionals-make-using-excel-data-in-powerpoint.

Schwabish, Jonathan A. 2021a. "The practice of visual data communication: What works." *Psychological Science in the Public Interest* 22(3): 97–109.

Schwabish, Jonathan A. 2021b. *Better Data Visualizations: A Guide for Scholars, Researchers, and Wonks.* New York City: Columbia University Press.

Schwabish, Jonathan A., Alice Feng, and Susan Popkin. 2022. Accessibility. Urban Institute report.

Smeeding, Timothy M. 2002. "Globalisation, inequality and the rich countries of the G-20: Evidence from the Luxembourg Income Study (LIS)." *Presentation given at the Reserve Bank of Australia Conference.* https://www.rba.gov.au/publications/confs/2002/smeeding.html.

Stone, Maureen. 2006. "Choosing colors for data visualization." *Business Intelligence Network.*

Wann, James. 2020. "Microsoft excel versus apple's numbers: Who prevails?" Excel with Business (blog), August 13, 2020. https://excelwithbusiness.com/blogs/news/microsoft-excel-versus-apple-s-numbers-who-prevails.

Wexler, Steve, Jeffrey Shaffer, and Andy Cotgreave. 2017. *The Big Book of Dashboards: Visualizing Your Data Using Real-World Business Scenarios.* Hoboken, NJ: John Wiley & Sons.

Wilkinson, Leland. 2013. *The Grammar of Graphics.* Berlin Heidelberg: Springer Science & Business Media.

World Wide Web Consortium. 2019. "Accessibility requirements for people with low vision." https://www.w3.org/TR/low-vision-needs/.

Index

Note: **Bold** page numbers refer to tables.

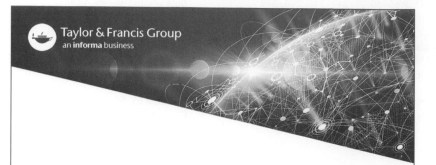